The Battle of Pavia 1525

From the Chronicles and the Tapestries of the Capodimonte Museum

Massimo Predonzani

Helion & Company Limited
Unit 8 Amherst Business Centre
Budbrooke Road
Warwick
CV34 5WE
England
Tel. 01926 499 619
Email: info@helion.co.uk
Website: www.helion.co.uk
X (formerly Twitter): @Helionbooks
Facebook: @HelionBooks
Visit our blog at helionbooks.wordpress.com

Published by Helion & Company 2025
Designed and typeset by Mary Woolley, Battlefield Design (www.battlefield-design.co.uk)
Cover designed by Paul Hewitt, Battlefield Design (www.battlefield-design.co.uk)

Text © Massimo Predonzani 2025
Illustrations © as individually credited
Cover illustration © Massimo Predonzani, 2025
Maps by George Anderson © Helion & Company 2025

Every reasonable effort has been made to trace copyright holders and to obtain their permission for the use of copyright material. The author and publisher apologise for any errors or omissions in this work and would be grateful if notified of any corrections that should be incorporated in future reprints or editions of this book.

ISBN 978-1-804518-34-2

British Library Cataloguing-in-Publication Data.
A catalogue record for this book is available from the British Library.

All rights reserved. No part of this publication may be reproduced, stored in a retrieval system, or transmitted, in any form, or by any means, electronic, mechanical, photocopying, recording or otherwise, without the express written consent of Helion & Company Limited.

For details of other military history titles published by Helion & Company Limited contact the above address or visit our website: http://www.helion.co.uk.

We always welcome receiving book proposals from prospective authors.

Contents

Foreword		v
Introduction		vii
1	Historical Background	9
2	The Attack on the Duchy of Milan	12
3	Towards Bicocca	14
4	The Arrival of Admiral Bonnivet	18
5	The Invasion of Provence	22
6	The Imperials Retreat to Lombardy	26
7	The Siege of Pavia	31
8	Bourbon Returns from Germany with Reinforcements	44
9	Sorties and Skirmishes Under the City Walls	50
10	Preparing for the Battle	55
11	The Beginning of the Battle of Pavia	58
12	The First Tapestry	66
13	The Intervention of the Spanish Arquebusiers	75
14	Second Tapestry	80
	The Defeat of the French Cavalry	
	The Imperial Infantry Captures the Enemy Artillery	
15	The Rout of the French Nobles and the Capture of the King	88
16	Third Tapestry	94
	The Capture of the King of France	
17	The Rout of the Swiss	101
18	Fourth Tapestry	103
	The Attack on the French Camp and the Flight of the Women and Servants of the Army of Francis I	
19	The Fifth Tapestry	107
	The Escape of Civilians from the French Camp. The Swiss refuse to advance despite the interventions of their leaders	
20	The Escape of the Duke of Alençon	113
21	Sixth Tapestry	115
	The Flight of the French Army and the Retreat of the Duke of Alençon across the Ticino	
22	The Sortie of de Leyva with the Garrison of Pavia	118

23	Seventh Tapestry The Sortie of the Besieged and the Rout of the Swiss, Who Drown in Large Numbers in the Ticino River	120
24	The Casualties of the Battle	125
25	The Aftermath of the Battle	130
26	The Heraldry of the Battle of Pavia	133
27	The Infantry in Pavia	151

Colour Plate Commentaries	156
Bibliography	158

Foreword

1525 marks the 500th anniversary of the Battle of Pavia, one of the most important—albeit little-known and little-understood—battles of early modern Europe. It is a great honour to be asked to write the foreword to Massimo Predonzani's second book for Helion on Pavia. His careful research, bringing together chronicles, official documents and, in the form of the Capodimonte tapestries, material culture, reveals the extraordinary complexity of pre-modern warfare.

This book is a wonderful example of the historian's craft. We possess only fragments of the past from which to weave our narratives, and the best histories reshape our understanding as new sources and new interpretative possibilities emerge. Battle histories are always works of interpretation: we can never fully capture the chaos of war or the myriad individual experiences that made up a battle. Yet Massimo's two books on Pavia together offer perhaps as complete a picture of any pre-modern battle as is possible at a distance of five centuries.

Pavia was, of course, part of the much wider conflict between the princely houses of Valois and Habsburg—a struggle that shaped European history for centuries to come. Although fought primarily by Italians, Spaniards, Germans and French, it also held special resonance for the English. Among the Imperial commanders was Richard de la Pole, 'the White Rose', nephew of King Richard III and the last Plantagenet claimant to the English throne. Contemporary newsletters spoke of the 'three kings' defeated at Pavia—Francis I, Henry II of Navarre and Richard de la Pole. In this sense, the battle is a defining chapter not only in European history but also in English history, and it deserves to be much better known. Massimo's book is an important contribution to that end.

Dr David Grummitt
The Open University and Research Officer, The Richard III Society

Introduction

The Battle of Pavia 1525 is the second book I have written on this battle. This volume updates and complements my previous work with additional chronicles and contemporary documents consulted in my research. Some of these texts were especially relevant for their detailed description of the siege of Pavia. Written by some city chroniclers present during the siege, they give detailed and timely information about the events from the point of view of the besieged.

In *The Battle of Pavia 1525*, I describe a different version of the Imperial attack that started the battle. In the previous book, the attack on the wall started from the east; in this volume, I chose to describe the entrance of the Imperials from the north. The documents are unclear, and the few chroniclers who report it point out two directions of the Imperial's nocturnal attack; not even modern scholars seem to agree. In these pages, I analyse this issue, explaining why the most probable approach was an attack from the north.

The Capodimonte tapestries were fundamental as they provided the most accurate iconographies of the course of battle. Executed by Flemish tapestry weavers, they depict clothing and architecture in a North European fashion rather than Italian. This North European vision also influences the scenes represented, such as the capture of the King of France, where the Flemish-Burgundian version prevails at the expense of the scholars' more accredited Italian and Spanish versions. The most important characters are easily identifiable thanks to the woven inscriptions on their figures and their numerous insignia. On the other hand, it is more difficult to identify many secondary characters, such as the four French cavalrymen with the King in the first tapestry, or the two Imperial cavalrymen marked by the inscriptions Monfort and Sucre in the last tapestry, or unknown coats of arms and emblems.

Thanks to research on sources and documents, I could recognise these characters and emblems with almost complete precision. Finally, as in my previous publications, this book includes various chapters on two contending armies' military heraldry, with precise and unpublished information on the captains' liveries and devices. For example, thanks to the texts by Scipione Ammirato, I've verified that Hernando de Avalos, the Marquis of Pescara and victor of the Battle of Pavia, had as many as eight devices during his military career.

THE BATTLE OF PAVIA 1525

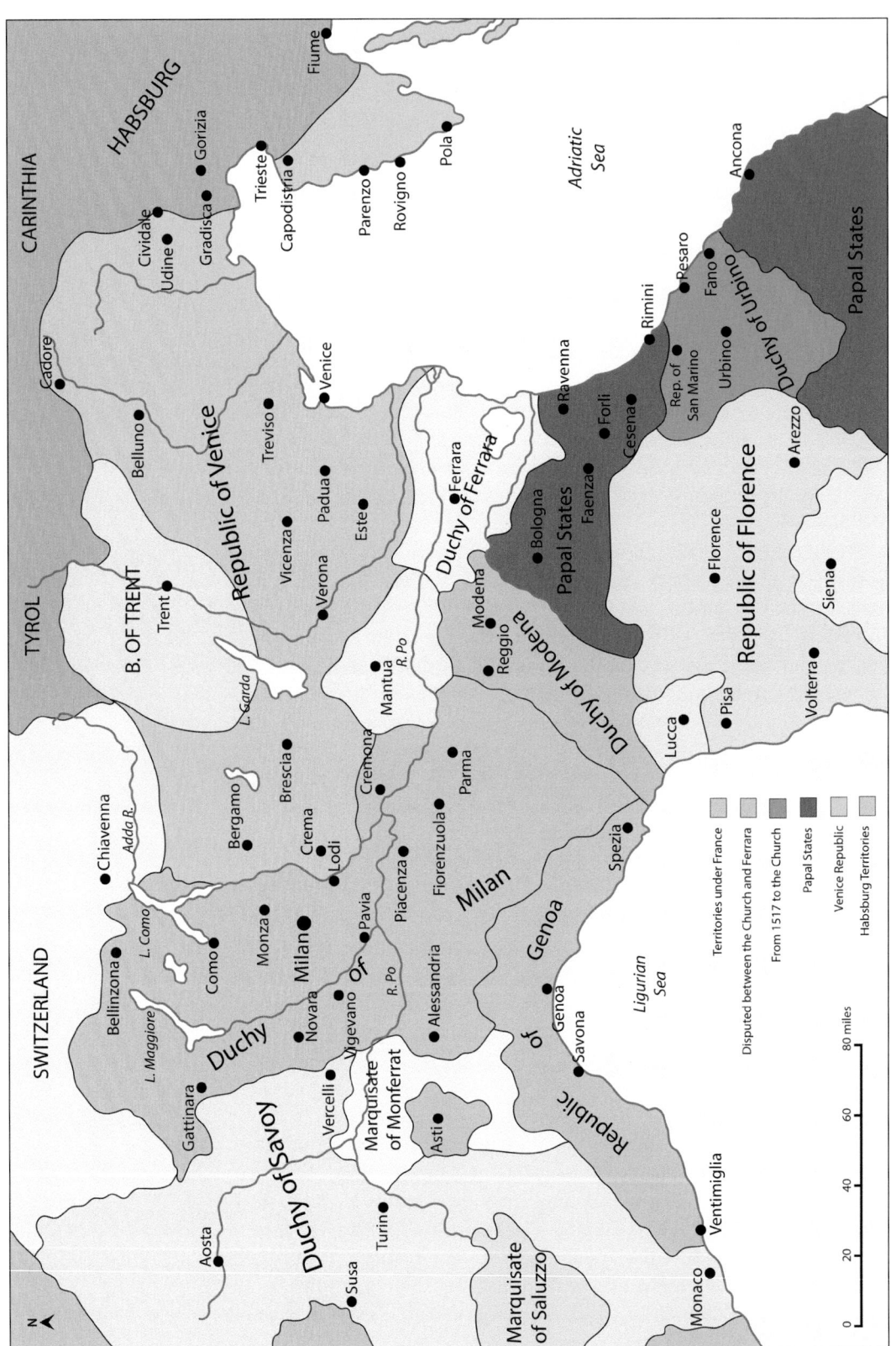

Northern Italy, 1516 after the Peace of Noyon.

1

Historical Background

The Peace of Noyon of August 1516 ended a long period of wars in Italy. These conflicts began in 1508 with the War of the League of Cambrai, followed by the War of the Holy League, and ended with the Battle of Marignano in September 1515.[1]

At the time, the Italian political situation was: the King of France, Francis I, had come into possession of the Duchy of Milan. With the War of Cambrai, the Republic of Venice had lost its territories in the Romagna and part of Friuli, but it still controlled the rest of the Italian North-East. Maximilian of Habsburg, Emperor of The Holy Roman Empire, controlled Trentino and the remaining part of Friuli, contested with Venice. In Southern Italy, the Kingdom of Naples was now under Spain with Ferdinand II of Aragon, and in 1516, under his grandson Charles I. The state of the Church, which under Julius II had endorsed all wars from the League of Cambrai onwards, had found in the new Pope, Leo X (Giovanni de' Medici), an heir to the aggressive policy of the Vatican State. These were the most powerful states.

There was also a myriad of independent and non-independent territories, such as the Republic of Genoa and the Duchy of Savoy, both under the influence of France. The Republics of Florence and Siena were also independent. The smaller duchies, such as Ferrara, Modena, Mantua and Urbino, were always ready to make alliances for their survival. The Swiss Cantons, which in Italy only included the Canton of Ticino, were a different matter. Swiss mercenaries were the best fighters of the time, and even after their heavy defeat at Marignano, they remained the most requested soldiers for service in foreign armies.

The Peace of Noyon brought a substantive balance between the most powerful states in Italy. The only one who reacted was Pope Leo X who, in May-June 1516, had ousted Francesco Maria della Rovere from the Duchy of Urbino in favour of his nephew Lorenzo dei Medici. However, change was in the air. Maximilian I, Emperor of The Holy Roman

---

1 See Predonzani, M. & V. Alberici, V., *The Italian Wars*, volume 2: *Agnadello 1509, Ravenna 1512, Marignano 1515*, (Warwick: Helion & Company, 2021)

Empire, feeling the end draw near, had to find an heir. The time-honoured tradition called for the German Prince-Electors to choose The Emperor. Charles I, King of Spain, was Maximilian's favourite and his grandson. Charles' election would unify the most powerful Kingdoms in Europe – Spain and Germany – creating a superpower with territories both in Central and Eastern Europe and the New World. However, this would have left the Kingdom of France isolated and surrounded by enemies. To prevent this situation, Francis I proposed himself as successor to the Imperial throne. In the autumn of 1518, the electors assembled in Augsburg, but Maximilian I died before an agreement was reached, leading in 1519 to a new diplomatic clash over the succession. Finally, Charles I, King of Spain, was elected Emperor as Emperor Charles V.[2]

When Charles V ascended the Imperial throne, his rivalry with the equally young and ambitious King of France, Francis I, was already bitter. The demanding payment of 100,000 ducats imposed by the Treaty of Noyon weighed on the new Emperor, whose coffers were certainly not full. This treaty established that Charles would marry the daughter of the King of France, Louise, and get her dowry. In exchange, The Emperor would have paid 100,000 ducats per year until Louise had come of age.[3]

Moreover, France and The Empire had a long-standing dispute over the Duchy of Burgundy, as well as the question of the Duchy of Milan – the King of France had never officially received the investiture. Francis I, for his part, wanted to reconquer the Kingdoms of Naples and Navarre, then under the Kingdom of Spain.

In April 1519, Pope Leo X, unsatisfied with having power only over the Duchy of Urbino, wanted to take Ferrara – ruled by Alfonso I d'Este. He entrusted this task to Alessandro Fregoso who, however, failed.

The year 1520 was relatively peaceful for Italy. The rest of Europe, however, was hit by the revolutionary wave surging from Martin Luther's ideas. While Charles V received the Imperial crown in Aachen on 23 October, on 10 December of the same year, Luther burnt the Papal bull *Exsurge Domine*, openly proclaiming his refusal of obedience to the Pope. On 3 January 1521, Leo X issued the famous bull *Decet Romanum Pontificem* to excommunicate Martin Luther, an action that would have a heavy influence for centuries to come.

The Pontiff, convinced that he had solved the problem, returned to his project of expanding his domains in Italy. His first step was to negotiate a military alliance with Francis I of France, who in the meantime, took advantage of the turmoil that broke out in Spain following Charles' ascension to the Imperial throne and sent André de Foix, Vicomte de Lautrec, to reconquer Navarre. At first, the campaign was successful, and de

---

2　Francesco Guicciardini *Storia d'Italia* , tomo II (Milan: Borroni e Scotti, 1843), pp.413–466.

3　At the time, Louise was a one-year-old. In constant poor health, she died two years later, thus avoiding a union with Charles.

HISTORICAL BACKGROUND

Foix took Pamplona and Fonterabia. However, on 30 June 1521, the French were defeated at Noàin and had to abandon Navarre.

Even the agreements with the Church were slow to be ratified since King Francis did not trust the Pontiff. Eager for conquest, the Pope abandoned the negotiations and turned to Charles V, signing an alliance with him in May 1521. This agreement established the conquest of Parma and Piacenza in the name of the Pope and the territories of Milan for The Empire. In addition, the Church would annexe Ferrara and, in the event of an enemy attack, there would be a combined defence of Florence and the House of Medici, of which Leo X was a part.

At first, the two allies' military actions were unsuccessful. The Church's Army attempted to seize Reggio, and an Imperial naval expedition against Genoa failed. Thus, the Pope and Charles V decided to attack the Duchy of Milan.

Meanwhile, Odet of Lautrec had arrived in Milan by order of King Francis to organise the city defences. He had with him 6,000 French, 4,000 Valais and 10,000 Swiss mercenaries. The latter were recruited thanks to the agreements following the Battle of Marignano of 1515 – perpetual reconciliation pacts rectified between the Swiss Diet and the King of France. In addition, France's ally Venice had promised an army to help.[4]

---

4 Francesco Guicciardini *Storia d'Italia* , tomo II (Milan: Borroni e Scotti, 1843), pp.255–264.

2

The Attack on the Duchy of Milan

Initially, the allies' forces focused on the city of Parma, which – other than satisfying the Pope's aims – was strategically fundamental for conquering the Milanese Duchy. According to Guicciardini's reports, Antonio de Leyva, Prospero Colonna and the Marquese di Mantua Federico Gonzaga, commanded the allies. Their force numbered more than 1,000 cavalry, 6,000 German infantry, 2,000 Spanish and the ever-present Italians.

The Papal-Imperial Allies approached Parma slowly, allowing Lautrec to lead a relief army that thwarted the conquest of the already partially occupied city. On 1 October 1521, Prospero Colonna attacked again, this time towards the Oglio River, but was promptly confronted by Lautrec and his fresh Venetian reinforcements.

This confrontation developed in a series of tactical movements of the two armies until November, when the Swiss mercenaries abandoned the French. Tired of waiting for the promised pay, the Swiss infantrymen left the camp and returned home, leaving the French commander in serious difficulties. Without such an important, and numerous, part of the army, the French were forced to retreat to Milan.

Lautrec tried to stop the enemies at the Adda River but was forced to retreat into Milan only to abandon the city shortly after. The position of the French in Lombardy quickly worsened. Once Milan was lost, the cities of Lodi and Pavia also hurried to open their doors to the new conquerors, followed shortly after by Piacenza, Parma and Como – which was captured by the Marchese di Pescara.

The French Army could not fight without the support of the Swiss, thus showing its dependence on those mercenaries.

However, in the decisive moment of this conflict, as can often happen, the tide changed – the Pope died. The strong emotions and the celebrations for the victory took a heavy toll on Leo X, already weakened by disease, who died suddenly. The anti-French League had not only lost its main supporter but also its largest financier of the campaign. Charles V, caught unaware and chronically short of funds, ordered Prospero Colonna to reduce the size of the army, since the French did not pose much of a threat anymore.

THE ATTACK ON THE DUCHY OF MILAN

The Florentine and German soldiers returned home, and Colonna remained at the head of only 1,500 infantrymen. Meanwhile, the Papal troops established a contingent in Modena and in Milan.

Throughout the month of December, the cardinals gathered in conclave disagreed on the election of the new Pontiff. Then, on 9 January 1522, they elected Adrian of Utrecht, Cardinal of Tortosa, who took the name of Adrian VII.

Portrait of Francis I by Titian (Wikipaedia)

3

Towards Bicocca

The stalemate created by the Pope's death led to a brief period of peace in Lombardy which, however, did not last long. The Swiss Diet, faithful to its agreements with Francis I, sent the King 15,000 Swiss infantrymen. These soldiers, led by the French captains La Palice and Montmorency, began their descent towards Milan in January 1522.[1]

Alarmed by the news, Charles V ordered Girolamo Adorno to go to Trento to hire landsknechts. From there, Adorno returned to Lombardy with 4,000 German soldiers, travelling quickly and undisturbed through the territories of Venice.

Meanwhile, Prospero Colonna had begun preparations for the defence of Milan, also sending detachments to protect the cities of Novara, Alessandria and Pavia. In Milan, Colonna stationed 700 men-at-arms, 700 light cavalry, and 12,000 infantry. He also encircled the castle, still occupied by the French, with a long, fortified trench.[2]

On the French side, Lautrec also reorganised his troops now reinforced by the Swiss, and the Venetian allies assembled their Army in Cremona under the leadership of Andrea Gritti and Teodoro Trivulzio.

In early March, the French Army crossed the Adda River and camped about two miles from Milan, in front of the castle of Porta Giovia. And so, the siege began. Prospero Colonna found himself holed up in the city, while the French and Venetians controlled and sacked the surrounding territory.

Meanwhile, another 6,000 German infantrymen left Trento under the leadership of Francesco II Sforza, the legitimate Duke of Milan and ally of The Emperor[3]. When Sforza arrived in Piacenza, 300 men-at-arms of Federico Gonzaga joined him, and later, also a contingent of 500 cavalrymen

---

1 R. de la Marck Florange, *Mémoires du Maréchal de Florange*, tome II (Paris: Renouard, H. Laurens, successeur, 1924), pp.55 & 56.
2 Francesco Guicciardini, *Storia d'Italia*, tomo II (Milan: Borroni e Scotti, 1843), p.322.
3 Antonio Grumello, *Cronaca* in *Raccolta di cronisti e documenti storici lombardi*, (Milan: Francesco Colombo, 1856), tomo I, p.286.

and 2,000 infantrymen of Giovanni de' Medici[4]. De' Medici, however, complained about the non-payment by The Emperor and switched sides, joining the French Army near Milan.

At the same time, Lautrec sent Captain Lescun to besiege Novara. In doing so, however, he denuded the garrison troops of the city. Francesco Sforza, who left 2,000 infantrymen in Pavia, took advantage of this and arrived in Milan on 2 April 1522, and was warmly welcomed by its citizens.

Lautrec, seeing that the garrison of the Lombard city had vastly increased, redirected his troops against Pavia and put it under siege. Prospero Colonna promptly moved to help the city, but a continual rain had fallen in the area. The Imperial and French Armies were greatly hindered by the bad weather, and both commanders decided to withdraw. Lautrec reached Monza, while Colonna settled in Bicocca, north-east of Milan.

The place was a manor estate a few miles from Milan and the property of Bishop Guido Antonio Arcimboldi. Colonna stationed his army in the middle of the estate, protected on all sides by a moat, and he built shelters and palisades around it to further fortify the area. To the north, from where he supposed the French would come, he erected an embankment at least three metres high and half a mile long.

Meanwhile, in the French Army, the Swiss threatened to abandon the campaign as they had yet to receive the agreed-upon money. They therefore proposed to Lautrec to give battle to the enemy, otherwise they would return home. The French commander had to accept in order not to lose the support of these formidable troops.

27 April 1522, the French Army moved from Monza and attacked the Imperial entrenched camp of Bicocca. The chroniclers disagree on the numbers of the two armies, especially regarding that of the Swiss. For some chroniclers, the Swiss mercenaries numbered 15,000, for others, they were a maximum of 8,000 men. In addition, the French had 400 heavy cavalry lances, 1,000 light cavalrymen and another 8,000 to 10,000 infantrymen – the Venetians, French and Italians of Giovanni Medici, plus the artillery. On the other hand, the Imperials had about 20,000 infantry – including landsknechts, Spanish and Italians – 400 to 600 heavy cavalrymen, 800 light cavalrymen and 28 pieces of artillery.

Lautrec planned to hit the Imperials with a heavy artillery bombardment and then attack their camp frontally with the Swiss, trying to blindside the enemy with part of the cavalry. The French cannon thus began to fire at the Imperials and their embankment, but the Swiss, eager to fight, launched the assault without waiting for the order.

On the embankment, Prospero Colonna had deployed artillery and 4,000 Spanish arquebusiers commanded by Hernando de Avalos, Marchese di Pescara. Behind them, there were 12,000 landsknecht pikemen commanded by Georg von Frundsberg.

---

4   Antonio Grumello, *Cronaca* in *Raccolta di cronisti e documenti storici lombardi*, (Milan: Francesco Colombo, 1856), tomo I, p.287.

THE BATTLE OF PAVIA 1525

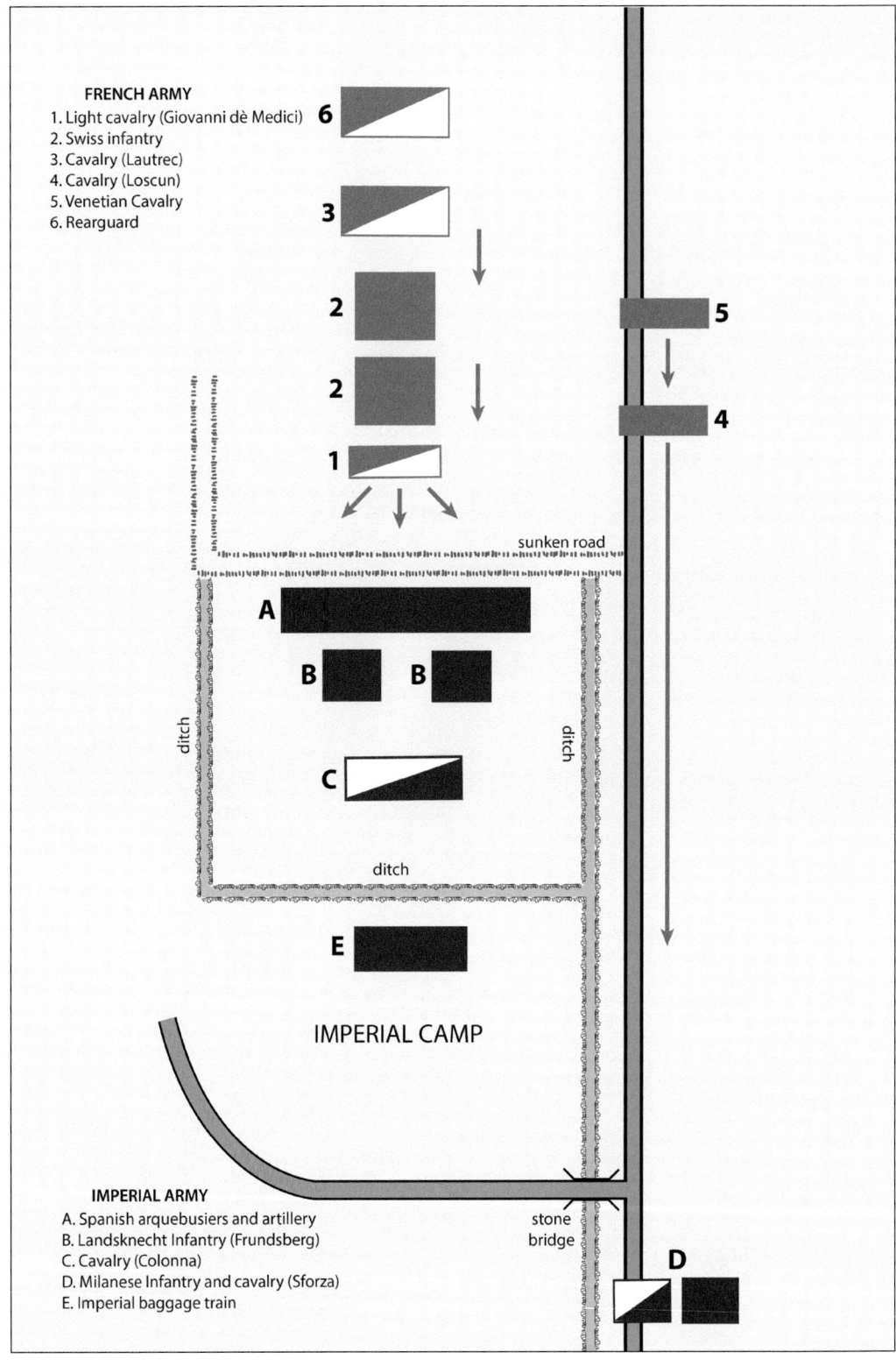

The Battle of Bicocca, 27 April 1522.

The Swiss were slaughtered. The artillery hindered their attempt to cross the moat and embankment, they were decimated and had to retreat after half an hour of combat, together with the entire French Army.

The chronicles report 3,000 to 4,000 casualties among the Swiss, including 22 captains and a few hundred casualties among the French and Venetians.

The day after this defeat, Lautrec withdrew with his troops to Bergamo and Cremona. Then, he left Northern Italy and returned to France, where he would have to explain to Francis I why he had returned with a defeated army instead of the Duchy of Milan.

The Venetian allies forded the Adda and set-up camp in Brembio, while the remaining Swiss took the road home.[5]

---

5   For a detailed description of the Battle of Bicocca see: M. Predonzani & V. Alberici, *The Italian Wars*, volume 3: *Francis I and the Battle of Pavia 1525* (Warwick: Helion & Company, 2022), pp.17–26.

4

The Arrival of Admiral Bonnivet

With the French Army out of Italy, Charles V now controlled Lombardy. The only thorn in the side of the Imperials was the city of Genoa, governed by Doge Ottaviano Fregoso, loyal to Francis I. Thus, Prospero Colonna aimed to take the city at the head of the Imperial Army. Genoa was defended by 2,000 Italian infantrymen, later reinforced by Pietro Navarro with two galleys of soldiers. After Pescara ordered a heavy bombardment which destroyed part of the city walls, the Imperial troops entered Genoa on 30 May 1522. A number of soldiers and citizens managed to save themselves on Navarro's ships, while Navarro and Doge Fregoso were taken prisoner.

The city was about to be burnt down, but the intercession of the Adorni brothers, noble citizens loyal to Charles V, avoided the worst.

Meanwhile, Venice remained on the defensive, but the constant threat of a return of the French Army forced the Imperials to maintain numerous troops on Italian territory. To afford its costs, Colonna forced the main Italian cities – Milan, Florence, Siena, Genoa and Lucca – to participate in the military spending.

In the meantime, The Emperor sent ambassadors to Venice to convince the Serenissima to enter the anti-French League. Although the negotiations were long, the Serenissima finally decided to support The Empire.

In the Papal States, Pope Adrian VI, who had taken the throne in August 1522, initially tried to reconcile the two antagonists – Charles V and Francis I. Later, however, the Imperial messengers convinced him to sign a new agreement against the French on 3 August 1523. Francis I did not remain idle and assembled a new army to return to Italy, but something unexpected happened. In April 1521, the *Connétable* of France, Charles III de Bourbon, lost his wife Susanna de Bourbon,[1] inheriting a huge patrimony that made him the richest noble in France. King Francis, fearing Bourbon's excessive power, ordered that all the fiefs inherited by his

---

1   Susanna de Bourbon, daughter of Peter II, Sieur de Beaujeu, and Anne of France.

THE ARRIVAL OF ADMIRAL BONNIVET

wife, originally included in the royal estate, became part of the estate of the Crown by right of devolution.

In this regard, in January 1522, the King promoted a trial in the parliament of Paris and in the meantime seized Bourbon's lands. Offended, Charles fled France and offered his military services to Emperor Charles, who gladly accepted them.

Despite this important defection, the King of France attempted a new invasion of the Milanese territory giving the command of the army to Guillaume Gouffier de Bonnivet, *Amiral de France* and his friend.

In August 1523, Bonnivet crossed the Alps with a powerful army of 1,800 lances, 6,000 Swiss infantry, 2,000 Grisons, 2,000 Valais, 6,000 Germans, 12,000 French and 3,000 Italians.[2] The admiral occupied Novara and Vigevano without encountering any resistance, and in a short time, the French conquered all the lands west of Ticino. At that point, Prospero Colonna gathered all his troops between Abbiategrasso, Boffalora and Turbigo to block the passage of the Ticino to the French.

Charles V, then, ordered Antonio de Leyva, stationed in Naples, to reinforce Colonna in Lombardy with his army. On 20 October 1523, de Leyva left Naples with 800 men-at-arms, Spanish and Italians, 500 light cavalrymen, 4,000 Spanish infantrymen and 10 pieces of artillery.[3]

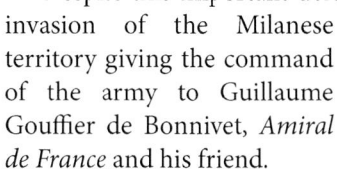

Guillaume Gouffier de Bonnivet. (Artwork by Massimo Predonzani)

---

2 Francesco Guicciardini, *Histoire d'Italie de l'année 1492 à l'année 1532,* tome 5 (Paris: A. Desrez 1837), p.72. Guicciardini reports a total of 31,000 infantry. P. Giovio in *La vita del s. Don Ferrante Davalo Marchese di Pescara* (Florence: 1556), p.136 gives the number of 30,000 infantrymen.
3 G. Passero, *Historie* (Naples: Vincenzo Maria Altobelli, 1785), p 307.

Nevertheless, the French managed to cross the Ticino near Vigevano and threatened Pavia. Prospero Colonna sent de Leyva to defend the city with 100 men-at-arms and 3,000 infantrymen, as he withdrew to Milan with the rest of the army, consisting of 800 men-at-arms, 800 light cavalrymen, 4,000 Spanish infantrymen, 6,500 German infantrymen and 3,000 Italian infantrymen.[4]

In 28 October 1523, the Marchese di Mantua also arrived in Milan with 300 lances, 500 light cavalrymen, 1,000 infantrymen and 2,000 hand gunners.[5]

The French lost three days gathering their troops after crossing the Ticino. Then, instead of attacking Milan, Bonnivet concentrated on occupying the neighbouring towns to cut the supplies for the enemy, wearing them down. However, it was the French troops who suffered from the lack of supplies due to the harsh climate in the region. The desertions and diseases in the army, in addition the pressing demands for payment by the Swiss, forced the French commander to lift the siege and retreat towards the Ticino.

Two major deaths affected the events. Pope Adrian VI died in Rome on 17 August 1523, and Cardinal Giulio de Medici replaced him on 19 November 1523, taking the name of Clement VII. Prospero Colonna died in Milan on 30 December of the same year.

At the beginning of January 1524, the situation for the French was that the army had been divided into two groups. One under the command of Bonnivet had taken positions in Abbiategrasso with 200 lances, 8,000 Swiss, 4,000 Italian infantrymen and 2,000 landsknechts. The other, much smaller, was stationed in Robecco sul Naviglio under the command of Bayard.

After the death of Colonna, the command of the Imperial Army passed into the hands of Alfonso d'Avalos, Marchese di Pescara. The new commander did not want to attack the French with the forces he had and waited for reinforcements. The reinforcements of 6,000 landsknechts arrived, brought by Bourbon, and also another army led by della Rovere, Duca di Urbino, of 6,000 infantry and 1,200 cavalry, including men-at-arms.

With these reinforcements, Pescara attempted an attack on the French. On the night of 27/28 January, the Imperial Commander left Milan with 3,000 Spanish infantrymen and attacked Robecco, taking it. Many defenders were taken prisoner, while Bayard managed to flee to Abbiategrasso. Then, d'Avalos occupied Vigevano while the Duca di Urbino and Giovanni Medici[6] occupied Garlasco, near Pavia.

---

4 Francesco. Guicciardini, *Histoire d'Italie de l'année 1492 à l'année 1532,* tome 5 (Paris: A. Desrez 1837), p.73.
5 G. Passero, *Historie* (Naples: Vincenzo Maria Altobelli, 1785), p.307.
6 De' Medici, after the clash at Bicocca, had again changed sides and joined the Imperials.

At this point, Bonnivet decided to retire to Novara and leave Abbiategrasso – Medici took it – while the bulk of the Imperial Army moved to Biandrate, west of Novara.

The months passed and the French in Novara began to suffer shortages of food and money, and disease spread among soldiers and citizens.

Fortunately, in mid-April came the news that two large Swiss contingents were coming to their aid from the Aosta Valley and Valtellina. Although Giovanni de Medici opposed them, the two Swiss forces sent by Pescara managed to reunite in Gattinara, on the right bank of the Sesia River. Then, to prevent them from joining Bonnivet, Avalos moved the army to Briona, just south of Gattinara.

The French commander could only leave Novara to join the Swiss allies and on 28 April he reached Romagnano, just north of Gattinara, on the left bank of the Sesia. The next day, Bonnivet had a bridge of boats built and ordered his army to cross the river. Throughout the morning, the Imperial light cavalry skirmished with the French crossing the bridge and captured part of the French artillery deployed there for protection. Bonnivet rushed with his men-at-arms and a group of Swiss to retrieve the guns, but had to face the arrival of Pescara, his light cavalry and 3,000 Spanish arquebusiers.

Once again, the Imperials' use of hand-held firearms was decisive. 400 Swiss infantrymen and numerous men-at-arms were killed. Bonnivet, wounded, entrusted the command of the retreat to the Marquis de Saint Paul and to Bayard.

The latter, in command of the rearguard, was killed by an arquebus shot in the back. However, his actions managed to enable the French Army to reach Gattinara.

The campaign was over, and Bonnivet had long been convinced to return to France. Taking advantage of the army's satisfaction with the recent victory, he resumed the retreat towards Ivrea and headed home through the Aosta Valley.

5

The Invasion of Provence

On 25 May 1524, Emperor Charles V and Henry VIII of England agreed an alliance against Francis I. The King of England, who had already attempted to invade France the year before, pledged to finance an Imperial attack on Provence led by Charles de Bourbon. Thanks to his popularity, Bourbon had convinced The Emperor that his army was capable of successfully invading France. The commander was sure that, with his intervention on French soil, the people would rebel against King Francis, paving the way for his victory.

The army would leave Genoa via the maritime Alps, as 12 ships would set sail commanded by Don Hugo de Moncada. The intention was to invade Provence relying on The Emperor's help, who would send an army from Spain into Roussillon, while from the north an English Army would attack Picardy. Bourbon did not have the command of the army, which was entrusted to Fernando d'Avalos, Marchese di Pescara, with the recommendation to follow the orders of the French Prince.

There are different sources regarding this army's strength. Giovio writes of 7,000 German infantrymen, 6,000 Spaniards, 2,000 Italians, 600 light cavalrymen and 1,000 men-at-arms. Guicciardini, instead, reports that there were 5,000 Germans, 4,000 Spaniards and 3,000 Italian infantrymen, then 800 cavalrymen and 500 heavy cavalry lances. Martin García Cereza reports 8,000 Germans, 5,000 Spaniards, 3,000 Italians, 500 cavalry lances and 500 light cavalrymen. Sandoval writes of 7,000 Germans, 5,000 Spaniards and only 500 Italians – similar to Guicciardini – and 500 men-at-arms. The French Florange reports higher figures: 8,000 landsknechts, 7,000–8,000 Spaniards, 4,000 Italians and 300 men-at-arms, thus around 19,000 to 20,000 men with 8 guns. Finally, the numbers for the Imperial Army from the Neapolitan chronicler Giuliano Passero are excessive: 25,000 infantrymen, 2,500 light cavalrymen and 1,000 lances. The number of soldiers of the lance – which at the time was of six men – multiplied by the number of lances results in the total number of 8,500 cavalrymen.[1]

---

1 P. Giovio, *Vite del Gran Capitano e del marchese di Pescara* (Bari: Gius, Laterza & Figli, 1931), p.347; Francesco Guicciardini *Storia d'Italia* , tomo III (Milan:

THE INVASION OF PROVENCE

I quote all these numbers to show the discrepancy in historical sources, while trying to explain the reason for these inconsistencies.

In the first days of July 1524, the Imperials arrived in Provence, and the meagre French forces posed little resistance. Throughout the month, Bourbon's Army occupied several places and castles, including the city of Aix-en-Provence, where the Bourbon was welcomed by joyous citizens.

After leaving a garrison in Aix-en-Provence under the command of La Motte des Noyers, in mid-August the Imperials reached and surrounded Marseille. The city was defended by the Roman Renzo da Chieri and Philippe de Chabot, Sieur de Brion, with 200 men-at-arms and about 4,000 Italian and French infantrymen. Marseille had strong and well-built walls, which Chieri reinforced with bastions, towers, terracing, moats and numerous artillery pieces. Moreover, thousands of Marseillais enlisted to defend their city, as Marseille was devoted to King Francis and hated the Spaniards – Alfonso V of Aragon had plundered it in 1423. Additionally, at sea, the French fleet under the command of Andrea Doria kept Hugo de Moncada's Imperial ships at a distance.

Hernando de Avalos, Marchese di Pescara (Wikipaedia)

The siege of Marseille lasted 40 days and saw, as the Marseille-born Honoré de Valbelle reported (not impartially) in his diary, several acts of heroism.[2]

The Imperial Army bombarded the walls west of the city and dug trenches to approach the walls and better emplace their cannons. The besieged responded with their own artillery and launched many sorties against the enemy camp.

On 23 August, Bourbon had the city bombarded with three large cannons and six smaller ones, opening a 10-metre-wide breach – however, its base was only two metres wide. Valbelle records that the

---

Borroni e Scotti, 1843), p.134; M. García Cerezeda, *Tratado de las campañas y otros acontecimientos de los ejércitos del emperador Carlos V en Italia, Francia, Austria, Berbería y Grecia,* tomo I (Madrid: Impresores de Cámara, 1873), p.76; P. da Sandoval,, *Historia del Emperador Carlos V,* tomo IV (Madrid: Madoz, 1846), p.100; R. de la Marck Florange, *Mémoires du Maréchal de Florange,* tome II (Paris: Renouard, H. Laurens, successeur, 1924), p.118; G. Passero, *Historie* (Naples: Vincenzo Maria Altobelli, 1785), p.314.

2 H. Valbelle, 'Histoire Journaliere d'Honoré de Valbelle,' Manuscrit fr 5072, 1501–1600.

Imperials fired 300 rounds which, other than knocking down the wall, killed a man-at-arms, two men and two children. He adds that the French artillery responded by destroying a large cannon, a smaller one and killing a gunner plus all the soldiers who stood near him.

The following day, Renzo da Chieri ordered the breach to be filled with stones, kindling, beams and ordered another bastion built behind the breach. In addition, the arquebusiers' line of defence made the Imperials desist from any attack. In the following days, Bourbon had tunnels dug to place mines under the walls, but Chieri had his soldiers dig countermines to destroy and blow-up the Imperials' tunnels.

The sorties continued. On 4 September, the Roman Vincenzo Tibaldo lost his life; he was a captain, who had distinguished himself several times in the victorious sorties against the Imperials. That day, he led 100 Marseillais against the enemy trenches but was confronted by three groups of Spanish infantrymen. Fewer in number, the Marseillais had to retreat, and Paolo Giovio reports that, upon the death of Vincenzo, all the others fled suffering many losses. Valbelle, on the other hand, writes that the gunners and arquebusiers of the city covered the French retreat, inflicting more than 40 casualties on the Spaniards and that the French suffered only two casualties – Tibaldo and another man.

However, both chroniclers agree that the two armies agreed a truce and recovered their fallen: Vincent, who died in front of the Imperial trenches, and a Spanish captain and standard bearer killed at the city gate.

The excavations of the Imperials' trenches towards the walls proceeded slowly, mainly due to the stony ground. The dirt from these excavations was used to fill the wicker gabions and protect the artillery and trenches from enemy fire. However, when hit by enemy artillery, these heavy gabions caused the death of infantrymen and artillerymen because of the stones that ricocheted among the soldiers.

The city's artillery caused further damage to the Imperials. Well positioned on the walls and on the monticello dei mulini (mound of the mills) that overlooked the city, the gunners could hit as far as the Imperial camp, firing randomly day and night. On 10 September, they hit the pavilion of the Marchese di Pescara. Giovio, who wrote the Marchese's biography and exalted his skills, reports that he was the only one to keep the lights on at night to show that he was not afraid of enemy fire. That day, the artillery fire killed two gentlemen and a chaplain during mass, then hit another pavilion and killed two horses. Valbelle cites the fact and mentions as a witness to the event a companion of the French, who was in Bourbon's camp and later reported the whole thing to Brione and Chieri. However, neither Valbelle nor Giovio say where Pescara was at the time of the explosion.

Still regarding these cannons, Giovio reports that in the siege, the artillery of Marseille alone killed about 200 soldiers – among the fallen, were captains Francesco Cantelmo, Guzmán and Louis Gallego.

In mid-September, Bourbon concentrated the bombardment on the walls near the gate and the San Paulo Tower. He had more artillery pieces now thanks to the large cannon taken from the Toulon Tower taken by the Imperials on 7 September.

Meanwhile, King Francis collected money and assembled a powerful army in Avignon by hiring Swiss, Germans, *provvisionati* (paid soldiers) and French troops. In addition, he gathered all his captains, such as La Palice, François de Lorraine, Richard de la Pole and many others.

On 24 September, Bourbon increased the rate of cannon fire against the San Paulo Tower. The artillery fired 403 shots and opened a breach 10-metres wide at the base – this time wide enough to launch an attack en masse. But when the smoke dissipated, the Imperials saw that behind the breach the besiegers had built another high bank with new trenches. In addition, thousands of defenders armed with arquebuses, crossbows and halberds were ready to resist and assault. The Imperials charged but were immediately stopped by heavy fire. The army retreated, and the landsknechts refused to advance, followed by the Spanish and the Italians. The commanders held counsel to decide what to do. Bourbon wanted to continue the siege, while Pescara and the other captains advised withdrawal because it had been reported that Francis I's Army had left Avignon heading south and that its vanguard was already in Aix. Furthermore, Emperor Charles had no funds and did not cross the border of the Pyrenees as he had promised; similarly, the King of England had made little progress in Picardy and had not advanced further.

Considering these facts, the Imperials decided to leave Marseille, and, on 29 September, they lifted the siege.[3]

---

3   Texts consulted on the siege of Marseille: P. Giovio, *Vite del Gran Capitano e del marchese di Pescara* (Bari: Gius, Laterza & Figli, 1931), pp.347–360; R. de la Marck Florange*, Mémoires du Maréchal de Florange*, tome II (Paris: Renouard, H. Laurens, successeur, 1924), pp.118–155; Francesco Guicciardini *Storia d'Italia*, tomo III (Milan: Borroni e Scotti, 1843), pp.133–136; P. da Sandoval, *Historia del Emperador Carlos V*, tomo III (Madrid: Madoz, 1846), pp.102–110; H. Valbelle, 'Histoire Journaliere d'Honoré de Valbelle,' Manuscrit fr 5072, 1501–1600, ff.78r–88v.

6

The Imperials Retreat to Lombardy

The Imperials quickly retreated towards Italy, aware of the danger they were in if the French reached the army. They had to leave part of the artillery behind: they buried a large howitzer, and other cannons were wrecked and destroyed. The French captured some cannons, but Pescara managed to take one back and massacred the enemy who had taken it. The Spaniards kept with them only the lightest and easiest pieces to move.

Bourbon's Army proceeded with a light cavalry vanguard followed by landsknechts, Italians and their luggage, the men-at-arms with other light cavalrymen, and finally the rearguard formed by Spanish arquebusiers.

The French Army was strong. According to Guicciardini, King Francis had 2,000 cavalry lances and 20,000 infantrymen, whereas Florange reports a total of 25,000 to 30,000 men.[1] The King had sent Montmorency to pursue the Imperials with his men-at-arms and numerous light cavalry. The cavalry frequently attacked the enemy rearguard, provoking bloody clashes – they were not always favourable to the French.

The Imperial commanders took the coast road reaching Nice and then Mantua, constantly attacked by the French cavalry. During the retreat, there were many desertions, especially among the infantry. In Nice, a company of landsknechts refused to move further and withdrew into a village. Pescara intervened, but he could not convince the Germans to resume their journey, so he ordered the houses to be set on fire. Many landsknechts died in the fires, and the others had to resume the march.

The Imperial Army managed to escape their pursuers, crossed the Alps, left the coast, and headed north.

Meanwhile, the bulk of the French Army was divided into two groups: *Maréchal* La Palice led the infantry and marched to the left of Montmorency

---

1   Francesco Guicciardini *Storia d'Italia*, tomo III (Milan: Borroni e Scotti, 1843), p.137; R. de la Marck Florange, *Mémoires du Maréchal de Florange*, tome II (Paris: Renouard, H. Laurens, successeur, 1924), p.152.

crossing Barcelonnette, Tenda and arriving in Cuneo. The King led his gentlemen and men-at-arms, crossed the Dauphiné in the direction of Briançon and, on 15 October 1524, crossed the Monginevro Pass. Francis intended to reach the Duchy of Milan before the Imperials.

The Imperial Army, warned of the King's move, had to march day and night and without stopping they arrived in Alba, in the Marquisate of Monferrato, on the same day that King Francis arrived in Vercelli.

The Imperial Army had also separated, and Charles de Bourbon with the landsknechts was a day's march behind Pescara. The latter, with the cavalry and the Spanish infantrymen, had not stopped or waited for Bourbon and, by a forced march, had arrived in Voghera, and the next day at Pavia, where he joined the forces of Charles de Lannoy, Viceroy of Naples.

The Swiss and the troops of La Palice joined the King of France; they arrived at Vigevano, near Ticino, on 23 and 25 October, and crossed the river to reach Abbiategrasso. On the same day, Pescara and the Viceroy left for Milan with weapons and supplies, leaving Captain Antonio de Leyva in Pavia with 300 men-at-arms and 5,000 infantrymen, mostly Germans.

On the same day, the French had their first success, thanks to Michel Antoine, Marchese di Saluzzo. The King had sent the Marchese and 300 men-at-arms to Novara on a patrol; 10 miles from the city, Antoine ran into an Imperial convoy of artillery and captured it. The French had lost the cannon in the previous campaign, and the enemy army had deployed them in Novara. Lannoy had ordered them to be deployed to Pavia and Lodi, but his plan had been in vain. These trophies comprised 17 heavy cannon, many of them culverins, plus powder and shot.

At the same time, La Palice with his men-at-arms and Florange[2] with the Swiss headed towards Binasco, halfway between Milan and Pavia, to intercept the Imperials marching to Milan. On the evening of 25 October, the Swiss vanguard of 5,000 men reached Binasco, already occupied by the Spaniards. The Swiss commander, Jean de Diesbach, decided to attack and sent his lieutenant, Louis d'Erlach, to warn Florange of the clash. Florange had stopped in Rosate for the night with the bulk of the Swiss and five artillery pieces, but as he had news of the impending combat, he immediately resumed the march with infantry and guns. The French commander sent relays to Abbiategrasso to warn Francis I as he was being joined by La Palice's troops.

The two captains arrived in Binasco in the dark, while the fighting was underway. The Swiss of Diesbach could do little against the large number of Spanish arquebusiers, and Florange put an end to the fighting and surrounded the village thanks to the light cavalrymen of Federico da Bozzolo.[3] In addition, he had fires lit to signal their positions to the

---

2   Robert de la Marck, Sieur de Florange, was the French commander of the Swiss mercenaries. He participated in the whole campaign that led to the Battle of Pavia, recounting the events in which he participated in his *Mémoires*.
3   Federico da Bozzolo belonged to a minor branch of the Gonzaga family. His father

delaying troops as well as to warm the men drenched by the rain that had been falling since the morning.

The following day, the Spanish left Binasco; Bourbon and Pescara had ordered the withdrawal of the rearguard, that had disengaged thanks also to the fires lit by the enemies that signalled their positions. The French immediately sent Bozzolo with the cavalry and Diesbach with 100 Swiss on horseback in pursuit. They reached the Imperials in Scanasio, halfway between Binasco and Milan, and started a violent clash. The Imperial rearguard consisting of Spanish harquebusiers and the Burgundian Succre's light cavalry[4] was defeated and retreated. Florange writes that they stole all the luggage, 40,000 loads of powder and killed a third of the Imperial arquebusiers. Additionally, they also threw the Imperial troops into utter disarray.

Florange and La Palice realised that victory was in their hands and perhaps also the outcome of the war.

The Imperial Army separated due to the march. The vanguard formed by cavalry and the commanders had lost contact with the rear, which was heading, in some disarray, towards Lodi. Thus, the French assmebled their strength for the final assault, about 8,000 infantrymen, Swiss and Italians, and 1,000 cavalrymen both heavy and light. But at that moment, the King ordered the retreat to Binasco to muster the army and attack Milan. Francis I did not know of the favourable chance at victory that had arisen, so Florange and La Palice thought of continuing the action anyway. However, upon receiving a second peremptory message from the King, they had to desist and return to Binasco.[5]

It is the French writer Jean Giono who reports this episode in a book about the Battle of Pavia, published 60 years ago. It is a well-written book, almost fictionalised, but unfortunately without footnotes.[6] In one chapter, he lists all the chronicles he consulted and which are, in his opinion, the most relevant. However, without footnotes, it is difficult to identify when he references which chronicle.

Still, Giono highlights the clash of Binasco which was, according to him, a missed opportunity that could have led the French to victory. Until then, King Francis had played this war by the book: he had crossed the Alps quickly with the army and had Milan within reach. If he had not so foolishly

---

was Gianfrancesco Gonzaga, and his mother was Antonia del Balzo, from a noble Neapolitan family. In his military career, he always sided with France, participating in the most important phases of the Italian Wars.

4   In other documents, this is also mentioned as Alvares Chuchar or Zucharo.
5   For sources on the Battle of Binasco: R. de la Marck Florange, *Mémoires du Maréchal de Florange*, tome II (Paris: Renouard, H. Laurens, successeur, 1924), pp.164–167; M. García Cerezeda, *Tratado de las campañas y otros acontecimientos de los ejércitos del emperador Carlos V en Italia, Francia, Austria, Berbería y Grecia*, tomo I (Madrid: Impresores de Cámara, 1873), p.91; Jean Giono (Franco Pierno, trans.) *Il disastro di Pavia*, (Milan: Ed. Settecolori, 2023), pp.130–133.
6   Jean Giono (Franco Pierno, trans.) *Il disastro di Pavia*, (Milan: Ed. Settecolori, 2023).

stopped Florange at Binasco, he would have won. As if that were not enough, Giono adds that the King had wasted three days in Turin to feast with Duca Charles III di Savoy, with the excuse of waiting for reinforcements. King Francis had many qualities but many flaws too – parties and women were among these latter.

But let us return to the recounting of the war.

The Imperial forces entered Milan under the command of Bourbon, Lannoy, Pescara, Sforza and his minister Girolamo Morone, the cavalry and part of the infantry. However, they were welcomed by the aftermath of a plague that had hit the city that summer. Other than a weakened population, they found the defences almost in ruins and a food shortage. The Imperials decided that stopping in the city was unwise, so they left a garrison in the castle and left Porta Romana in the direction of Lodi. Almost at the same time, the Marchese di Saluzzo entered through the gate of Porta Ticinese, chasing the Imperials as far as Marignano.

Arriving at the gates of Milan, King Francis did not enter with the entire army to prevent looting. He sent a garrison to control the city and a contingent of troops to besiege the 700 Spanish infantry garrisoned in the castle. According to Florange, the King's Lieutenant General of Milan tasked Louis de la Trémoille with besieging the castle. With Trémoille, were *Maréchal* de Foix,[7] the Sieur de Saint-Pol, and the Sieur de Vaudemont[8] with their companions, 500 men-at-arms and 4,000 franc-archers led by a Burgundian captain named Aubigny. Trémoille had trenches dug below the castle and opened the siege.[9] Guicciardini writes that, at that time, the French had 2,000 lances, 8,000 German infantry, 6,000 Swiss infantry, 6,000 mercenaries of various kinds and nationalities and 4,000 Italians.

The King convened a meeting of captains to discuss what to do. Most lords – including La Palice, Trémoille, Florange and Montmorency – thought it best to attack Lodi, where the demoralised and disorganised Imperial troops had taken refuge. Bonnivet and a few others advised instead the siege of Pavia, where there were many landsknechts who, according to Bonnivet, tired of their long and useless contract could be bribed with money.

Francis had known Bonnivet from an early age and was good friends with him, so he decided to besiege Pavia, thus marking his destiny. Trémoille remained in Milan – Teodoro Trivulzio would replace him later – with several thousand French and Italian infantry and 500 light cavalry. The rest of the army marched to Pavia where it arrived on 28 October 1524.[10]

---

7   Thomas de Foix, Sieur de Lescun, known as 'The Shield', brother of Odet de Foix.
8   Louis de Vaudemont, fourth son of René II of Lorraine.
9   R. de la Marck Florange, *Mémoires du Maréchal de Florange*, tome II (Paris: Renouard, H. Laurens, successeur, 1924), pp.151–152.
10 Francesco Guicciardini, *Storia d'Italia* , tomo III (Milan: Borroni e Scotti, 1843), pp.139–140; P. Giovio, *Vite del Gran Capitano e del marchese di Pescara* (Bari: Gius, Laterza & Figli, 1931), pp.370–371.

THE BATTLE OF PAVIA 1525

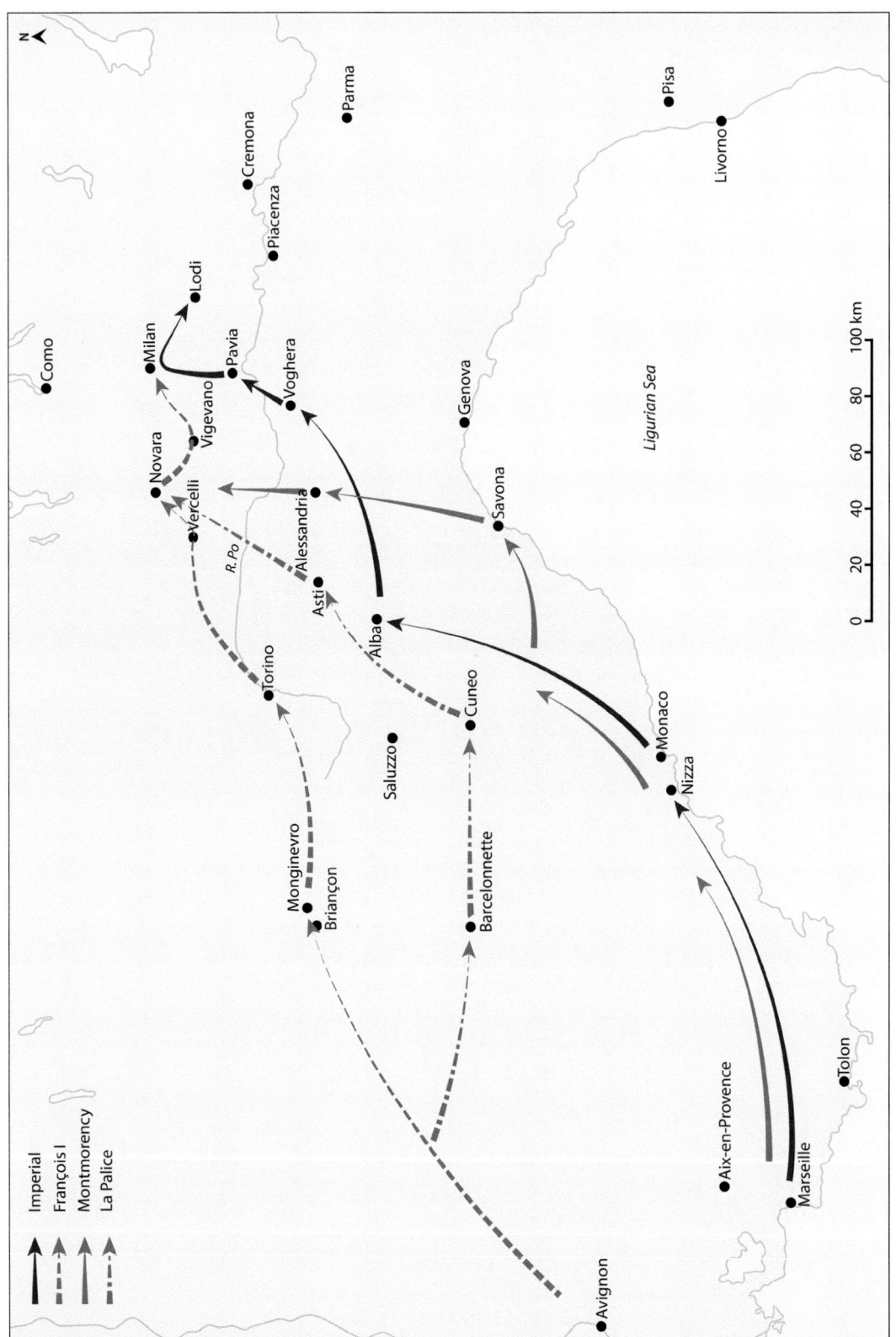

The French invasion of Italy, 1524.

7

The Siege of Pavia

Paolo Giovio wrote that it was the Lombards who named the city Pavia, but in ancient times it was called Ticino, taking its name from the river that flows south and bathes the city walls. The river is crossed by a beautiful, covered stone bridge, protecting those who cross it from inclement weather. To the north, the city is protected by a superb castle facing the Parco Vecchio, built by Galeazzo Visconti as a hunting reserve. The park, surrounded by a high wall, stretches for 16 miles to the north with gardens, woods, and open country. It is also crossed by canals, streams and moats.

Jean Giono wrote that that winter was particularly rainy and cold. This hindered the troops that were crossing the Alps and the rivers in flood, causing many deaths among men and horses. The same problem would occur in the park, where the frequent rains reduced much of the terrain to a swamp, making it difficult for the cavalry to manoeuvre, which we will see in the chapter on the battle.[1]

King Francis and Henri d'Albret, King of Navarre, stayed in San Lanfranco, west of the city. A little further south, the landsknechts of the Black Band stopped in San Salvatore with their commanders: the Comte de Lambesc, François de Lorraine; the Duke of Suffolk, Richard de la Pole, called 'the White Rose', and the German Captain Graf Wolf von Lupfen. There were also Commander Galiot de Genouillac, Sieur d'Acier, with the artillery and the Spanish Captain Pedro de Guevara, who had passed into the service of the King of France with 1,000 Spanish infantry. The Marchese di Saluzzo and Federico da Bozzolo stopped south of the Ticino River with Italian and French soldiers. At their right, the Maréchal de Montmorency marched with 200 men-at-arms and 6,000 German, Italian and Corsican infantry, stopping in Borgo Ticino, in front of the city and its bridge. On the other side, east of Pavia, Florange and the Swiss stopped in the five abbeys: San Pietro, San Giacomo, Santo Spirito, San Paolo and San Giuseppe. John

---

1   P. Giovio, *Vite del Gran Capitano e del marchese di Pescara* (Bari: Gius, Laterza & Figli, 1931), p.372; Jean Giono (Franco Pierno, trans.) *Il disastro di Pavia*, (Milan: Ed. Settecolori, 2023), pp.141–142.

THE BATTLE OF PAVIA 1525

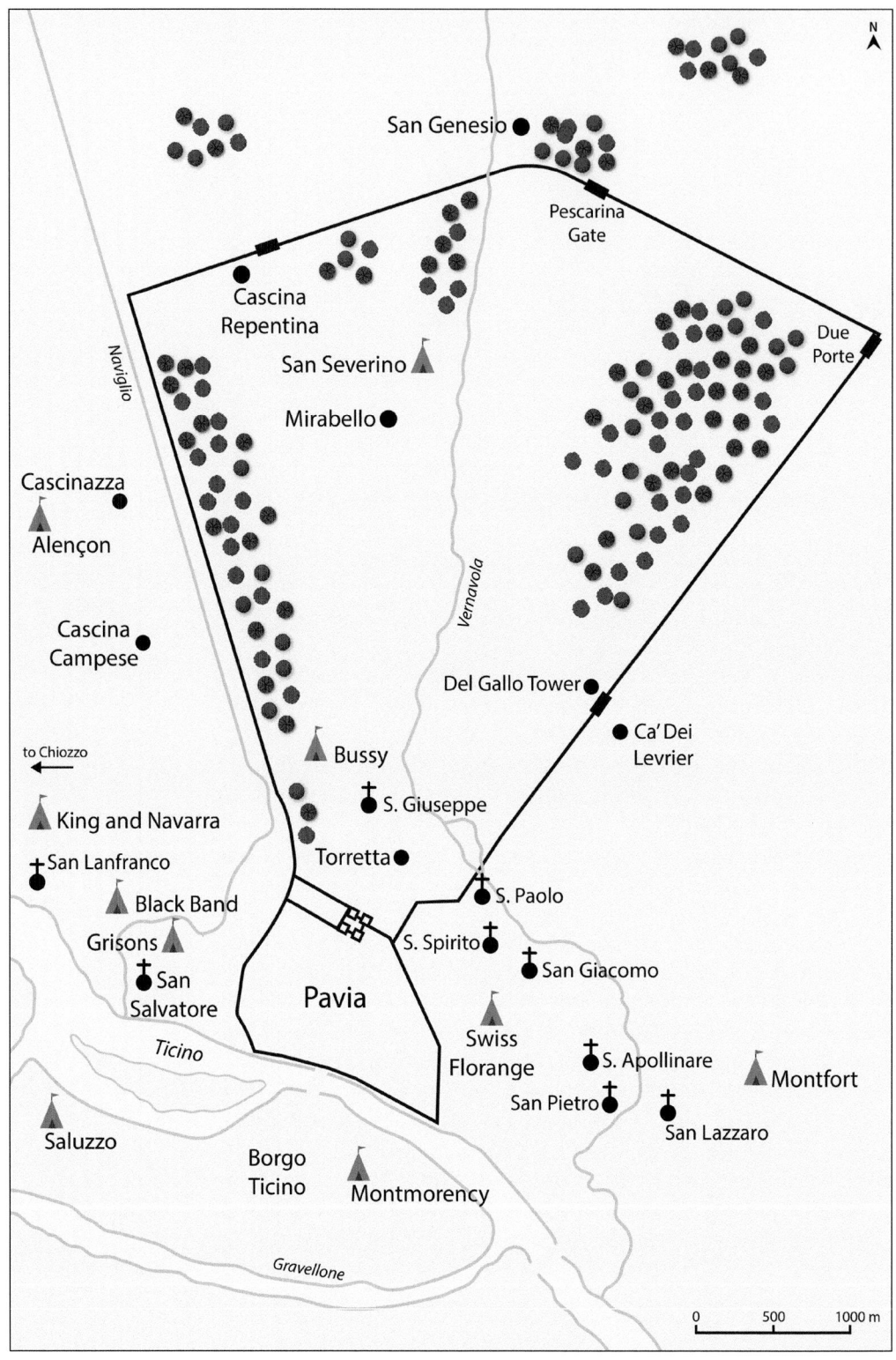

Pavia, the park, and the French camps.

Stewart, Duke of Albany, and Jacques de Chabannes, Sieur de La Palice, and their soldiers were also camped with the Swiss. At the Abbey of San Pietro, was the church of Sant' Apollinare, occupied by the Provençals led by captain Monfort. Jacques Amboise, Sieur de Bussy and commander of the French troops, camped north of San Giuseppe to act as a link between the Swiss and the King, thus completing the encirclement of Pavia. Charles Valois, Duc d'Alençon, set-up camp with the rearguard in Cascinazza near the Naviglio, at the height of Mirabello Castle. This castle, dating back to the fourteenth century, was in the middle of the park, where Galeazzo da Sanseverino, Grand écuyer de France, stayed with his men-at-arms and French infantry. The rest of the *gendarmerie*, of little use in a siege, was sent to positions in the surrounding villages.

This deployment of French troops around Pavia was taken from Florange's chronicle and the Pavian chronicler Francesco Taegio, the only ones who mention the entire arrangement of the French quarters in a quite similar way.

Taegio witnessed the siege from within the city and his almost daily chronicle cannot be said to be impartial. In fact, in addition to increasing the strength of the enemy army – he reports Francis I to have had 36,000 men in total, 7,000 more than the strength reported by Guicciardini, in his reports – he also exaggerates the number of their losses. In addition, he reports a smaller number of the besieged. According to him, there were 200 men-at-arms, 200 light cavalry, 500 Germans and 500 Spaniards defending Pavia.[2]

Other chroniclers agree on the number of cavalry but report higher infantry numbers. The Spaniard Cerezeda writes that the defenders were 4,000 landsknechts and 1,000 Spanish; according to the German, Schertlin von Burtenbach, there were 6,000 German infantry and 500 Spanish; for the Frenchman, du Bellay, there were 6,000 Germans and 1,200 Spanish; the only one with larger figures was Florange, who wrote of 7,000 Germans, 3,000 Spanish and 10,000 citizens of Pavia who volunteered to defend their city.[3]

Several captains assisted the commander of Pavia, de Leyva. One of them was Heitel Fritz, Graf Hohenzollern and commander of the landsknechts, who died in January 1525, whereupon the command passed to a nobleman

---

2   For the French Army deployment around Pavia: F. Taegio, *Rotta e prigionia di Francesco primo re' di Francia sotto Pavia l'anno 1525. Composta dal Taegi, e dal latino tradotta dal Cremonese Cambiago* (Pavia: 1655), p.7; R. de la Marck Florange, *Mémoires du Maréchal de Florange*, tome II (Paris: Renouard, H. Laurens, successeur, 1924), pp.177–178.

3   M. García Cerezeda, *Tratado de las campañas y otros acontecimientos de los ejércitos del emperador Carlos V en Italia, Francia, Austria, Berbería y Grecia*, tomo I (Madrid: Impresores de Cámara, 1873), p.90; M. Jähns, *GeschichtlicheAufsätze* (Berlin: Verlag von Gebrüder Paetel, 1903), p.241; M. Du Bellay, *Memoires* (La Rochelle: 1573), p.188; R. de la Marck Florange, *Mémoires du Maréchal de Florange*, tome II (Paris: Renouard, H. Laurens, successeur, 1924), p.174.

from Trentino, Battista di Lodron. Additionally, there were the German captains Martin Pfaff, Michael Alting, Graf Ehriftop von Lupfen, Eitelek von Reischach and Conrad Glures, and finally the Spanish captain Tomaso Sancen Baetia.

Taegio writes that on the evening of the French arrival in Pavia, Montmorency attacked the bridge over the Ticino – in front of his camp – with a company of infantry. At first, the French prevailed against the landsknecht garrison, but alerted by the clamour of the battle, many citizens immediately intervened alongside Lodron and other Germans and managed to repel the attackers. In the clash, Albizio died carrying the Colours of Antonio de Leyva. The same night, de Leyva had the last arch of the bridge destroyed to prevent any attack from that side. The following day, Montmorency had trenches dug in Borgo Ticino, in front of the bridge, and deployed the artillery to bombard the city walls.

On 30 October, the French destroyed the mills on the Ticino with artillery fire. Thus, De Leyva ordered mills to be built in various parts of the city, and for horses and men to turn the millwheels. On the same day, Montmorency had his cannon fire at Torre Gravellona, which stood on an eyot on the Ticino and Gravellone Rivers. In the tower, there were 30 to 40 Spanish who, after a useless struggle, surrendered; Montmorency had them all hanged. This action greatly angered de Leyva, who swore to do the same with every one of Montmorency's soldiers that he captured. On 31 October, the French armed Torre Gravellona with some cannon and fired at the city, causing a great deal of damage, de Leyva therefore ordered his artillery to eliminate the cannon tower and it was done, destroying the tower completely.[4]

The French Storm

While these things were happening in Pavia, the Imperials had to reorganise the army. The Marchese di Pescara was in Lodi with the infantry and had to refortify the city, as he had found its defences lacking. Charles de Lannoy, Viceroy of Naples, Francesco Sforza and the cavalry had moved to Soncino, on the other side of the Adda River. Other contingents of troops were stationed in Alessandria, Como and Trezzo.

Meanwhile, Bourbon had left for Germany to hire additional landsknecht infantrymen and ask for the help of The Emperor's brother, Ferdinand. The newly hired landsknechts were paid with the 50,000 ducats that The

---

[4] For the initial events of the siege see: F. Taegio, *Rotta e prigionia di Francesco primo...* pp.16–19; R. de la Marck Florange, *Mémoires du Maréchal de Florange*, tome II (Paris: Renouard, H. Laurens, successeur, 1924), pp.178–179; P. Giovio, *Vite del Gran Capitano e del marchese di Pescara* (Bari: Gius, Laterza & Figli, 1931), p.373; M. Verri, Relazione delle cose successe in Pavia dal 1524 al 1528, in Raccolta di cronisti e documenti storici lombardi inediti, Milan 1857, tomo II, pp.206–209.

Emperor had sent to Genoa for the war in Provence. However, Bourbon did not have additional money, and he could not obtain any from the Duchy of Milan. His only hope was the Kingdom of Naples – the Imperials had asked for its revenues. Then, they asked for help from Florence, which stalled, and from the Pope. However, Pope Clement VII did not wish to participate in a conflict between France and The Empire. Venice, which had previously joined the League against France, agreed with the Church, since it viewed with fear the rise of Imperial power in Italy, and thus the Venetians chose to remain neutral.[5]

Back to the siege. In the first days of November, the French built some bridges over the River Ticino to connect the quarters of the King, who was in San Lanfranco, with those of La Palice on the opposite side in the five abbeys. In addition, some parts of the park wall were demolished to allow the movement of troops. From 3 to 5 November, the French deployed artillery batteries to the east and west of the city, and on the following two days, the King ordered the bombardment of the walls. On the east side, that of the abbeys, the fire concentrated on the bastion of Porta Santa Maria della Pertica, near the castle. On the other side, the cannon bombarded a square tower called Mezzabarba, located roughly opposite the royal quarters.

Although the Imperial artillery countered the French guns effectively, the French fire still opened large breaches in the city walls. However, the French supply of gunpowder ran short and the King had to suspend the bombardment. Antonio de Leyva, then took advantage of the truce and repaired the damage to the walls with gabions and trenches. He also had ditches dug behind the walls and with the resultant earth had mounds and shelters erected for his infantrymen and arquebusiers.

The day after, on 8 November, the Marchese Alfonso di Ferrara, a French ally, supplied them with gunpowder, and the bombarding of the city resumed. After five hours of bombardment, the Torre Mezzabarba – on the side of the King's camp – collapsed to the ground, and the signal for the assault was given. Florange writes that on that side there were 5,000 to 6,000 French troops and Italian mercenaries who, at the order of Sieur de Forges, attacked through the breach. Maréchal de Foix and Montmorency followed them with 200 men-at-arms, followed by the landsknechts led by the Duke of Suffolk and Graf Wolf. Even the King and his knights joined the assault. However, the attack went badly. De Leyva had deployed 5,000 to 6,000 men flanked by gendarmes on the rubble of the breach, several cannon on the walls and the small ramparts surrounding, which had not been destroyed by the French fire. Although the King's soldiers attacked bravely, many fell under the defenders' fire. Some soldiers managed to reach the top of the breach but were repulsed by the Germans with pikes and arquebuses. Given the losses, the King ordered the retreat. According to Florange, the French

---

5   Francesco Guicciardini *Storia d'Italia* , tomo III (Milan: Borroni e Scotti, 1843), p.140.

had 300 to 400 casualties, including the standard bearer of the King's Gardes Écossaise.

Taegio writes that, among the defenders, were Graf Lodron, Enrico di Castelalto, Bucardo di Beransen, Michael Mertel, Gaspard Schegler, Volfang Honel, Matteo Beccaria and Bartolomeo Eustachio.

Simultaneously, the French had attacked from the east the bastion of Porta Santa Maria della Pertica. Florange writes that Jacques d'Amboise, Seigneur de Bussy, led 5,000 mercenaries together with the Seigneir de Donzy and Jean du Mex, Seigneur d'Aubigny, at the head of many gentleman volunteers[6]. The Duke of Albany followed behind them with 200 men-at-arms, Florange and the Swiss. Despite the losses, Aubigny initially managed to cross the breach with his men but had to stop at the ditches, which had also been dug behind the rubble. Cannon and arquebuses massacred the mercenaries, who had to retreat dragging the Swiss and the men-at-arms with them. Florange writes that about 800 men died in this assault, including the Lord of Bussy and seven captains. On the Imperial side, there were barely 10 or 20 losses. Taegio mentions the captains of the besieged who distinguished themselves in this action: the Graf Hohenzollern, John d'Au, Michael Alting, George di Ostan, the Spanish officer, Baetia, Francesco Sermiente and Marchese Francesco Malaspina Scaldasole.[7]

The count of the losses in these two French assaults is from Florange's chronicle, which gives a total of about 1,100 men. It is peculiar how Taegio cites fewer losses among the assailants – 300 dead – and among the besieged, seven Germans and three Spanish. Sandoval reports a loss of 3,000 infantry and 300 French men-at-arms, and Passero gives 5,000 men killed in the assaults.[8]

Regarding these attacks on the city walls, the Austrian painter and printmaker Wolf Huber, one of the leading members of the Danube School, made an interesting drawing on the Battle of Pavia, dated 1530. In his work, in addition to the combat of February 1525, Pavia is seen from the north, from the park, probably with Mirabello in front of the city. Then, there are the castle, walls, bastions and buildings such as houses, palaces, and towers. Architecturally, all buildings are in North European style – imposing, with

---

6 Aubigny belonged to the Mex family of Franche-Comté, not to be confused with the Stewart, Dukes of Aubigny.
7 For the assault, I consulted: P. Giovio, *Vite del Gran Capitano e del marchese di Pescara* (Bari: Gius, Laterza & Figli, 1931), pp.373–374; R. de la Marck Florange, *Mémoires du Maréchal de Florange*, tome II (Paris: Renouard, H. Laurens, successeur, 1924), pp.180–188; F. Taegio, Rotta e prigionia di Francesco primo re di Francia sotto Pavia l'anno 1525. Composta dal Taegi, e dal latino tradotta dal Cremonese Cambiago, (Pavia 1655), pp.20–24; Martino Verri, Relazione delle cose successe in Pavia dal 1524 al 1528, in Raccolta di cronisti e documenti storici lombardi inediti (Milan: 1857), tomo II, pp.209–210; Jean Giono (Franco Pierno, trans.) *Il disastro di Pavia*, (Milan: Ed. Settecolori, 2023),.146–154.
8 P. da Sandoval, *Historia del Emperador Carlos V*, tomo IV (Madrid: Madoz, 1846), p.144; G. Passero, *Historie* (Naples: Vincenzo Maria Altobelli, 1785), p.316.

bell towers, and with churches without crosses. There is no cross in the whole city, which gives a Protestant view of the work.

Behind the city, in the background, is the Ticino River with the Gavellone tributary, which together form the eyot of the same name. All waterways are crossed by wooden bridges. The image below is my copy of a detail of the eastern part of Pavia, beyond the castle. It should be the Santa Maria in Pertica gate, the one attacked by the Sieur de Bussy, still bearing the signs of the assault. In front of the round bastions is the French line with cannon protected by gabions and, between them, the moat. Inside the moat, are numbers of ladders to climb the bastions or to descend into the moat, in which there are a large number of dead. Behind the bastions, the city walls and buildings are damaged or have collapsed from artillery fire. It is an effective representation of a siege, dramatically accentuated by a hanged man hanging from a high tower.

Pavia from the north, from an engraving by Wolf Huber. Copy by the author.

The French Try to Divert the Course of the Ticino and Send an Army Against the Kingdom of Naples

Although King Francis had a number of pieces of artillery, he realised that taking Pavia would be difficult due to the enemy's courage and his own chronic lack of gunpowder. Given the considerable loss of soldiers in recent assaults, he convened a council of war to discuss the options.

It was thus decided to deploy sappers to dig trenches and create embankments to bring the infantry closer to the walls and later to emplace cannon and dig mines. In addition, the Duc d'Alençon proposed to divert the course of the Ticino River, which flanked a good part of city walls to the south. This side of the city walls was older and weaker than others, and the Duc thought that, without the protection of the river at its base, it would have been easier to take.

Jean Giono explains how this difficult work, which began on 20 November, was accomplished. A little further west of San Lanfranco, at the height of the village of Chiozzo, there was an old canal that flowed into the Gravellone River. There, the French sank boats loaded with stones and built a barrier of rocks and earth over it. Then, they reinforced the dam with timber, skins and oiled canvas and anchored it to the bottom with lead. Slowly part of the water of Ticino began to pour into the Gravellone, but due to heavy rain the barrier gave way during the night, and the dam had to be rebuilt. After six days of torrential rain, the water washed away the entire dam, and the idea was abandoned.[9]

The besieged had to face different hardships. The landsknechts protested because they had not received the promised wages and clothes for the winter. On 22 November, tired of waiting, they threatened to leave the city. De Leyva decided to use his own silverware to make coins bearing his name. When this proved insufficient, the city council borrowed money from the patrician and noble citizens and woollen clothes from the merchants, momentarily solving the problem.

Although the landsknechts had been paid, there were still desertions among the army. A German and a Spanish soldier were caught while trying to leave the city and de Leyva had them posted in the front of his army to make an example out of them, according to Giovio, and he added that there was a rumour about the Graf Hohenzollern, commander of the Germans, who intended to pass over to the French side, flattered by the King's promises. When de Leyva heard the rumours, he invited the German commander to dinner and poisoned him. Later, de Leyva claimed that Hohenzollern had died from overdrinking. Guicciardini and Sandoval also

---

9   P. Giovio, *Vite del Gran Capitano e del marchese di Pescara* (Bari: Gius, Laterza & Figli, 1931), pp.161–162.

wrote about this fact, but some historians have doubted the treason and poison story and asserted that Hohenzollern died of natural causes.[10]

While these things were happening in Pavia, Pope Clement VII, concerned about the long war, sent two of his ambassadors – Gian Matteo Giberti, Bishop of Verona, and Niccolò Schonberg, Archbishop of Capua – to King Francis and the Imperial captains to negotiate peace. The ambassadors proposed a truce and that each of the two contenders keep the cities and lands held at that time. However, the King disagreed since he hoped to take Pavia. The besieged were also against it, as they were waiting for Imperial help, and so the negotiations failed.

King Francis, the Pope and Venice held another negotiation, but this meeting was kept secret. The two Italian states promised not to help Charles V, and in exchange, the King of France would protect the Venetians and attack the Kingdom of Naples – a too-powerful neighbour for the Church's taste.

In addition, Francis hoped that an attack would force Viceroy de Lannoy to leave Lombardy to defend Naples. To this end, in December 1524, the King sent an army south under the command of John Stewart, Duke of Albany.[11] The duke set out at the head of 200 lances, 600 light cavalry, 4,000 German and Italian infantry, and a dozen pieces of artillery. He had to join Renzo da Chieri in Emilia, who had another 4,000 infantry, and together they would reach the Papal States to recruit and hire another 4,000 infantry with the help of the Pope.[12]

The French captains disagreed with the King on this reduction in the number of men, although the French Army remained strong. According to the Spaniard, Prudencio de Sandoval, the King had 50,000 men at Pavia, excluding the forces led by the Duke of Albany. Cerezeda disputes these numbers and reports that the French had 36,000 men: 12,000 Swiss, 5,000 Germans, 7,000 French troops, 5,000 Grisons, 7,000 Italians, 1,500 lances and 2,000 light cavalry. Pedro de Guevara also served with the French with 1,000 Spanish infantry.[13]

The number of Italian soldiers had increased in mid-November with the arrival of Giovanni de' Medici, who had left the service of The Emperor and the Duca di Milan because he had not been paid. Giovanni had 400 light cavalrymen and 4,000 infantrymen, of whom 2,000 were arquebusiers. The

---

10 P. Giovio, *Vite del Gran Capitano e del marchese di Pescara* (Bari: Gius, Laterza & Figli, 1931), p.378.
11 John Stewart was Regent of Scotland from 1515 to 1524 and a proponent of the traditional alliance between France and Scotland.
12 Francesco Guicciardini *Storia d'Italia*, tomo III (Milan: Borroni e Scotti, 1843), p.143; R. de la Marck Florange, *Mémoires du Maréchal de Florange*, tome II (Paris: Renouard, H. Laurens, successeur, 1924), pp.190–191.
13 P. da Sandoval, *Historia del Emperador Carlos V*, tomo IV (Madrid: Madoz, 1846),, p.148; M. García Cerezeda, *Tratado de las campañas y otros acontecimientos de los ejércitos del emperador Carlos V en Italia, Francia, Austria, Berbería y Grecia*, tomo I (Madrid: Impresores de Cámara, 1873), p.96.

arrival of this contingent greatly cheered King Francis, who held the Medici in high esteem, and made him stay near his camp in San Lanfranco, on the way to Milan.

Meanwhile, the siege of Pavia continued, with the construction of trenches and continual artillery fire against the city. There was a square tower near Porta Calcinara, south of the city, from which the Imperials fired on the eyot of Gravellone and the camp of Montmorency. Galiot, commander of the French artillery,[14] had a platform built on the banks of the Ticino and from there, he began to counter the enemy fire from the tower. The French continually had a shortage of gunpowder, but this time they were supplied by Giovanni Medici, and so their artillery fire succeeded in demolishing the tower.

What ended badly, however, were the French assaults on the walls. One of these, on the night of 16 December, saw Medici's infantrymen attempt to break in using ladders against the defences. The landsknecht guards, although taken by surprise, thwarted the attack by throwing the Italians down the ladders and hitting them with stones.

Meanwhile, the Duke of Albany had arrived in Fiorenzuola d'Arda, about halfway between Piacenza and Parma. Alerted by scouts and French patrols, Pescara and Lannoy immediately organised a strong contingent of troops in Lodi to intercept the duke. While the Imperials were on their way to Piacenza, Francis I, fearing a defeat of the Duke of Albany, sent Giovanni de' Medici with his troops, flanked by the Swiss led by Jean de Diesbach and the Florange to Albany's aid. Once reunited near Fiorenzuola, the two forces organised an entrenched camp and awaited the Imperial troops.

The Imperials had crossed the Po River, but approaching Fiorenzuola they ended up in the swamps around the river, which hindered their advance. However, the landsknechts took two prisoners and discovered the true destination of the Duke of Albany's Army – the Kingdom of Naples. The Viceroy, like other Imperial captains, thought that the French were only looking for powder, but alarmed by the news, wanted to leave for Naples. However, the Marchese di Pescara convinced him to abandon the idea. Avalos claimed that this war could only be won in Lombardy and that rushing to Naples would mean losing Pavia and the entire duchy, without the certainty of saving the Kingdom from its enemies. Thus, the Imperials sent the Duca di Traietto to Naples with the order to collect as much money as possible and, together with Ascanio Colonna and the nobility of the Kingdom, organise the defence. Then, the Imperials took the road back to Lodi; crossing the Po River gave them some trouble, and they lost several men to the snow and the wear and tear attacks of the Swiss and the Medici. As many as 2,000 dead, according to Jean Giono.[15]

---

14 Galiot de Genouillac, Sieur d'Assier, *Grand Maître d'Artillerie*.
15 Jean Giono (Franco Pierno, trans.) *Il disastro di Pavia*, (Milan: Ed. Settecolori, 2023), pp.163–165 ; R. de la Marck Florange, *Mémoires du Maréchal de Florange*, tome II (Paris: Renouard, H. Laurens, successeur, 1924),.pp. 199–203.

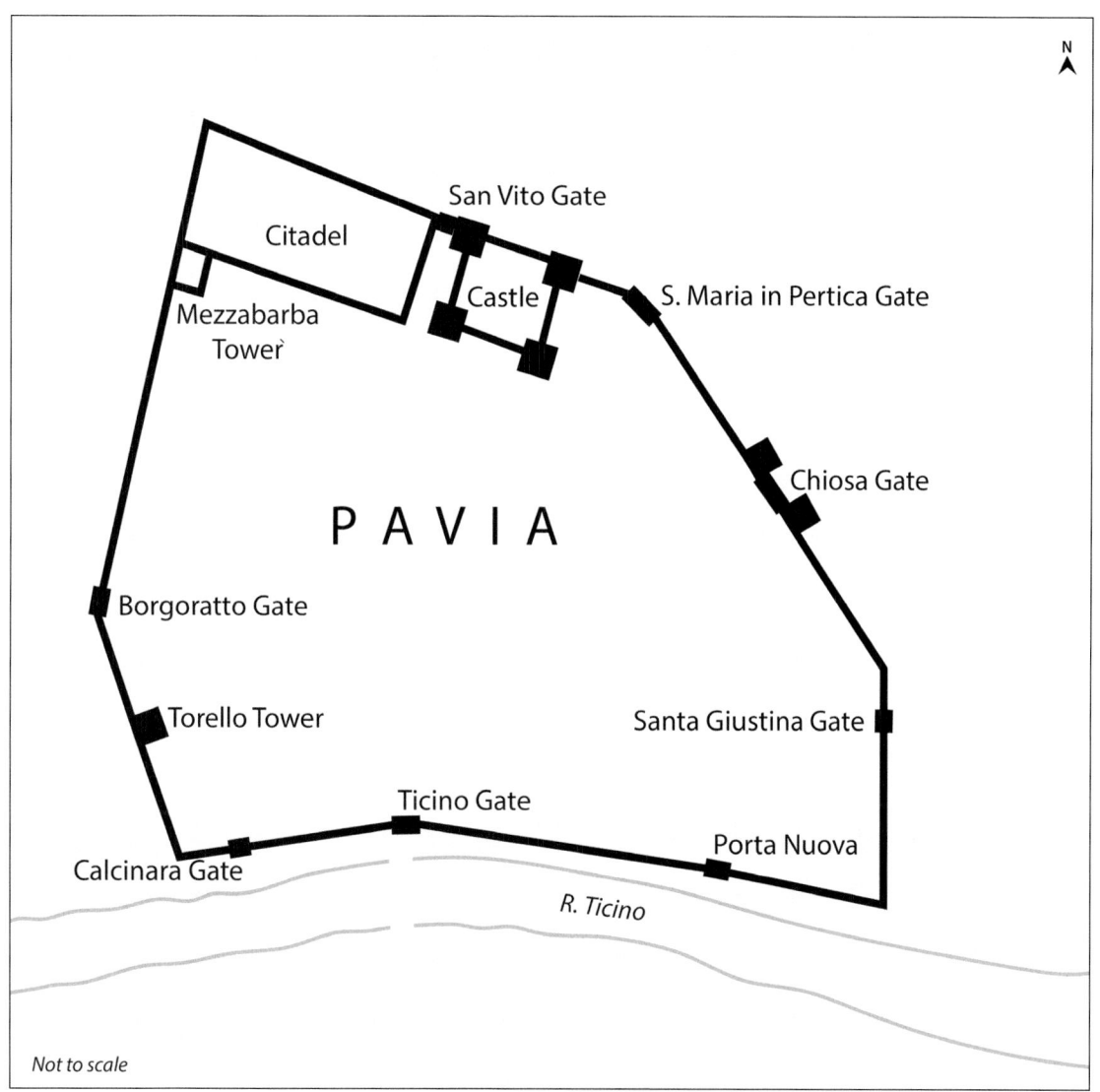

The city gates of Pavia.

De' Medici, the Swiss and the French contingents returned to the camps near Pavia, while the Duke of Albany continued towards the Papal States. The duke passed through Reggio and entered Tuscany through Garfagnana, arriving in Lucca and then Siena, where he imposed taxes in both cash and provisions for his army. He proceeded slowly and arrived in Rome only on 13 February 1525, where the Pope received him with honours. After the news of the defeat of Pavia and the capture of the King, he would return to France without ever reaching Naples.

Taegio writes that, on 23 December in Pavia the soldiers raised their voices about the lack of pay. This time, they were paid partly with the money made available by the canons of the Duomo and partly with the silverware of the university, used to mint more coins. Still, in the city, there was a general shortage of goods.

On Christmas Eve, a messenger arrived with over 40 letters from the Imperial captains, including Duca Sforza, the Viceroy of Naples, Duc de Bourbon and the Marchese di Pescara. In these letters, they promised to free the city no later than 12 January. This news brought happiness and comfort to the besieged soldiers and population. It was not Taegio who reported this, but an anonymous chronicler from Pavia. In his chronicle, he reports the events almost daily, giving details omitted by Taegio. Often, however, the chroniclers report different dates, and in any case, the two share the tendency to exaggerate the efforts of the besieged. In the first days of January, the Duca di Ferrara sent 130 mules loaded with powder to the French camp, closely escorted by Giovanni Medici. With this ammunition, on 3 January, the French bombed the walls on two sides of the city; to the west against the Torello Tower and to the east against the towers of Porta Chioza, which stood between Porta Giustina and Porta Santa Maria della Pertica. The following day, they continued firing until one of the towers of the Chioza gate collapsed, but at night, the citizens of Pavia managed to close the breach, making the assault impracticable.

Then, the French targeted the already-damaged Torello Tower; Taegio writes that the cannon shot 320 cannonballs of 100 pounds each against this tower. Finally, half of the tower came down, but it did not crumble. Instead, it fell intact, resting on the walls and making the assault even more difficult. This fact is confirmed by the anonymous chronicler, and both chroniclers cite the event as a prodigious miracle of the Almighty.

On 7 January, the bombardment resumed against the same targets. The French had a good artillery park in Pavia with 55 cannon, 32 of which were siege guns. Thanks to this strength, they destroyed another tower at Porta Chioza, and the same night, the men of Giovanni de' Medici stormed the walls but were repulsed once again.[16]

---

16 F. Taegio, Rotta e prigionia di Francesco primo re' di Francia sotto Pavia l'anno 1525. Composta dal Taegi, e dal latino tradotta dal Cremonese Cambiago (Pavia: 1655), pp.37–39; A. Bonardi, L'Assedio e la battaglia di Pavia. Diario inedito (Pavia: Poulailler,1895), pp.8–9.

On 9 January, at midnight, the French stormed a bastion in the eastern part of the city. One force tried to climb the walls using ladders, while others aimed at the embrasures with crossbows and arquebuses. The Spanish and Germans defended the bastion for three hours, repelling the assault but suffering nine deaths among the landsknechts and six among the Spaniards, as well as many wounded. Still, Taegio writes that when dawn came, the citizens of Pavia saw with satisfaction that numerous enemies lay dead in the moat and under the bastion.

On the same day, two French prisoners said that the King no longer intended to take Pavia by assault, which had proven unsuccessful so far, but preferred to besiege the city. He had been told that there was a great famine in the city, which made him hope for an early surrender. Taegio confirms the famine and reports that Pavia lacked hay and many horses died of hunger and the little barley that remained was reserved for the strongest horses. In the stables, some horses ate mud or wood out of hunger, but sometimes they even nibbled the manes and tails of the other horses. The anonymous chronicler of Pavia recounts the lack of food and carefully lists the remaining provisions:

> We have wine for 15 days, wheat and cheese for two months, but there is no meat. There are some chickens for an écu each and peacocks for four ecus each. Donkey meat costs five soldi a pound, and horse meat costs four soldi and is much requested. Wine is worth two ducats per brenta [wine vat], wheat six lire per sack. You can find some eggs at 16 soldi each and lard at 40 soldi a piece.'

The accuracy of this list suggests that this anonymous chronicler was – as Bonardi who published his chronicle at the end of the nineteenth century, suggests – a civilian food merchant. Still, this list suggests that, unlike animals, humans – or rather, the wealthy and the military – were not starving at the time.[17]

---

17   A. Bonardi, L'Assedio e la battaglia di Pavia. pp.8–9; F. Taegio, Rotta e prigionia di Francesco primo… pp.40–41.

8

Bourbon Returns from Germany with Reinforcements

In those days, Bourbon returned from Germany with reinforcements. Some chroniclers report that he arrived in Lodi on 10 January, others on 14 January. According to the sources, he had 10,000 to 12,000 landsknechts under the command of Georg von Frundsberg assisted by Marck Sittig von Ems and Jacob von Wernau, with captains Urban von Landeck and Albrecht von Freiberg. There were also some Swabian nobles: Friedrich von Ems, Veit Vehinger von Glurns, George Stral, Hans von Stamm, Heinrich Flizinger, Philipp von Landeck, Hans von Bibrach, Daniel von Werth and Kaspar von Waldsee. At the time, some German nobles often fought alongside the landsknechts, even Emperor Maximilian joined them in battle in their pike square.

The cavalry formed by men-at-arms from Burgundy and Upper Austria was led by Graf Nikolaus von Salm with the noble Merander Fraf von Ortemburg, Lasla Graf von Haag, Johann Graf von Virneburg, Sebastian Losenstein, Nicolaus Fleckenstein and many others. The cavalry numbered around 500 men. Frundsberg reports that they were 2,000 strong, probably also counting their camp followers or the light cavalry. Finally, there were a dozen artillery pieces with the army.[1]

The landsknechts of Pavia protested again in the middle of the month about their non-paid wages. Taegio writes that this time Leyva paid them with money borrowed from the wealthiest citizens. A few days later, however, two Spanish soldiers from Lodi managed to enter the city with 3,000 ducats, putting the accounts in order.

Later, there were various sorties against the French camp. On 23 January, several Germans left for the eastern part of the enemy lines and killed 60 Swiss, without a loss. On 25 January, it was the turn of 20 Spaniards who

---

1   F. W. Barthold, *Georg von Frundsberg und das teutsche Kriegshandwerk zur Zeit der Reformation* (Hamburg: Perthes, 1833), pp.272–274.

BOURBON RETURNS FROM GERMANY WITH REINFORCEMENTS

went out to the west, where they killed many artillerymen and captured four arquebuses.

The war continued even outside Lombardy. Francis I learned of an Imperial expedition to Liguria. In that area, the city of Genoa was in the hands of the Imperials, while Savona was held by the French. Even the Genoese noble families were split: the Adorni had sided with Charles V, and the Fieschi with Francis. The Fieschi warned the King that an Imperial fleet with 6,000 to 7,000 men under the command of Don Hugo de Moncada, Viceroy of Sicily, was about to raid French-held Varazze. This town on the Ligurian Coast and located between Savona and Genoa, was surrounded by weak walls and had only a small garrison of infantry. According to Florange, the King of France sent Michel Antoine, Marchese di Saluzzo, with 400 men-at-arms, 6,000 Italian infantry and a few bands of Spaniards to help Varazze. Other chroniclers report that Saluzzo was already in Savona with an army, and a fleet led by Andrea Doria.

Starting from Genoa, Moncada arrived in front of Varazze on 24 January, while Saluzzo was approaching by land. After a bombardment with the cannon of the ships, the Imperials docked and began the difficult approach towards the castle. Some 7,000 Spanish and Genoese infantrymen had disembarked, but Saluzzo's infantry intercepted and attacked them with the help of Varazze's garrison. On the ships, there were another 10,000 men – sailors and infantry – who, however, failed to aid Moncada because of the arrival of the French Fleet commanded by Doria. Doria's galleys put the Spanish Fleet to flight, while on land the Imperials could not stand up to the French assault. When Saluzzo's men-at-arms arrived, the infantry on the land scattered and fled. Many Imperial soldiers died, and 2,000 were taken prisoner. Moncada was also captured along with the brothers Giorgio and Barnaba Adorno.

The Marchese di Saluzzo, to please the King, sent Moncada with the gentlemen of his entourage also taken captive, to France.[2]

King Francis was satisfied with this victory since, in the same days, the imperials had captured the stronghold of Sant'Angelo. This important location was six miles from Lodi and 24 from Pavia, a perfect placement to intercept imperials' supplies to and from Lodi.

According to Garcia Cerezeda, on 27 January, the imperial army left Lodi with 800 lances, 700 light cavalrymen, 14,000 Landsknechts, 5,000

---

2 Francesco Guicciardini *Storia d'Italia*, tomo III (Milan: Borroni e Scotti, 1843), p.149; R. de la Marck Florange, *Mémoires du Maréchal de Florange*, tome II (Paris: Renouard, H. Laurens, successeur, 1924), pp.197–199; M. García Cerezeda, *Tratado de las campañas y otros acontecimientos de los ejércitos del emperador Carlos V en Italia, Francia, Austria, Berbería y Grecia*, tomo I (Madrid: Impresores de Cámara, 1873), pp.112–113; P. Giovio, *Vite del Gran Capitano e del marchese di Pescara* (Bari: Gius, Laterza & Figli, 1931), pp.382–383; Vincenzo Promis, 'Memoriale di Gio. Andrea Saluzzo di Castellar dal 1482 al 1528' in *Miscellanea di storia italiana* (Turin: dalla Stamperia Reale, 1869), volo VIII, pp.593–594.

Spaniards, 4,000 Italians and artillery. These forces headed for Marignano, making the French believe that their target was Milan.

Warned of the enemy's movements, King Francis moved his camp from San Lanfranco to San Paolo, where La Palice was. That way, the king was closer to the enemy army and, in the event of an attack, could quickly help Milan or more easily defend the camp, if the imperials turned towards Pavia. Charles Valois, Duke of Alençon, arrived in San Lanfranco with the rearguard in place of the king.

However, the enemy's march towards Milan was a trick devised by Pescara. The following day, the army changed direction and arrived at Sant'Angelo, skirting the Lambro River to the south.

The town, defended by solid walls, was under the command of Pirro Gonzaga, brother of Federico da Bozzolo, with 200 cavalrymen and 800 infantrymen. The bulk of the Imperial army stopped and set up camp two miles from Sant'Angelo, while Pescara with the infantry, the Spaniards, the Italians and the artillery went under the city. In the night, he prepared the attack and placed the defence gabions and artillery in front of a square tower.

Paolo Giovio is the only chronicler who gives an accurate description of the assault on Sant'Angelo. The following day, on 30 January, Avalos ordered to aim at the tower front and flanks, where it connected to the city walls. After a couple of hours, the tower collapsed, and a large breach opened in the walls. Pescara ordered the moat in front of the walls to be filled with fascines and led the assault in person. Galvanized by his presence, the Italian and Spanish infantrymen competed to climb the breach. Many were wounded in the assault and some died, hit by the arquebuses of Pirro's infantrymen. Marco Antonio Capece, a Neapolitan nobleman, died of a blow to the chest. Pescara was also shot in the ribs, but the blow was miraculously stopped by his jacket, while another shot grazed his leg. As he often does in the biography of Hernando d'Avalos, Giovio does not miss the opportunity to exalt the commander's courage and, as in this case, allude to his divine protection.

The tower was taken and the defenders retreated into a trench prepared as a second defence behind the walls. Giovio writes that, however, Pirro's men began to feel discouraged after the hundred deaths suffered at the hand of Spanish arquebuses and cannons. Thus, the marquis' second attack made them finally give in and flee; their commander took refuge in the fortress with other nobles.

The victorious imperials sacked Sant'Angelo, while Pescara sent the Marquis del Vasto to negotiate the surrender with those who had taken refuge in the fortress. Gonzaga surrendered at the discretion of the winners. The imperials took many provisions, wheat and wine, as well as about 700 horses and all the weapons of the defeated. Chronicler Juan de Oznayo, who was with the troops of Marquis del Vasto during the war, wrote that the enemies had lost 700 infantrymen, 300 light cavalrymen and 50 men-at-arms between dead and prisoners. In addition to Pirro Gonzaga, the nobles Pirio Locque, Emilio Cavriana and three sons of Phoebus Gonzaga were

BOURBON RETURNS FROM GERMANY WITH REINFORCEMENTS

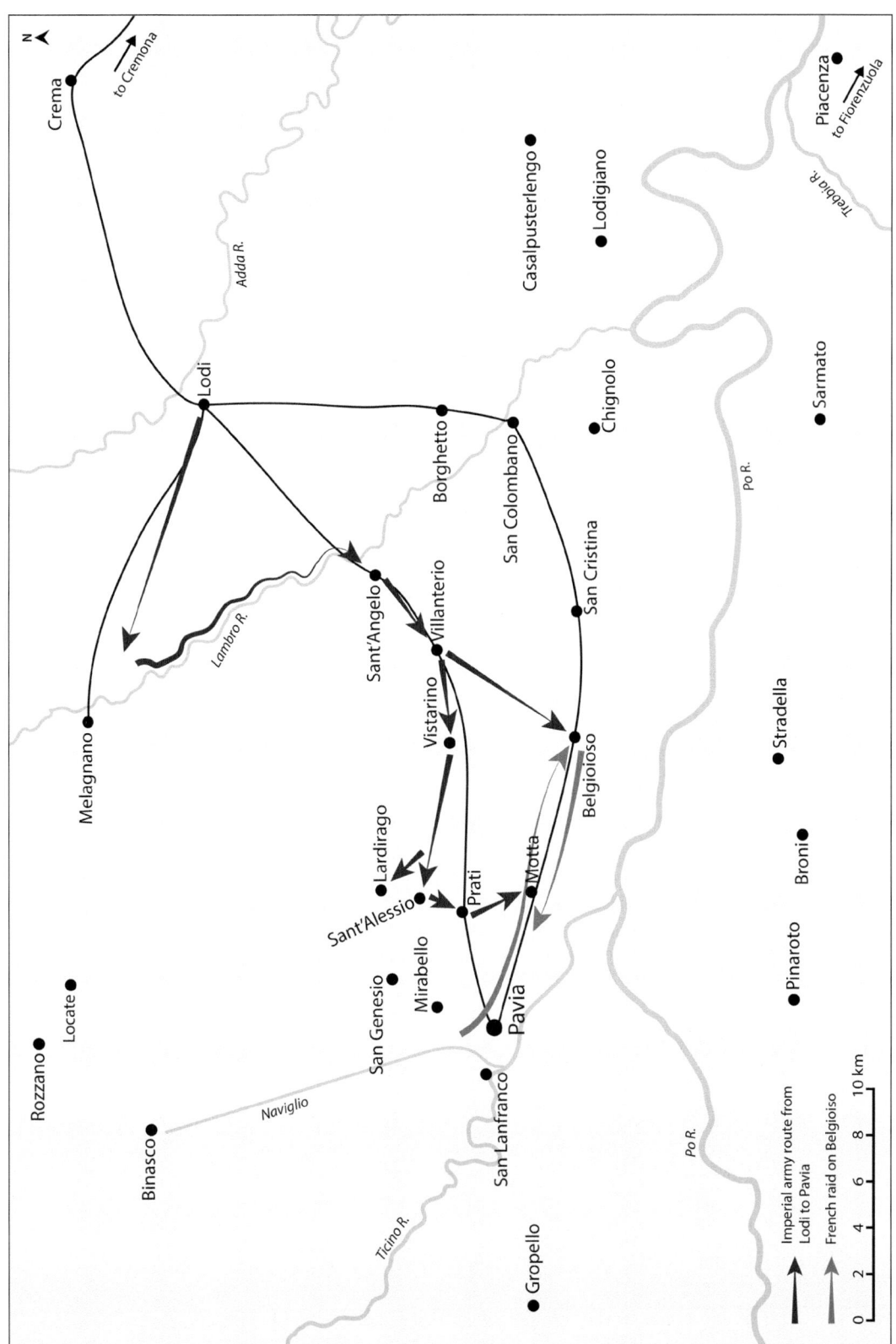

The advance of the Imperial Army from Lodi and the French counter-attack.

taken prisoner. They were all sent to the fortress of Pizzighettone, while the soldiers were released without weapons or horses on condition that they did not fight against the emperor for two months. According to the anonymous chronicler, the French in Sant'Angelo had lost 2,000 men, twice as many as Gonzaga's forces. However, these numbers are clearly biased narratives[3].

Alerted of the loss of Sant'Angelo, King Francis ordered the wall of the Park to the east — where the five monasteries were located — to be reinforced with additional shelters, and he deployed there most of the artillery. Then, he had the wall of the Park broken down in three places, so that the cavalry — it was mostly stationed in the Park — could easily pass through. With these wide gates, the army could quickly pass from San Lanfranco in the west to San Lazzaro in the east.

In addition to Sant'Angelo, the imperials had taken Belgioioso. Thus, the king summoned a captains council to plan a strong response against the imperial army. Most of the captains wanted to leave a small array around the city and give battle to the enemies with the whole army — this was the opinion of La Tremoille, La Palice, Florange, Montmorency, Galiot, Sanseverino and many others. However, Bonnivet and the king disagreed. They organized an expedition with part of the gendarmes led by Bonnivet, Tremoille, La Palice and the king himself to attack Belgioioso. With them, there were the light cavalrymen of Giovanni Medici and 3,000 Swiss of Florange. On the morning of 31 January, the king of France chose to make this bet. Bonnivet put a department of imperial heavy cavalrymen to flight, and Medici captured Belgioioso and chased the Landsknechts who defended it. Rather than fighting, there were insignificant skirmishes that, thanks to the imperial artillery, had the only result of letting the besieged people of Pavia understand that aid was on its way. After a couple of hours of skirmishes, the king, satisfied with the good day, ordered to return to the quarters, abandoning Belgioioso to the imperials.

On 1 February, the imperials resumed their approach to Pavia, first occupying Vistarino and the next day Lardirago and Sant'Alessio, four miles from Pavia. On 3 February, they moved to Prati and placed their accommodations from there to Motta and in a forest next to San Lazzaro. They were two and a half miles from Pavia and half a mile from the defences and trenches of the French camp. The two armies were so close that they targeted each other with artillery. Giovio writes that a large iron ball hit the Bourbon's housing, fortunately without causing any deaths since the council had just finished and the captains had left.

Meanwhile, in Pavia, de Leyva had freed the Santa Maria in Pertica and Porta Nuova gates, which had previously been obstructed, so that he could

---

3 F. Guicciardini, cit. pp. 155-156; P. Giovio, cit. pp. 393-396; R. de la Marck Florange, cit. pp. 206-208; M. García Cerezeda, cit. pp. 113-115; F.W. Barthold, cit. p.280; F. Taegio, cit. pp. 43-44; A. Bonardi, cit. p.12; J. De Oznajo, Batalla de Pavia y prison del rey de France Francisco I, in Coleccion de documentos inéditos para la historia de Espana, Madrid 1846, volume IX, p. 442.

BOURBON RETURNS FROM GERMANY WITH REINFORCEMENTS

leave in case of battle. (See the illustration on page 56.) On the morning of 6 February, there was a big skirmish between the French and the Imperials at Ca' dei Levrieri, east of the Park. Bourbon had placed batteries of cannons there. On the other side, there was Torre del Gallo with the ducal chicken coop, where the Swiss and Savoyards had built a fort and defended it with four pieces of artillery. From these two points, the two armies bombarded each other almost daily, often leading to skirmishes.

Taegio writes that de Leyva took advantage of the French engaged with the Imperials of Ca' dei Levrieri to send Captain Francesco di Ponte out of Porta Nuova with 100 light cavalrymen. Di Ponte was accompanied by the Spanish captains Beregano and Bracamonte with their infantrymen and four more companies of Germans. They headed west to San Salvatore, where they found and attacked four companies of Grisons. The Grisons made little resistance and fled, and the Spaniards pursued, killed and captured many of them. Taegio writes that, unlike the Spaniards, the Germans did not take prisoners and plundered all their quarters, taking away calves, sheep and game. In addition, they took 10 barrels of powder and two pieces of artillery.

The captain of those Grisons, Paolo della Selva or Sylvia[4], was not in the camp but had gone to the king to ask for his soldiers' wages. When he learned of the defeat of his men, he asked Francis for help, who gave him 400 men-at-arms and two companies of infantrymen. However, his rescue attempt was useless. Upon his arrival in San Salvatore, the enemies had already returned safely to Pavia.

No French chronicler reports this fact. On the imperial side, other than Taegio, the anonymous chronicler reports something, although slightly different. The imperials attacked with 50 light cavalrymen and 2,500 infantrymen a band of 500 Grisons; 50 of them were cut into pieces and the others threw themselves into the Ticino River to save themselves, but most of them drown. The anonymous adds that the loot was grand, rich in wagons, crates, tents, clothes and prisoners. In addition, the Imperials captured two falconets and a larger cannon, thrown into the river for its weight. They also took 15 barrels of powder and 168 horses. A third version comes from chronicler Cerezeda: according to him, the Grisons in San Salvatore were 2,500 with three pieces of artillery and they resisted sternly. Still, 600 of them died, with only a few losses on the Spanish side. Due to the arrival of the French cavalry, the three pieces of artillery were not brought into the city but thrown into the ditch under the walls[5]. The three chroniclers report the same feat of arms, victory and loot, it is the numbers of artillery pieces, enemies and casualties that vary.

---

4   Captain Dietingen von Salis.
5   F. Taegio, cit. pp. 47-48; A. Bonardi, cit. pp. 14-15; M. García Cerezeda, cit. pp. 103-104.

9

Sorties and Skirmishes Under the City Walls

Over the following days, the exchange of fire and skirmishes between the two armies continued. At the end of each clash, the soldiery returned to their respective camps which, being close to each other, were constantly under enemy fire. Cannon fired day and night causing many deaths on both sides. King Francis and his nobles went every day to Florange's camp to watch the Imperial forces' camp. The King watched the artillery duels and drank wine with his captains. One day, however, the enemies noticed his presence and pointed their guns at him, firing two shots that killed about 30 of the Swiss around the King but without hitting him.

There were also skirmishes; the following are some excerpts from various chronicles. Florange writes that, on 10 February, Bourbon sent the Spanish to attack the Swiss guns deployed near the five abbeys. The first attack failed but the second, made at night, succeeded completely. The Spanish occupied the position of Captain Marc-Antonie Métivier and massacred 400 Swiss. According to Florange, however, the French counter-attack massacred many more Spanish – about 1,000!

The Spaniard García Cerezeda recounts a night time attack against a bastion of the park by the Marchese di Pescara, together with Captain Don Alonso de Córdoba. They led 1,000 Spanish infantry and landsknechts wearing white shirts for the encamisada, in order to recognise their friends in the dark. They killed 500 Frenchmen from newly arrived reinforcements. The Imperials threw nine large cannon, that they could not carry off, into the ditch under the bastion. Alerted by the clamour, King Francis, who was in Mirabello that night, immediately sent help, but it arrived when the enemy had withdrawn without suffering losses.

However, these two night attacks by Florange and Cerezeda seem to be the same episode.

The anonymous chronicler mentions another sortie from the city on 12 February. Taking advantage of an artillery duel, 500 infantry and 50 light cavalry attacked the Swiss of Santa Pollinare, looting, and killing 50 Swiss but losing only 10 of their own men.

SORTIES AND SKIRMISHES UNDER THE CITY WALLS

These are just some events reported in the contemporary documents.

On 16 February, there was a major clash with Giovanni Medici's men. The relevant sources give a mix of dating, but even more controversial is actual event and its consequent actions. That day, de Leyva led 100 men-at-arms out of the west gate[1] with 50 other cavalry led by Captain Francesco da Ponte and Gracimandrico with two cannon in tow. De Leyva and Matteo Beccaria followed them with two squadrons of Spanish infantry led by captains Beregano and Bracamonte, and three companies of Germans led by Captain Eitelek von Reischach – 1,500 infantry in total. The formation marched along the waterway towards San Lanfranco and arrived at the Campese farmhouse, surrounded by a high wall, where there were five infantry bands of Giovanni de' Medici. The captain was absent at the time because he was with his cavalry. That day, Medici was in Stradella south of Pavia – Sanudo reports this in his Diarii – where he joined with the light cavalrymen of Captain Zucaro,[2] from whom he took 60 cavalry and some prisoners.

The Castle of Pavia
(Author's collection)

Taegio writes that, in Campese the Italian infantry fought valiantly, and many died in the battle on both sides. The Imperials, however, broke the wall at three points with their guns and entered, killing all of the defenders except for two captains, who begged for their life on their knees. Taegio concludes by saying that the Italians suffered a loss of 500 men, lost four Colours, many oxen, provisions, weapons and a lot of wine, all of which was brought back into Pavia in triumph. According to the anonymous chronicler, the Italians lost 600 men, four Colours and 42 oxen, while the attackers lost about 12 men. These disproportionate losses between attackers and defenders – the latter were protected by a wall – is striking. Even more exaggerated is Cerezeda's report; the Spanish chronicler writes that Giovanni lost 800 men and as many more were wounded, while the Spanish only had six wounded. In a nutshell, according to these losses, Giovanni's bands must have been utterly defeated. Even Sanudo reports

---

1   It should be the Borgoratto Gate.
2   Second in command of the light cavalry under Sant'Angelo.

THE BATTLE OF PAVIA 1525

300 dead among the Italians in Campese, while Jean Giono, somewhat parochially, mentions only 20 casualties among Giovanni's men.

Giovio writes that upon his return, Giovanni Medici was angered and pained and vehemently scolded the French of Alençon, who had not intervened to help his men, although they were near Cascinazza. Then, he swore revenge on the enemy and, two days later, he drew de Leyva's soldiers out of Pavia with a stratagem provoked by a few Italian cavalry. The Imperials chased them, falling into the ambush prepared by Giovanni. Giovio writes that many Imperial soldiers were killed, and the others fled back into the city. Florange, on the other hand, says that 300 to 400 Imperial troops were killed, the same number as the Italian casualties two days before. However, during this fight, the Italian captain suffered a severe wound – an arquebus shot in the knee. Immediately rescued and brought back to camp, he had to leave the siege.

Giovanni Medici's knights chase women and children. (Artwork by Massimo Predonzani)

SORTIES AND SKIRMISHES UNDER THE CITY WALLS

The two chroniclers of Pavia, however, describe this last event differently, and Medici does not get an honourable mention. Firstly, they disagree on the date: one cites 18 February, and the other 20 February. They report that, in the middle of the day, many women, children, some soldiers and other poor people came out of the western gate, perhaps 2,000 people in all. These people went into the gardens to collect herbs and wood or just to get some air, but Giovanni de' Medici, who wanted to avenge the assault on his men in Campese, saw them. The captain arrived with 300 cavalry and a large body of infantry and charged with great fury at these poor people, who fled. Taegio writes that many pregnant women and children were cruelly killed. The Anonymous reports 30 deaths; seven of them soldiers but the rest women, boys and the elderly. Then, he concludes: 'This fact caused more shame than honour to the captain, but fate punished his evil deed. When he withdrew, he took an arquebus shot to the leg.'

Antonio Bonardi, who published the chronicle of the Anonymous, focuses on this unfortunate fact and compares it with other writings that, instead, report the fight to have happened against soldiers and not defenceless civilians. Still, Bonardi states that the two chroniclers, being in Pavia, were certainly more informed than others, who often had to rely on second-hand sources. Thus, he concludes with a criticism on the general opinion that saw the Italian leader as a warrior with a noble soul.[3]

The Marchese di Pescara was asked to issue a pass in Giovanni's name so that he could be taken to Piacenza, where he could receive better care. Although de' Medici had turned his back on him two months earlier, the Marchese willingly granted the pass. Giovio writes that this deprived the French camp of a valuable and indomitable soldier. In fact, since his arrival in Pavia, there had been numerous mentions in the chronicles of his clashes with the enemy.[4]

Over the same days, the French lost yet another asset: the Grisons infantry. The Duca di Milan, Francesco II Sforza, had sent his captain Gian

---

3   For the sources about these skirmishes: R. de la Marck Florange, *Mémoires du Maréchal de Florange*, tome II (Paris: Renouard, H. Laurens, successeur, 1924), pp.215–220; M. García Cerezeda, *Tratado de las campañas y otros acontecimientos de los ejércitos del emperador Carlos V en Italia, Francia, Austria, Berbería y Grecia*, tomo I (Madrid: Impresores de Cámara, 1873), pp.116–117, n. p.103; A. Bonardi, L'assedio e la batalla di Pavia. Diario inedito (Pavia: Poulailler, 1895), pp.17–21; F. Taegio, Rotta e prigionia di Francesco primo re' di Francia sotto Pavia l'anno 1525. Composed by Taegi.., (Pavia: 1655), pp.51–53; M. Sanudo, I Diarii (Venice: M. Visentini, 1893) tomo XXXVII, pp.623 and 626; Jean Giono (Franco Pierno, trans.) *Il disastro di Pavia,* (Milan: Ed. Settecolori, 2023), pp.178–179; P. Giovio, *Vite del Gran Capitano e del marchese di Pescara* (Bari: Gius, Laterza & Figli, 1931), pp.403–405.

4   I have devoted several pages to this individual in my previous book: M. Predonzani & V. Alberici, *The Italian Wars*, volume 3: *Francis I and the Battle of Pavia 1525* (Warwick: Helion & Company, 2022), pp.109–114. In these pages, I focus on the term Giovanni 'delle Bande nere', a name given to his company after the death of the condottiero.

Giacomo Medici[5] against the territory of the Grisons, who had managed to occupy the city of Chiavenna and its fortress. This place was strategically important for the control of the mountain passes into Switzerland and the State of the Three Leagues, that is, the country of the Grisons. Frightened of a possible attack, the Grison infantry decided to return to their homeland, even refusing the offer of double pay to stay. The chronicles report that 5,000 Grisons left, and some Swiss who were in the League with them.[6] This happened about five days before the Battle of Pavia.

Seeing his army decrease in number, King Francis requested help from Saluzzo who was in Savona. Saluzzo sent him 2,000 Italian infantry who, however, were intercepted by Gaspare del Maino. Cerezeda writes that del Maino came from Alessandria and surprised the King's reinforcements as they crossed the Bormia River, which flows south of the city. The victorious Sforza troops captured the main captains, many Colours and a large amount of plunder.

Having lost this help, the King sent for Trémoille. The captain came from Milan with his men-at-arms and most of the infantry, who had been besieging the castle held for months by the soldiers of Sforza. Teodoro Trivulzio and Louis de Chandio remained in Milan with a few thousand infantrymen. Then, Francis ordered Montmorency, who was in Borgo Ticino, to join him with his best cavalry and infantry and leave the others in the quarters under captain Clermont. Other than the constant decrease in his forces, King Francis was also caught between the city and the enemy army, playing the role of besieger and besieged at the same time.

---

5   This officer, called Medeghino, belonged to the modest Milanese Medici family, which had no ties to the more famous Medici of Florence.
6   P. Giovio, *Vite del Gran Capitano e del marchese di Pescara* (Bari: Gius, Laterza & Figli, 1931), pp.405–406; M. Du Bellay, *Memoires* (La Rochelle: 1573), p.207; Blaise de Monluc, *Commentaires et lettres* (Paris: Mme Ve J. Renouard, 1864), tome I, p.70; R. de la Marck Florange, *Mémoires du Maréchal de Florange*, tome II (Paris: Renouard, H. Laurens, successeur, 1924), p.241; F. W. Barthold, George von Frundsberg und das teutsche Kriegshandwerk zur Zeit der Reformation, (Hamburg: Perthes, 1833), pp.294–295; M. Jähns, *GeschichtlicheAufsätze* (Berlin: Verlag von Gebrüder Paetel, 1903), p.262.

10

Preparing for the Battle

The King summoned the council of war and proposed to send part of the cavalry behind the enemy in San Colombano, south of Sant'Angelo, to cut off the Imperial Army's supplies. The rest of the army would focus on besieging Pavia. He trusted in the arrival of reinforcements from the Pope and the Venetians and the success of the Duke of Albany in Naples. Still, the senior captains disagreed with his plan. Among others, Maréchal Jacques de La Palice proposed to lift this tedious siege and move the whole army to Binasco, halfway between Pavia and Milan. The Maréchal believed that the Imperial landsknechts would return home, once freed from the siege and left without pay and food. The French were aware of the lack of money in the enemy army, and that only the Spanish and Italians had promised to remain for a month without pay; that month had passed. Moreover, La Palice was convinced that moving to Binasco would favour aid in arms and food from France and friendly states.

Trémoille, Sanseverino and René of Savoy, experienced captains, liked the idea but not Bonnivet, who was greatly trusted by the King. The admiral described the plan as acceptable only to old captains in their seventies devoid of fighting vigour. Giovio, who reports the speeches of the council, suggests that the admiral expressed his opinion more moderately and not in these almost offensive words towards those captains. He exhorted them to stay at Pavia with courage and without fear, because it was customary for the French to win when the King was with the army.

King Francis was uncertain. He considered the opinions of his captains but, in the end, followed Bonnivet's advice, considering it closer to his warrior spirit.[1]

Meanwhile, the Marchese di Pescara painstakingly prepared the Imperial Army for the upcoming battle. He tirelessly went to the guards and to the ramparts to try to find a weak point in the opposing lines. He saw that a direct attack on the King's quarters was not feasible, at least

---

[1] P. Giovio, *Vite del Gran Capitano e del marchese di Pescara* (Bari: Gius, Laterza & Figli, 1931), pp.407–412.

THE BATTLE OF PAVIA 1525

not without heavy losses. Thus, he planned to enter the park by breaking through the wall and reaching Mirabello by a short detour. Giovio writes that, at that time, Mirabello was used for birding and hunting but now housed part of the cavalry and a mishmash of merchants and officials. Strategically speaking, it was an excellent location, almost in the centre of the park, and the flat terrain made it suitable for an infantry and cavalry manoeuvre battle. Furthermore, holding Mirabello closed the way to Milan to the French, and made it easier to send reinforcements to the city.

The Imperial captains, especially Bourbon and Lannoy, approved this plan. The marquis ordered the preparations and, on the night of 21 February, sent some patrols beyond the northern wall of the park to gain intelligence on the enemy. The French surprised and killed many of them, but the survivors reported that the wall on the side of Porta Pescarina was undefended. So, the marquis decided to open some breaches on that side.

Clarification regarding the precise entry point of the Imperials into the park is essential. Firstly, most chroniclers do not say where the wall was broken but only mention the fact that it was, and those who do, cite two different places. Grumello and Antonio Numaio write that the Imperials went to Due Porte, east of the wall. Sandoval, du Bellay, and Capino de Capo, instead, write that the breach was made on the side of the Certosa, towards Milan, others towards Mirabello. The shortest way would have been from the North, as Pescara wanted. Looking at the map of the route from Porta Pescarina to Mirabello is free, with the only obstacle being the Vernavola stream. On the east side, Due Porte, on the other hand, is further away and

Pavia, after the painting preserved at the Royal Armouries in Leeds. 1, The bridge over the Ticino. 2, Church Bell Tower. 3, Count Lodron's lodgings. 4, Signal tower. 5, Marchioness de Viresol's lodgings. 6, Cathedral. 7, De Leyva's lodgings. 8, Blocked gate. (Artwork by Massimo Predonzani)

gives way to the largest forest in the park. Historians tend to favour the version of the entrance being near Porta Pescarina, which I agree with.[2]

After identifying the point of attack, Pescara sent Captain Arriano to Antonio de Leyva to advise him of his intentions and to be ready with the army to leave the city. At the right time, he would be warned by two cannon shots.

Arriano left one night and, taking the long way around, arrived on the other side of the city. There, he met some French sentries, but he managed to deceive them by using the white cross of the French Army instead of the Imperial badge. Thus, posing as a soldier of Giovanni Medici, he managed to enter the city. De Leyva informed Pescara that the messenger had arrived safely by lighting a beacon on a tower.

On the night of 23/24 February, the Imperial Army left the Ca' dei Levrieri camp and took the road to Lardirago. To confuse the French, Pescara had ordered three captains – Luis Viacampo, Gayoso and Juan de Herrera – to go to different places with their companies, near the French shelters in Torre del Gallo, and alarm them by the noise of weapons and drums. Then, to make the French believe they were retreating, he ordered the waggons with the baggage, escorted by a body of light cavalry, to take the road to Lodi.

Meanwhile, the Spanish sappers had been sent forward and arrived at the wall at midnight. They were two companies, the pikemen led by Captain Salsedo and the arquebusiers led by Captain Santa Cruz. Santa Cruz's men had large beams with iron-reinforced tips, poles and picks. Giovio writes that the baked-brick wall of the park was sturdy, and the sappers struggled all night to break it.

---

2   In M. Predonzani, & V. Alberici, *The Italian Wars*, volume 3: *Francis I and the Battle of Pavia 1525* (Warwick: Helion & Company, 2022), we analysed the entrance from Due Porte.

11

The Beginning of the Battle of Pavia

Towards dawn, Salsedo and Santa Cruz managed to breach the wall in three points. Capino da Capo writes that they made three large holes, two near Mirabello and the third half a mile away, towards Milan.[1] The breaches were 60 paces wide, although some chronicles report that there was only one breach.

The first to pass through was Alfonso d'Avalos, Marchese di Vasto, with a vanguard of 2,000 landsknechts and 1,000 Spanish. Pescara had ordered them to reach and occupy Mirabello quickly. Behind them followed the entire army, and Juan de Oznajo accurately listed its composition:

The heavy cavalry was divided into three bands: in the vanguard was Viceroy Charles de Lannoy with 200 lances; in the centre, Bourbon with 300 lances (Oznajo also mentions del Vasto with them); in the rearguard was Hernando de Alarcón with another 200 lances. Overall, the heavy cavalry counted 700 lances, which roughly coincides with the data Cerezeda and Guicciardini report. However, it should be noted that the two chroniclers recorded those figures when the army was stationed in Lodi. However, these numbers are still much lower than those reported by Schertlin de Burtenbach of 1,000 Imperial men-at-arms, and Caspar Wintzerer of 2,000 men-at-arms.[2]

Then, Oznajo lists 500 light cavalrymen led by Ferrante Castriota, Marchese di Sant'Angelo, however, the actual number was certainly twice

---

1   C. de Capino, 'Relazione del 28 febbraio 1525' in *Bollettino della Società pavese di storia Patria* (Pavia: 1907), tome 7, p.215.
2   J. de Oznajo, 'Batalla de Pavia y prison del rey de France Francisco I' in Coleccion de documentos inéditos para la historia de Espana, (Madrid: Imprenta de la Viuda de Calero,1846), volumen IX pp.454–457; M. Jähns, *GeschichtlicheAufsätze* (Berlin: Verlag von Gebrüder Paetel, 1903), p.251; J. Baader, 'Die Schlacht bei Pavia, nach dem Bericht eines Augenzeugen' in Anzeiger fur kunde der deutschen vorzeit, November 1868, p.350.

THE BEGINNING OF THE BATTLE OF PAVIA

that. Then came the infantry: 6,000 Spanish infantrymen under Pescara, 12,000 Germans led by Georg von Frundsberg and 2,000 Italian infantrymen under captains Caesar of Naples and under Papacoda – according to the accounts, they also had seven guns with them. The rest of the artillery remained at Ca' dei Levrieri.

The total number of Imperial infantry recorded by Oznajo, thus, reaches 20,000 men, including the 3,000 infantrymen of the vanguard of del Vasto. Schertlin reports 17,000 men, while Wintzerer writes of 24,000 infantry in total. This is Pescara's army before the fighting started, to which we must add the about 5,000–6,000 infantry under de Leyva in Pavia.

Calculating the strength of the French Army is much more difficult because the relevant primary sources were written by Imperial chroniclers, who exaggerated the number. For example, Neapolitan chronicler Giuliano Passero reports that the King of France had a total of 70,000 men; Oznajo, copied by Sandoval, mentions 67,000 men; Schertlin reduces the number to 39,000, and Cerezeda writes of 35,000 soldiers. However, all of these figures are exaggerated, and as such unreliable. Certainly, at the beginning of the campaign, the French Army was more numerous than the opponents – about 40,000 men – but 9,000 men had left for the Kingdom of Naples with the Duke of Albany, and several thousand were stationed in Milan as a garrison, and about 5,000 Grisons returned home shortly before the final battle. It is also important to consider that there were a number of movements within the army and also the arrival of various reinforcements, as well as casualties, wounded and deserters. These factors reduced the number of the French Army and make it difficult to determine its size.

However, starting from the figures published by Guicciardini during the siege and comparing them with those of scholars Paolo Pieri and Jean Giono, I hypothesise these numbers for the French Army before the battle: 1,200 lances, 1,500 light cavalry, 8,000 Swiss, 5,000 Germans, 4,000 French and mercenaries, 4,000 Italians and about 50 artillery pieces.[3]

Returning to the battle, it must have been 6 in the morning, when the Imperial Army followed the vanguard and began to enter the park. The soldiers were ordered to wear the encamisada, that is, a white shirt over their clothes and armour. Some chroniclers report that large white paper squares were sewn on jackets, or landsknecht clothing. They also had red bands or crosses over their shirts as a field sign. According to Frundsberg's report, only the vanguard wore white shirts.

The signal was given – two cannon shots – to warn those in Pavia that the action had begun. That year the winter had been cold and it was a foggy day, with the ground icy and muddy.

---

3 Francesco Guicciardini *Storia d'Italia*, tomo III (Milan: Borroni e Scotti, 1843), p.152; P. Pieri, Il Rinascimento e la crisi militare italiana, Einaudi editore, 1952, p.558; Jean Giono (Franco Pierno, trans.) *Il disastro di Pavia*, (Milan: Ed. Settecolori, 2023).204–205.

The Imperial vanguard had driven back some bodies of French troops guarding the wall, who fled and gave the alarm – they were commanded by the Genoese, Greco Giustiniano. The French had been on high alert for a long time. Roche du Maine, Sieur de Tercelin, had already patrolled the park that night with his light cavalry, aware of the noise made by the Spanish beyond the wall on the east side.

After midnight, Florange had moved from the Torre del Gallo camp, alerted by the enemy's attempt to break down the wall to the north. Florange himself wrote in his chronicle that he took with him the Seigneurs de Isselstain and de Gisse, 3,000 Swiss and four culverins to move into the woods between the camp and the Two Gates to understand the origin of that noise, although not without difficulty due to darkness and fog.[4]

Meanwhile, King Francis was warned that Imperial troops had entered the park and he alerted the entire army. The King had left Mirabello on 19 February to set his main camp in Cascina Repentina. He had most of his men-at-arms and their captains with him: Bonnivet, Trivulzio, La Palice and Trémoille, as well as part of the cavalry and the light artillery, all of the landsknechts, and 2,000 Picard and Italian infantry.

The rest of the army was at Torre del Gallo, with the heavy guns, 1,000 Swiss and the rest of the French infantry, under the command of Galiot de Genouillac. At the camp of the five abbeys, were the remaining Swiss, about 4,000 men, while in San Salvatore and Borgo Ticino were about 5,000 French and Italians and the men-at-arms of Alençon to block any sorties by the besieged.[5]

While the Imperial Army formed up after crossing the park wall, Alfonso d'Avalos, with his infantry and a force of light cavalry, rushed towards Mirabello and, after fording the Vernavola River, joined the King.

In the castle, there were few soldiers but a large number of civilians – merchants, sutlers, camp followers, sick soldiers, magistrates, women – and a large amount of provisions. The Imperials slaughtered all those who failed to escape and sacked the city. There, they also found Cardinal Girolamo Aleandro, Pope Clement's Ambassador to the King of France, and took him prisoner.[6]

It was now daylight, but the fog persisted, making visibility difficult. The entire Imperial Army had entered the park: the right wing consisted of Pescara's Spanish infantry, the centre of the landsknechts, and the left wing of the Italians with the artillery. From what chroniclers recount, the heavy cavalry was divided into three groups: the Viceroy on the right of the Spanish, Bourbon near the landsknechts, and Alarcón in the rearguard.

---

4   R. de la Marck Florange, *Mémoires du Maréchal de Florange*, tome II (Paris: Renouard, H. Laurens, successeur, 1924), p.223.
5   F. Taegio, Rotta e prigionia di Francesco primo re' di Francia sotto Pavia l'anno 1525. Composta dal Taegi… (Pavia: 1655), p.57.
6   P. Giovio, *Vite del Gran Capitano e del marchese di Pescara* (Bari: Gius, Laterza & Figli, 1931), p.418.

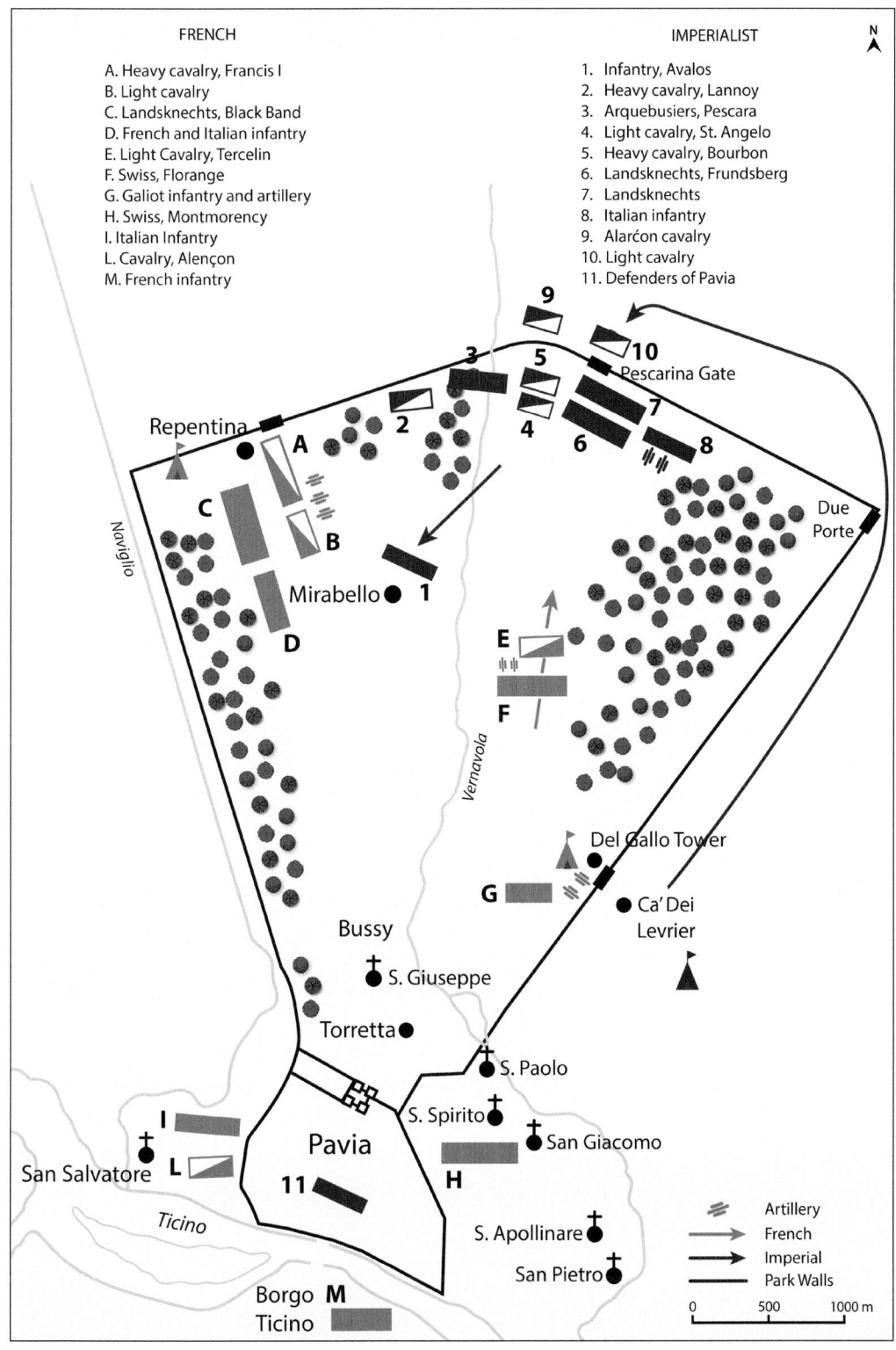

Map of the battle.

The light cavalry was also divided into three groups: Sant'Angelo was with the main army, another group was with del Vasto, and the third group had remained beyond the breach. Finally, Pescara and his guard were with the Spanish infantry. This army was directed southwest, towards Mirabello to join with del Vasto.

On the Imperial left wing, small clashes had already begun between the Imperial light cavalry and that of La Roche du Maine.

On the left wing, was the Italian infantry, commanded by Cesare Maggi and Papacoda, of 2,000 Neapolitan infantry supported by 600 Spanish arquebusiers and artillery pulled by oxen. The cannon slowed them down and got stuck in the mud and were left behind by the bulk of the troops. According to Paolo Giovio, while trying to free the artillery, the infantry was attacked by Federico di Bozzolo and Philippe de Chabot, Sieur de Brion, and their men-at-arms with some light guns. Other sources report that the French cavalry were supported by the Swiss of Florange, who charged at the Italians after firing their culverins. Maggi's infantrymen defended themselves well but were cut down by the combination of artillery, cavalry and infantry and had to retreat into a nearby forest, where they were slaughtered. Giovio writes that Sebastiano Squarcia and four entire companies of infantry were killed. From the writings of the same chronicler, an infantry company consisted of 200 men. The French cut off the legs of the oxen pulling the guns and spiked the pieces, making them useless. Sources vary even in the number of artillery pieces: for some, they were four pieces, for others five, seven or even fifteen. Thanks to the help of the Imperial cavalry, Cesare Maggi and the survivors managed to disengage, finding refuge among Frundsberg's German units.[7]

Detail of the Battle of Pavia by Ruprecht Heller, with the French attacking the Imperial cannons. This captures perfectly this action. (Courtesy of Nationalmuseum, Stockholm)

7   P. Giovio, *Vite del Gran Capitano e del marchese di Pescara* (Bari: Gius, Laterza & Figli, 1931), p.421; J. de Oznajo, 'Batalla de Pavia y prison del rey de France Francisco I' in Coleccion de documentos inéditos para la historia de Espana, (Madrid: Imprenta de la Viuda de Calero,1846), volumen IX, p.459; J. Da Nocera, 'Relazione' in D. Testi, La batalla de Pavia, Fuentes historiograficas y epistolares del siglo XVI, (Madrid: Ministerio de Defensa 2024), p.64; L. Contile, De fatti di Cesare Maggi da Napoli, (Milan: 1565), pp.15–16; R. de la Marck Florange, *Mémoires du Maréchal de Florange*, tome II (Paris: Renouard, H. Laurens, successeur, 1924), p.225; A. Varillas, Histoire de François I (Paris; 1685), tome I, p.403.

THE BEGINNING OF THE BATTLE OF PAVIA

Paolo Giovio writes that both sides witnessed the defeat of Cesare Maggi, and that King Francis rejoiced in anticipation of his victory. On the contrary, Pescara immediately sent dispatch riders to Bourbon, Frundsberg and Lannoy with the order to advanced towards Mirabello and engage the enemy.

Del Vasto left Mirabello as well and was also on his way to join the main army. Meanwhile, a body of Imperial light cavalry attacked the landsknechts of the Black Band, who repulsed them and they fled.

At that point, the French artillery opened fire against the Imperial Army. These were the cannons that the King had with him in the main camp at Cascina Repentina – the accounts speak of about 30 pieces pulled by horses to move them easily. Some chroniclers report that it was the great artillery master Galiot de Genouillac who ordered the guns to open fire, but actually these were in Torre del Gallo, too far from battle to be effective. Moreover, from their position they risked hitting the men of Florange and Tercelin.

Jean Giono writes that by this time it had to be 8 in the morning, the fog was thinning and the Imperial forces headed towards Mirabello offered their support against the French. There are various different opinions about the damage inflicted by the French fire. According to du Bellay, it was deadly: it opened gaps in the Imperial ranks, sending arms, heads and pieces of armour flying. Max Jähns, who reports the account of Schertlin de Burtenbach, captain of the landsknechts in Pavia, writes that the Imperials lost 1,000 men to the bombardment in a short time. Frundsberg, on the other hand, declares that the French guns did little damage to his landsknechts, as he ordered them to lie on the ground to avoid the fire. Pescara did the same, writing in his report that he ordered the Spaniards and Germans to take shelter in the depressions in the ground. According to Giovio, the cavalrymen of Lannoy and Alarcón suffered most of the losses, until they had to retreat behind a peasant house to take shelter. Finally, Taegio writes that, 'many Imperial soldiers were killed.'[8]

King Francis witnessed from afar the casualties being caused by his guns, and seeing the enemy troops in disarray, he ordered the attack, impatient to confront the enemy. The King was at the head of the men-at-arms, all the nobles and a strength of about 900 lances. At this period, the French lance consisted of six men: the man-at-arms, two archers, a coustiller (light cavalryman) and two pages or valets. Leaving aside the last two non-combatants, the King would have had about 3,600 French cavalry.

---

8   M. Du Bellay, *Memoires* (La Rochelle: 1573), p.211; M. Jähns, *Geschichtliche Aufsätze* (Berlin: Verlag von Gebrüder Paetel, 1903), p.271; 'Reports on the battle of Frundsberg and Pescara' in D. Testi, La batalla de Pavia, Fuentes historiograficas y epistolares del siglo XVI, (Madrid: Ministerio de Defensa 2024), pp.48 and 51; P. Giovio, *Vite del Gran Capitano e del marchese di Pescara* (Bari: Gius, Laterza & Figli, 1931), p.422; F. Taegio, *Rotta e prigionia di Francesco primo re' di Francia sotto Pavia l'anno 1525. Composta dal Taegi, e dal latino tradotta dal Cremonese Cambiago* (Pavia: 1655), p.57.

The sources report that the Sieur de La Palice, Henri d'Albert (King of Navarre), François Comte de Saint-Pol and Amiral Bonnivet were in the vanguard with the King. Some sources also mention Montmorency as being with them, while others say that he was still in San Lanfranco. The French preferred way of fighting was the charge of the heavy cavalry, whose shock power and impact was considered decisive in battle. However, the Battle of Pavia demonstrated that this concept was outdated…

The French guns stopped firing so as not to hit the King's men, and even the infantry, the landsknechts of the Black Band and the Swiss on the right wing remained behind, unable to support the cavalry charge. According to Giovio – and he is not alone – it was this choice that determined Francis' defeat.

On the other hand, the Imperial cavalry immediately charged against the French. They were the 500 light cavalry (ginetes) of Ferrante Castriota, Marchese di Sant'Angelo, and some men-at-arms. Some chroniclers write that the men-at-arms were under Bourbon, others that they were under Viceroy Lannoy, but the most believe them to have been under both commanders. In total, there had to be 500 lances – about 2,000 Spanish, Neapolitan and Burgundian cavalry, the latter belonging to Nikolaus von Salm. Added to the ginetes of Castriota, there were 2,500 Imperial cavalry against 3,600 French. The Imperial cavalry were heavily outnumbered.

The French cavalry were superior not only in number but also in weight of weapons, horses and skill in jousts. The Emperor's cavalry was thrown into disarray at the first impact. King Francis killed Sant'Angelo with a thrust of his lance. According to chronicler Alfonso de Valdés, on the other hand, it was an estoc thrust into the open visor of his helmet that killed him.[9] This event is shown on the first Capodimonte tapestry, which is analysed below. The light cavalry of Sant'Angelo scattered.

Another contingent that suffered the French fury was that of von Salm's Burgundian men-at-arms, although there were also Austrians and Bavarians among them. They lost two Standards, and some sources write that the King himself killed one of the standard bearers. One of these Standards bore the badge of Burgundy of two crossed ragged staffs, the other could have displayed the Imperial Eagle.[10]

The King also wounded Jean d'Andelot of Franche-Comté in the cheek with a sword blow. An anonymous chronicler of Villersexel wrote that only 20 cavalrymen of the company of the Bailly d'Aumont, also of the Franche-Comté, survived.

---

9   All chroniclers agree that Castriota was killed by the King except Jacomo da Nocera. According to him, the Castriota was killed by Swiss soldiers. See M. Sanudo, I Diarii (Venice: M. Visentini, 1893) tomo XXXVIII, p.12.

10 Gabriel Pita Da Veiga Joyanes & Joaquin Pita Da Veiga Subirates, 'La prison del rey de France: consideraciones sobre la captura de Francisco I y sus verdaderos protagonistas' in *Revista de Historia Militar*, no. 12 (2020), pp.160–162.

Paolo Giovio writes that the French were especially eager to find the traitor Duc de Bourbon. In order not to be recognised, Bourbon had given his emblems to his comrade Pompèran, while he was dressed as a simple cavalryman. Hugo of Cardona, lieutenant of Pescara, was also killed by the King's guard, while the Lannoy and Bourbon squadrons were pushed back a long way and had to take shelter in the woods near Porta Pescarina. Jean Bouchet, who wrote the biography of Trémoille, says that in this clash the Imperials lost 300 men-at-arms. Taegio, instead, simply mentions that there were 'many Imperial casualties.' Oznajo emphasises the prowess of the Imperial commanders, such as Bourbon and Lannoy, in this clash. Then, he mentions Alarcón, who unsaddled a Frenchman but was unsaddled in return. Left without a horse, he would have been overwhelmed, but some Spanish arquebusiers intervened to help him. Among them, there was a Jorge de Sevilla, who killed a French cavalryman and gave the horse to Alarcón. (cf colour plate B, 'Cardone falls from his horse'.)

After defeating the enemy cavalry, the French stopped to let the horses rest. King Francis, satisfied, turned to Thomas de Foix, Seigneur de Lescun, and said with joy, 'Monsignor, now I want to be called Lord of Milan.'[11]

---

11 Other sources on the French cavalry charge: P. Giovio, *Vite del Gran Capitano e del marchese di Pescara* (Bari: Gius, Laterza & Figli, 1931), pp.422–423; R. de la Marck Florange, *Mémoires du Maréchal de Florange*, tome II (Paris: Renouard, H. Laurens, successeur, 1924), pp.226–227; Jean Bouchet, 'Panégyric du chevallier sans reproche, Louis de La Trémoille' in Mémoires pour servir a l'Histoire de France, tome quatrieme (Paris: J.L.F. Foucault, 1837) p.477; A. de Valdés, 'Relazione sulla battaglia' in D. Testi, La batalla de Pavia, Fuentes historiograficas y epistolares del siglo XVI, (Madrid: Ministerio de Defensa 2024), p.74; J. de Oznajo, 'Batalla de Pavia y prison del rey de France Francisco I' in Coleccion de documentos inéditos para la historia de Espana, (Madrid: Imprenta de la Viuda de Calero,1846), volumen IX, p.462; A. Gautier, 'Personaggi della Franca Contea alla battaglia di Pavia del 1525' in Pavia 1964 n. 1 & 2-3, pp.21 & 24.

12

The First Tapestry

As mentioned in the introduction, I have used the Capodimonte tapestries to describe the battle. These works of art accurately represent – or so it is believed – the events and people involved in the clash, other than illustrating interesting details of the battlefield and the city of Pavia. In this chapter, I will try to refute their accuracy with the support of historical sources. Moreover, one must not forget that these tapestries were made in Flanders.

First Tapestry: 'Advance of the Imperial Troops and Attack of the French *Gendarmerie* Led by Francis I' (See Plate I.)

First tapestry (Reproduced with the permission of the Ministero della Cultura, Museo e Real Bosco di Capodimonte)

THE FIRST TAPESTRY

This tapestry depicts various moments of the initial clash. Above: the entrance of the Imperial Army into the park. Below: King Francis I with his men-at-arms; on the right side, the combat between the two bodies of cavalry and, in the corner below, the Spanish wearing their shirts for the *encamisada*.

The King's group, larger than the other soldiers, is in the foreground to underline its importance, although it contrasts visibly with the grandeur of the Imperial Army, represented as the winner. The troops move out of a forest on the left: first, the infantry with numerous arquebusiers, followed by the pikemen. They are German landsknechts, with their characteristic dress: caps with slashing, puffed sleeves and thigh coverings, and an exaggerated codpiece. They carry two-handed swords and the characteristic sword called a *katzbalger*, about 80cm long with a wide blade and a distinctive S-shaped guard.

The numerous firearm armed men among the landsknechts, notoriously represented with few firearms in iconography, made me think initially of Pescara's Spanish arquebusiers. Almost all artwork on the Battle of Pavia, such as this one, are of Flemish-German craftsmanship and depict the infantry dressed in landsknecht fashion. Thus, not only Germans and Swiss but also Spanish, French and Italian soldiers are represented with the same style of clothing. Indeed, the landsknechts had influenced the fashion of

Spanish arquebusiers. (Reproduced with the permission of the Ministero della Cultura, Museo e Real Bosco di Capodimonte)

the time across Western Europe. Italians, French, Spaniards and other Europeans all added slashing to their clothes, but they did it less frequently than the Germans and also maintained their national fashions.

The Spanish arquebusiers, by contrast, are those on the far right who wear white shirts over their clothes. They differ from the previous ones for their tighter sleeves and longer swords with straight cross-guard.[1] However, their clothes also remain landsknecht in style.

To return to the Imperial Army, the infantry carry Colours with the red St Andrew's cross – called the Cross of Burgundy – one of the Imperial identification badges that foot soldiers also sported on their clothes. There are four Colours, three with the red cross on a field striped white and yellow, yellow and blue and yellow and green. The fourth, on the left, displays an almost-black St Andrew's cross on a red field.

Probably, these colours were to differentiate the infantry bands (see colour plate G.2 'Landsknecht Colours from the Tapestries').

On the right of the infantry, the Imperial cavalry is depicted with the park wall in the background. The men-at-arms carry heavy lances and wear full armour with robes or tabards on top – most with the yellow or golden livery, but others with the red or crimson livery. They wear white and red shoulder scarves as a recognition sign. Some cavalry sport only one scarf, while others wear two. Amidst the cavalrymen, is *Connétable* Charles de Bourbon, with his family coat of arms on the front barding of his horse: three golden lilies on a blue field with a red bend (azure, three fleurs-de-lys or, a bend gules). BOURBN on his horse's reins is another recognition sign. Identifying personalities by such inscriptions is a constant in the Capodimonte tapestries. Over his armour, Bourbon is wearing a yellow skirt – his livery colour, as Brantôme and Sanudo mention in their texts.[2] The cavalrymen in yellow around him are his company, and the soldiers following him are his personal guard. They carry a shorter spear than others – with a wide iron tip, reminiscent of the tip of a winged spear. They wear sallets and their plumes recall the colours of Bourbon's panache – red and yellow.

To analyse the cavalry Standards. Two are large and stand out from the rest but are devoid of colours and symbols. Due to the tapestry's poor state of conservation, in the 1998 restoration, the restorers replaced these two Standards with a neutral fabric.[3] Thanks to previous publications, such as Casali's, we know the original colours of these Standards. The first square Standard on the left had yellow, red and white vertical bands, which were

---

1   I noticed this difference between German and Spanish infantrymen thanks to, Luigi Casali, *Gli arazzi della battaglia di Pavia nel Museo di Capodimonte a Napoli* (Pavia: Edizioni ViGiEffe, 1993), pp.15–16.
2   Pierre Brantôme, *Oeuvres complètes*, tome I (Paris: R. Sabe, 1864), p.286; M. Sanudo, *I Diarii* (Venice: M. Visentini, 1889), tomo XXV, p.413; M. Sanudo, *I Diarii* (Venice: M. Visentini 1890), tomo XXIX, pp.78–79.
3   N. Spinosa, *Gli arazzi della battaglia di Pavia* (Milan: Bompiani, 1999), p.110.

THE FIRST TAPESTRY

Knights of Bourbon. (Reproduced with the permission of the Ministero della Cultura, Museo e Real Bosco di Capodimonte) See Plate P for great detail in colour.

the colours of the Habsburg Emperor, Charles V. This livery is also on the other large triangular Standard. Its lower part was white with a double yellow and red border, and in the white lower, towards the staff, was a Cross of Burgundy.

Behind these Standards, still visible, are smaller ones of various sizes. The field of one square Standard is divided into stripes of The Emperor's three colours. Just above, another one displays the Pillars of Hercules in gold, and in the middle, there is a gold Cross of Burgundy with gold flint steels. The Pillars were the impresa of Charles V, usually accompanied by the motto *Plus Ultra* (Further Beyond). On the other hand, the St Andrew's cross with the steel is a Burgundian symbol inherited by the Habsburgs – firstly, by Emperor Maximilian I, then by his nephew Charles V. On a final note, the fringes on the edge of the Standards are in the colours white, red and gold.

On the far right, there is another Standard similar in field and fringe colours, with the golden Pillars and the Cross of Burgundy. The only difference is its split-tail fly.

The last Standard displays the impresa of *Connétable* Charles Bourbon, the winged stag. The Standard has a red or crimson field; the Stag is a natural colour with white wings and a cartouche bearing a motto that is not

THE BATTLE OF PAVIA 1525

Bourbon's Standard. (Reproduced with the permission of the Ministero della Cultura, Museo e Real Bosco di Capodimonte)

visible. Bourbon primarily used the motto *Esperance*.[4] The Standard has a white and gold fringe.

These Standards are in the middle of a myriad of cavalry spears, many of which have banners or pennons on top. These insignia are of various shapes and colours. Many have stripes in the three colours of The Emperor or the red St Andrew's cross over these colours. Others display the white cross on a red or yellow field otherwise they are all red, all white or all yellow. The artist clearly wanted to highlight The Emperor's colours and emblems in these insignia, apart from the winged stag. The same thing happens with the French insignias. However, in battle at the time, cavalry flags usually displayed the colours and impresa of the various captains.

Immediately below the Imperial cavalry on the right, the scene represents a fight between two bodies of cavalry. The French men-at-arms led by King Francis clash with the Imperial vanguard of light cavalry. The Imperial vanguard, which attacks to the right, wears armour and helmets similar to burgonets, and the horses have only harnesses – unlike the opponents' horses with caparisons. To the far left of the group, there is the fight between the King and Ferrante Castriota, Marchese di Sant'Angelo and Commander of the Imperial light cavalry. On the bridle of the Sant'Angelo's horse, there is an inscription – MAR SAN ANGE – and the Marchese is about to be overcome by the King.

To focus on the composition at the bottom of the tapestry, representing the most relevant group: the King with the French cavalry. These figures are the ones fighting against Castriota's cavalry. The King is recognisable by the three lilies of France on the front barding of his horse. Over his armour, he wears a silver surcoat and has tall plumes on his helmet of white, red and

---

4 For other Bourbon's mottos see: M. Predonzani & V. Alberici, *The Italian Wars*, volume 3: *Francis I and the Battle of Pavia 1525* (Warwick: Helion & Company, 2022), pp.94–96.

THE FIRST TAPESTRY

tenne.⁵ A detailed analysis of the King's dress can be found in the chapter describing the tapestry depicting his capture.

Alongside the King, there is a cavalryman with his visor raised, sword in hand. He has a peculiar impresa on his tabard and horse barding depicting several clouds with golden rain. Unfortunately, the cavalryman does not have any other identification symbols. He is depicted in the clash and in the tapestry of the King's capture, where he dies from a blow at the throat by two enemy cavalrymen. His closeness to the King in the composition of the tapestry and his death have led various scholars to think that he may be Guillaume Gouffier de Bonnivet, *Amiral de France* – a trusted friend of the King. Paolo Giovio writes that Bonnivet saw the French Army fleeing and realised he was to blame for its defeat. So, he raised his visor and met the enemies head on, offering his throat to their blades. More precisely, others say that he threw himself with open arms against the landsknechts' pikes, thus finding his death.⁶ Be it swords or pikes, however, the difference is that the cavalryman's impresa does not correspond to that of the *Amiral*. Bonnivet used the anchor, the dolphin and the bosun's whistle, all emblems compatible with his lineage.⁷ The depicted impresa represents straight golden rays descending from blue clouds and among them countless dots or drops. It is a golden rain, symbolically manna, which fed the children of Israel.

Just, Conte de Tournon. (Reproduced with the permission of the Ministero della Cultura, Museo e Real Bosco di Capodimonte)

---

5   For the devices or liveries of Francis I see: M. Predonzani & V. Alberici, *The Italian Wars*, volume 3: *Francis I and the Battle of Pavia 1525* (Warwick: Helion & Company, 2022), pp.76–81.
6   P. Giovio, *Vite del Gran Capitano e del marchese di Pescara* (Bari: Gius, Laterza & Figli, 1931), p.429; M. Jähns, *GeschichtlicheAufsätze* (Berlin: Verlag von Gebrüder Paetel, 1903), p.288.
7   A. Seillier, *Maison Gouffier de Bonnivet in Mémoires de la Société Académique de l'Oise*, Beauvais 1892, Tome XV, p.116; M. Sanudo, *I Diarii* (Venice: M. Visentini, 1890) tomo XXIX, pp.23, 79, 242.

THE BATTLE OF PAVIA 1525

It was the de Tournon who carried this impresa, from a noble family of the Auvergne, as documented by the Flemish humanist Giacomo Tipozio.[8] At the time, Cardinal François II of Tournon was one of Francis I's main counsellors on foreign policy, but he did not participate in the Battle of Pavia, where his brother Just, Comte de Tournon, was killed. Just was adviser and chamberlain to Francis I, lieutenant general in Languedoc, and in 1524, commander of 50 lances.[9] He died in the Battle of Pavia saving the King. Varillas records: '*Le Comte de Tournon abbatu sous son cheval, fut étouffé dans la presse*,' (The Count of Tournon fell from his horse and died crushed by its weight.) Paolo Giovio, on the other hand, wrote that the body was never found, others simply mention him as among the French casualties.[10]

The other three men-at-arms with the King each have their names written on their swords or bridles. The first on the left wears a crimson red skirt over his armour, has a sword in hand, and his horse is protected by a richly worked shaffron and a plate peytral. Scholars have thought this man-at-arms to be Galeazzo da Sanseverino from the name MONESAR on his sword – standing for MONsigneur Ecuyer SARseverin. Since 1896, when Luca Beltrami first mentioned this name in his published list of words woven into the individual tapestries, all publications on this topic have since followed this idea.[11] Identifying this man-at-arms with Sanseverino would be fitting both for his lineage and death in battle, were it not for the name on the sword. The real name is MONTPESAR, as can be clearly see in the enlarged detail below. The line above the O stands for the letter N.[12]

Montpezat (Montpesar). (Reproduced with the permission of the Ministero della Cultura, Museo e Real Bosco di Capodimonte)

---

8   J. Typotii, *Symbola Divina & Humana, Pontificum, Imperatorum, Regum* (Prague:1601), tomus I, pp.45 & 48; C. Paradin, *Devises heroiques et emblems* (Paris:1614), p.66.

9   Michel Pol Potier de Courcy, *Histoire généalogique et chronologique de la Maison Royale de France*, Paris: Firmin Didiot Frères, 1882), tome IX, p.580; J. D'Auton, *Chroniques de Louis XII*, (Paris: Librairie Renouard, 1889), tome I, p.50.

10   A. Varillas, Histoire de François I (Paris; 1685), tome I, p 407; P. Giovio, *Vite del Gran Capitano e del marchese di Pescara* (Bari: Gius, Laterza & Figli, 1931), p.432; P. Charles Fleury, *Histoire du cardinal de Tournon* (Paris: 1728), p.48.

11   Luca Beltrami, *La battaglia di Pavia illustrata negli arazzi del Marchese del Vasto nel Museo Nazionale di Napoli*, (Milan: Publisher unknoiwn, 1896): S. di Giacomo, *I sette arazzi della battaglia di Pavia*, in *Emporium, rivista illustrata d'arte*, (Bergamo: 1897), tomo V, p.306; Luigi Casali, *Gli arazzi della battaglia di Pavia nel Museo di Capodimonte a Napoli* (Pavia: Edizioni ViGiEffe, 1993), p.15; Carmine Romano (ed.), *Art & War in the Renaissance: The Battle of Pavia Tapestries* (New York: Rizzoli International 2024), p.105.

12   I saw the error thanks to high-resolution photographs of the tapestries from the

Thus, the man-at-arms can no longer be identified with the Galeazzo da Sanseverino, but instead with Antoine de Lettes des Pres, Seigneur de Montpezat. He was a Gentleman of the Chamber of King Francis I, and Brantôme describes him as a man-at-arms of the company of *Maréchal* de Foix. According to some, he was captured in Pavia with his King, whom he followed and served in captivity in Spain. He had become his confidante. De Montpezat later served as ambassador to England and distinguished himself in many battles, becoming a *Maréchal* in 1543.[13]

The cavalryman to the right of Montpezat has an M on the crimson harness of the horse and his name on the bridle – unfortunately, it is not completely readable. It reads MONTEP, but the two other letters could be E N, E R or I G. Some studies identify this man as Montpezat – as I thought before I studied the high-resolution photos. Others have identified him as the Sieur de Montpensier. The Montpensier estates located in central France, however, at the time belonged to *Connétable* Charles de Bourbon,

Montepen. (Reproduced with the permission of the Ministero della Cultura, Museo e Real Bosco di Capodimonte)

Capodimonte Museum. I do not know why this has not been noted in another publication, even the most recent Carmine Romano (ed.), *Art & War in the Renaissance: The Battle of Pavia Tapestries* (New York: Rizzoli International 2024) noted this mistake. Perhaps earlier scholars did not have such accurate photos?

13 R. de la Marck Florange, *Mémoires du Maréchal de Florange*, tome II (Paris: Renouard, H. Laurens, successeur, 1924), pp.125, 234 e 238; P. da Sandoval, *Historia del Emperador Carlos V*, tomo IV (Madrid: Madoz, 1846), p.234; Pierre Brantôme, *Oeuvres complètes*, tome V (Paris: R. Sabe, 1867), pp.240–241; F.W. Barthold, *George von Frundsberg und das teutsche Kriegshandwerk zur Zeit der Reformation* (Hamburg: Perthes, 1833), p.343.

THE BATTLE OF PAVIA 1525

and in 1523, after he betrayed the crown of France, it passed to his sister Louise. So that does not seem possible either.

I think this horseman is René de Montejan or Montigend, knight of the King's Order. Alonso de Santa Cruz, instead, believes him to be a court butler. In Pavia, René de Montejan (or Montigend) was wounded in the leg and taken prisoner. He became a *Maréchal* in 1538 for military merits[14]. The name MONTEPEN would be a good fit for Montejan.

The last cavalryman on the right wears a white or beige surcoat decorated with several tassels over his armour. He displays his name on his sword scabbard: POMEREUT. This is Jean Pomereux or Pommereu, Seigneur de Plessys; for some, he was a squire of the King, for others, the master of artillery. He, too, was captured in battle.[15]

Usually, in iconography such as this tapestry, it is logical to think that the men close to the King are the important commanders who distinguished themselves in the fight. However, this is not the case. The four men described in this paragraph are not commanders but nobility from King Francis's court elite who, for various reasons, were close to him – a squire, a butler or a confidante. Cf colour plate C.

Pomereut. Detail of the scabbard. (Reproduced with the permission of the Ministero della Cultura, Museo e Real Bosco di Capodimonte)

---

14 Alonso de Santa Cruz, *Cronica del Emperador Carlos V*, (Madrid: Impr. del Patronato de Huérfanos de Intendencia é Intervención Militares 1920), volumen II, p.99; R. de la Marck Florange, cit. p.238; M. Du Bellay, *Memoires* (La Rochelle: 1573), p.213; P. Anselme, *Histoire genealogiqueet chronologique de la Maison Royale de France* (Paris: 1712), tome I, p.624; Pierre Brantôme, *Oeuvres complètes*, tome V (Paris: R. Sabe, 1867), pp.292–298.

15 Alonso de Santa Cruz, *Cronica del Emperador Carlos V*, (Madrid: Impr. del Patronato de Huérfanos de Intendencia é Intervención Militares 1920), volumen II, p.99; R. de la Marck Florange, *Mémoires du Maréchal de Florange*, tome II (Paris: Renouard, H. Laurens, successeur, 1924), p.238; G. Guiffrey, *Cronique du Roy François premier de ce nom*, (Paris 1860), p.45.

13

The Intervention of the Spanish Arquebusiers

After its victorious charge, the French cavalry was at the woods to the southeast of Porta Pescarina, on ground flooded by the water of the Vernavola Stream. The fight with the enemy cavalry was not over and continued on the peripherals and into the woods against stubborn groups of Imperial cavalry. The landsknechts of the Black Band had fallen far behind and were proceeding slowly. Florange with part of the Swiss was in the eastern corner of the park, but the bulk of the Swiss was still in Torre del Gallo.

The King's heavy cavalry was isolated, and the Spanish arquebusiers commanded by captain Quesada, sent by Pescara to help the Imperial cavalry, attacked them on the left flank. Once again, the sources disagree on the number of these infantry. Paolo Giovio writes that there were 800 arquebusiers and, as the action progressed, they increased in number. According to historians, they reached 2,000 men, including a body of pikemen.

The sixteenth-century historian Pedro Mejía writes that the first volley of fire from the Spanish killed more than 200 men-at-arms. Paolo Giovio writes more realistically that 'after terrible volleys of arquebus fire, they killed a large number of men and horses,' meaning that they fired a number of times. The French, seeing that a tight formation made them more vulnerable, had to divide into smaller groups, but even this was useless. Then, they reformed into a tight formation again and charged the arquebusiers, but the lightly armoured Spanish retreated and dispersed, evading the attack.

Although they were on horseback, the French were hampered by the weight of their armour and harness, and the water-soaked ground made it increasingly difficult for them to move. Meanwhile, other Spanish arquebusiers and pikemen arrived and, as well as surrounding the cavalrymen, crept in between them, firing and attacking them point-blank.

About the effectiveness of the arquebuses, Giovio writes that they were deadly due to their calibre, greater than that of the hand cannons in use at the time. The chronicler writes that the arquebus could pierce not only men-at-arms' armour but often also two soldiers or two horses at a time. Martin du Bellay writes that the Spaniards had arquebuses à croq, that is, with a forked rest, which were particularly heavy and therefore more effective.

However, in the numerous iconographies of the battle, there is no trace of these arquebuses, only representations of the lighter ones. However, these arquebuses are depicted with a long barrel – about one-metre-long – which, according to scholars, would help to increase the velocity and power of the bullet. Oznajo offers another explanation of the lethal effect of the Spanish arquebusiers at Pavia, believing that it was because of the tactic they adopted: 'Now, our arquebusiers in the front line were advised to light two or three matches each to shoot more freely and each carried four or five bullets in their mouths to load more quickly.' Rapidly reloading their weapon would ensure a volume of fire unsustainable to the opposing cavalry. Thus, the role played by the arquebus was certainly fundamental.[1]

Meanwhile, on the right, to the east of the park, Maréchal Montmorency had arrived with 100 men-at-arms and a few thousand infantrymen to help the King. He had moved from San Lanfranco as soon as he heard the cannons fire, but there del Vasto confronted the vanguard and a body of cavalry. François de Scépeaux in his memoirs wrote that Montmorency managed to defeat a band of landsknechts but then the arquebusiers of del Vasto scattered his cavalry. Giovio recalls that in the clash the Maréchal and the Marchese di Vasto duelled for a while. Then, the Italian captain Giovan Battista Castaldo killed Montmorency's horse. The Maréchal fell to the ground and was taken prisoner by captain Herrera.[2]

The sources report the actions that followed differently and at varying times. Some chroniclers say that Florange, seeing his sovereign in danger, urged his Swiss to the aid of the gendarmerie but was confronted by del Vasto, galvanised by his recent victory against Montmorency. Florange managed to defeat the Imperial cavalry but was soon attacked by the Spanish arquebusiers, who targeted the Swiss. The Swiss had no arquebuses with them and had to retreat, abandoning their cannon. 700 or 800 Swiss fell, along with captain Tormer Hannequin de Fribourg, and even Florange was wounded.[3]

---

1   P. Giovio, *Vite del Gran Capitano e del marchese di Pescara* (Bari: Gius, Laterza & Figli, 1931), pp.424–425 & 429; M. Du Bellay, *Memoires* (La Rochelle: 1573), p.791; Juan De Oznajo, *Batalla de Pavia y prison del rey de Francia Francisco I*, in *Coleccion de documentos inéditos para la historia de espana* (Madrid: Imprenta de la Viuda de Calero,1846), volumen IX p.467; Pedro Mejía, 'Relazione' in D. Testi, La batalla de Pavia, Fuentes historiograficas y epistolares del siglo XVI (Madrid: Ministerio de Defensa 2024), p.148.

2   Report by François de Scépeaux in D. Testi, La batalla de Pavia, Fuentes historiograficas y epistolares del siglo XVI, (Madrid: Ministerio de Defensa 2024), p.161; P. Giovio, *Vite del Gran Capitano e del marchese di Pescara* (Bari: Gius, Laterza & Figli, 1931), p.425.

3   R. de la Marck Florange, *Mémoires du Maréchal de Florange*, tome II (Paris: Renouard, H. Laurens, successeur, 1924), pp.227–228; P. Giovio, *Vite del Gran*

Meanwhile, to the left of this clash, the landsknechts in the pay of France were advancing. They were 5,000 strong supported by about 1,000 French and Italian infantry. Their commanders were Richard de la Pole Duke of Suffolk, the head of the House of York and its claimant to the English throne, and François de Lorraine – brother of the Duke of Lorraine – Count Wolf von Lupfen, and captain Monfort for the French infantry. Two squares of landsknechts marched against them, one led by Georg von Frundsberg and the other by Marck Sittig von Ems, a total of about 10,000 men. They were joined by several thousand Spanish infantry commanded by the Marchese di Pescara.

Giovio writes that the Germans of the Black Band and Germans in Imperial service had long hated each other. The latter reproached the Black Band for having disobeyed Emperor Maximilian when, in 1512, he became an enemy of France and ordered all Germans fighting for the French to abandon the French Army. In addition, the men of the Black Band were accused of infamy because they had attacked and besieged their brothers in Pavia. The Black Band said that they were honoured to serve the King of France, who had always paid them, and did not want to break their oath.

These two groups of landsknechts had different origins. The Black Band came from Rhenish Germany, Flanders or Swabia, as did their captains Hans von Brandeck and Wolf von Lupfen. The Imperial landsknechts came from southern Germany, the Tyrol and the Principality of Trento. Though in different factions, many knew each other and had fought under the same flag in other battles. Some of them were even related to each other, such as the two Swabian captains, who had relatives among the Imperial landsknechts.

Giovio, who wrote extensively about this battle, says that the two bands approached in silence, without any cries of incitement or anger. A captain of the Black Band, Georg Langenmantel of Augusta, preceded the others and raised his hand and voice, challenging the commanders of the opposing ranks, Frundsberg and Sittig, to a duel. The Imperial commanders, angered, refused with loud cries, and Langenmantel fell to the ground struck by their pikes. A landsknecht cut off his hand, adorned with precious rings, and showed it defiantly to the enemy. The Imperial troops, galvanised, attacked the Black Band.

In an instant, the clash harshened, and there was no mercy for an opponent. Both sides opened large gaps among the opposing ranks with their pikes – more than 5 metres long. The two formations began to merge and interlock until pikes and halberds became useless at such a close distance. Then, the infantrymen began to use short swords, axes, knives or their bare hands. The resentment was so strong that some stories report

---

Capitano e del marchese di Pescara (Bari: Gius, Laterza & Figli, 1931), pp.425–426; Relazione di Paulo Luzascho in D. Testi, La batalla de Pavia, Fuentes historiograficas y epistolares del siglo XVI, (Madrid: Ministerio de Defensa 2024), p.68.

that even the wounded fought to the end, even using their teeth. (Cf colour plate D)

Some sources report that Pescara fought in this clash on horseback, not armed as a man-at-arms as would be expected, but as an infantryman. While spurring his horse against the enemy, he was wounded in the face by a pike, and his horse was killed immediately after. He fell to the ground in the middle of the fight and was hit by a halberd in the left leg; without the intervention of his companions, he would have died. According to the report of the battle by the Marchese di Pescara himself, he was wounded not while fighting against the landsknechts of the Black Band, but the Swiss.

Finally, a manoeuvre of the Imperial Army – stronger in number – put an end to the fighting between landsknechts, which had been going on for some time. With Pescara's Spanish, the Imperial troops numbered twice as many as their opponents. By expanding their wings, they managed to surround the Black Band and slaughter them, leaving them no way out. Among the fallen, were the Duke of Suffolk, François de Lorraine, the Graf von Nassau, Baron Dietrich von Schomberg, Georg Langenmantel, captains Longman and Bunau, and 50 other German nobles. Graf Wolf von Lupfen, Hans von Brandeck and Graf Otrtenburg were wounded and taken prisoner, while some nobles and servants were given quarter. Many sources report that almost all the landsknechts on the French side were killed.[4] Finally, the Imperial landsknechts captured the French cannon brought by the King from the main camp of Cascina Repentina.

Spanish sources give a different version of this clash between landsknechts: according to them, it was the Spanish who defeated the Black Band, and Oznajo gives the following account:

> Pescara got off his horse wielding a pike; he ordered his continos [comrades-in-arms] to do the same, and together they entered the Spanish square. They placed themselves in the third rank since the first was reserved for captains, the second to lieutenants and the third to gentlemen. Then, they faced the landsknechts of the Black Band who, according to Oznajo, were as many as 15,000 strong with a vanguard of 4,000, all protected by light armour and supported by 200 arquebusiers. When the latter opened fire, the Spanish knelt and suffered no casualties. It was then for the Spanish to fire. They had 600 skilled arquebusiers, able to hold two to three lit fuses in

---

4   P. Giovio, *Vite del Gran Capitano e del marchese di Pescara* (Bari: Gius, Laterza & Figli, 1931), pp.427–428; C. Wintzerer, 'Die Schlacht bei Pavia' in *Anzeiger Deutsciien vorzeit organ des Germanischen Museums*, 1868, p.348; M. Du Bellay, *Memoires* (La Rochelle: 1573), 211–212; R. de la Marck Florange, *Mémoires du Maréchal de Florange*, tome II (Paris: Renouard, H. Laurens, successeur, 1924), p.229 ; F. W. Barthold, *George von Frundsberg und das teutsche Kriegshandwerk zur Zeit der Reformation* (Hamburg: Perthes, 1833), pp.324–326; J Max, *Geſchichtliche Duffätze* (Berlin: 1903), pp.282–284.

their hands and four to five bullets in their mouths. Oznajo points out that these arquebusiers fired with such rapidity that they seemed to be 6,000 men and not 600. In about 15 minutes, they had killed 5,000 Germans.[5]

However, it is evident how the Spanish chronicler exaggerates in his recount.

---

5 'Relazione sulla battaglia del Pescara' in D. Testi, La batalla de Pavia, Fuentes historiograficas y epistolares del siglo XVI, (Madrid: Ministerio de Defensa 2024), p.49; J. de Oznajo, 'Batalla de Pavia y prison del rey de France Francisco I' in Coleccion de documentos inéditos para la historia de Espana (Madrid: Imprenta de la Viuda de Calero,1846), volumen IX, pp.466–467.

14

Second Tapestry
The Defeat of the French Cavalry
The Imperial Infantry Captures the Enemy Artillery See Plate J

As per the chapter title, this tapestry depicts the defeat of the French men-at-arms, and the landsknechts capturing their artillery. The scene is set inside the park walls, depicted in the upper and bottom parts of the tapestry. Beyond the wall in the background, there are two opposing camps protected by artillery. The artist may have wanted to represent the Imperial camp of Ca Levrieri on the left, and the French camp of Torre di Gallo on the right.

In the foreground on the left are the Spanish arquebusiers. Several scholars consider them one of the main factors that contributed to the Imperial victory. Here, they are depicted in the act of defeating the French cavalry. Their imposing Colour bears a red St Andrew's Cross on a yellow and white field.[1] (Cf colour plate G.5, 'Spanish Colours at Pavia'.)

On the left of the banners is Hernando de Avalos, Marchese di Pescara, mounted – the horse has MAR.sc DI PES on its neck. Pescara wears a crimson jacket, infantry armour on top richly inlaid with gold, and a pair of yellow hose. He uses a chapeau to keep his hair tidy, and a flat black beret embellished with white plumes. In his right hand, he holds a long spear as if about to strike an enemy. Chronicler Juan de Oznajo describes Pescara immediately before battle as:

---

1 At first glance, the Colour seems to have a yellow field, but enlarging the image there are three white-grey stripes, one in the centre and two on the edge of the Colour.

SECOND TAPESTRY

Pescara wore a burgonet and rode a beautiful tordillo[2] horse named Mantuano. Hernando wore cochineal hose, a crimson satin jacket and a rich shirt adorned in gold and pearls. He sported no other device aside from the common one,[3] and his continos [gentlemen] rode with him.[4]

The Second Tapestry. (Reproduced with the permission of the Ministero della Cultura, Museo e Real Bosco di Capodimonte)

To the right of the Colour in the centre of the tapestry, the words MAR. is DV VASTE appear on the ground between the French cavalry and the Imperial Army. It is right above two Imperial soldiers, probably officers; one wears armour and holds a pike, the other holds a halberd and wears a burgonet. The inscription should identify, probably the latter, as Alfonso d'Avalos, Marchese di Vasto.

All around them, are the Spanish arquebusiers; the front ranks are firing against the French gendarmes, killing many and scattering the rest. The back ranks are reloading, while others with the weapon already loaded and pointed are changing with those in the front rank. The scene gives a sense of confusion, but the sequence of movements of the Spanish soldiers is effective.

The Spanish wear a white shirt over their clothes, each with a red cross or scarf. They carry long swords with straight cross-guards, a horn for powder across the shoulder or a bandolier of bottles for the charge of powder – often they had both – and some wear iron vambraces. Many arquebuses have the

---

2   Tordillo: reminiscent of the colour of the thrush, grey with white spots.
3   The common device was the red scarf or cross, the Imperial badge.
4   Juan de Oznajo, *Batalla de Pavia y prision del Rey de Francia Francisco I* in *Coleccion de documentos inéditos para la historia de Espana* (Madrid: Imprenta de la Viuda de Calero,1846), volumen IX, p.456.

THE BATTLE OF PAVIA 1525

Spanish arquebusiers fire at the French cavalry and at Pescara. (Reproduced with the permission of the Ministero della Cultura, Museo e Real Bosco di Capodimonte)

barrel embossed in the middle or at the muzzle, at times with elaborate designs. As was mentioned in the first tapestry, the Spanish clothes are too landsknecht in fashion, a fault found in much iconography of the period. For example, in the Battle of Pavia by Jörg Breu, by Ruprecht Heller and by Wolfgang Huber, all infantry is dressed like landsknechts, whether they are Spanish, French or Italian.

There is only one painting of the battle in which the Spanish are recognisable by their clothes: the Battle of Pavia painting in the collection of the Birmingham Museum in Alabama, by an anonymous Flemish author. In this work, the arquebusiers wears a white shirt that covers their jackets, hose of various colours without slashing, and knee-length breeches with slashing. They have small, flattened caps on their heads, all decorated with feathers.

An excellent document on Iberian customs is the Trachtenbuch, a book of drawings by German painter Weiditz Christoph executed between 1528 and 1529 during a trip to Spain. They are mainly illustrations of traditional dress, but the album also illustrates male clothing of tunics, doublets, jackets and hose. There is, in addition, a depiction of *zaragüelles*, a kind of wide knee-length breeches worn by commoners. There are hats and caps (*bonete* or gorre) with turn-ups. Among the drawings, there is one soldier with the words 'Basque warrior' (cf image 'Basque warrior' below). He is depicted wearing tight-fitting red hose without slashing but with a codpiece. He has a sleeveless jacket and a puffed beanie with a hem. Ultimately, all the clothing in the Trachtenbuch has no cuts or slashing.

Plate A: King Francis I defends himself against the attack of Imperial troops.
(Illustration by Massimo Predonzani © Helion & Company 2025)
See Colour Plate Commentaries for further information.

Plate B: A French gendarme unseats Don Hugo of Cardona.
(Illustration by Massimo Predonzani © Helion & Company 2025)
See Colour Plate Commentaries for further information.

Plate C: Three knights accompanying the King in the first Capodimonte tapestry.
(Illustration by Massimo Predonzani © Helion & Company 2025)
See Colour Plate Commentaries for further information.

Plate D: Combat between Imperial landsknechts and the French Black Band.
(Illustration by Massimo Predonzani © Helion & Company 2025)
See Colour Plate Commentaries for further information.

Plate E: The Spanish arquebusiers defeat the French gendarmes.
(Illustration by Massimo Predonzani © Helion & Company 2025)
See Colour Plate Commentaries for further information.

Plate F: The French and Swiss infantrymen escape, pursued by a stradiot and a jinete.
(Illustration by Massimo Predonzani © Helion & Company 2025)
See Colour Plate Commentaries for further information.

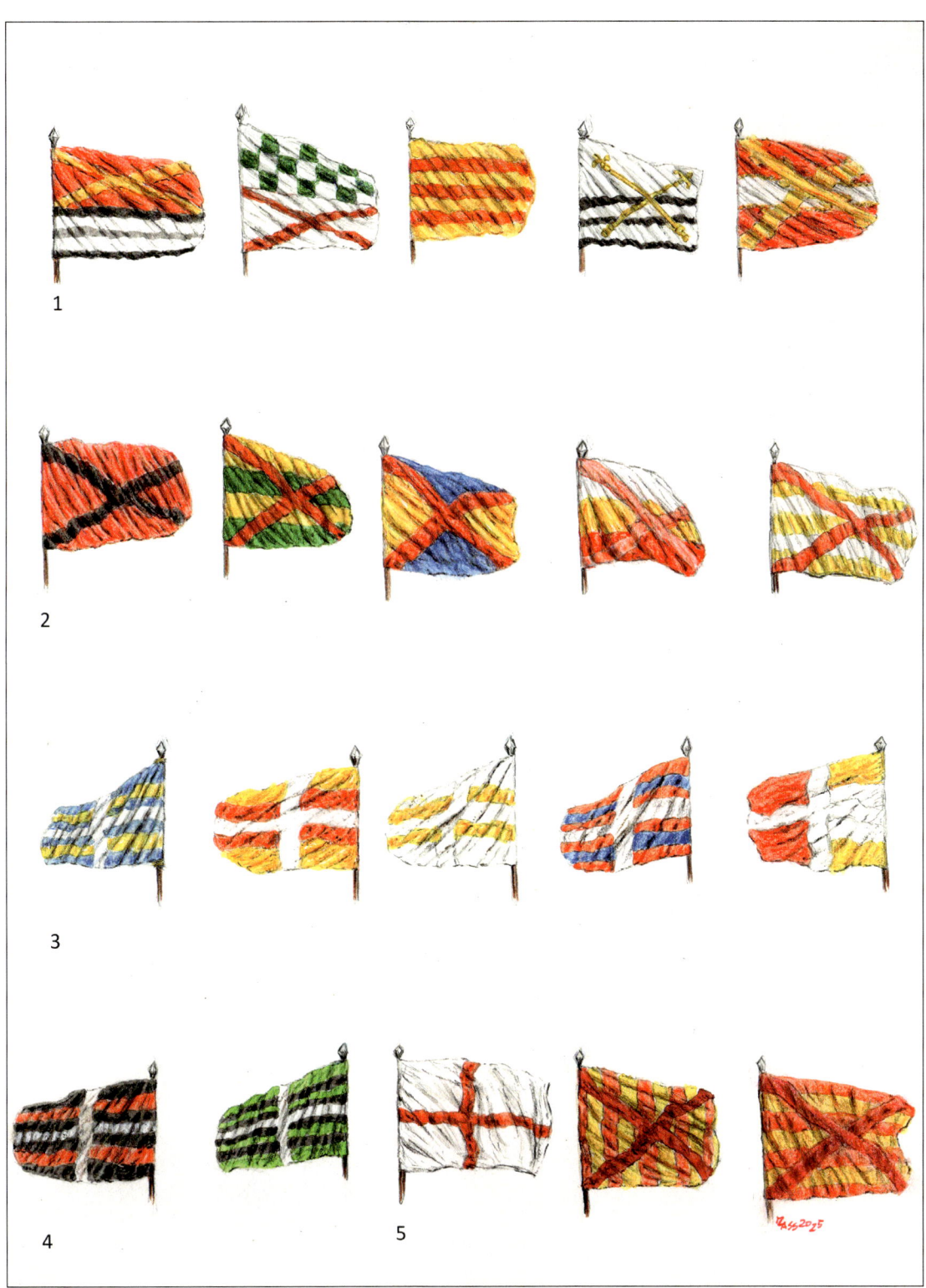

Plate G: Infantry Colours.
(Illustration by Massimo Predonzani © Helion & Company 2025)
See Colour Plate Commentaries for further information.

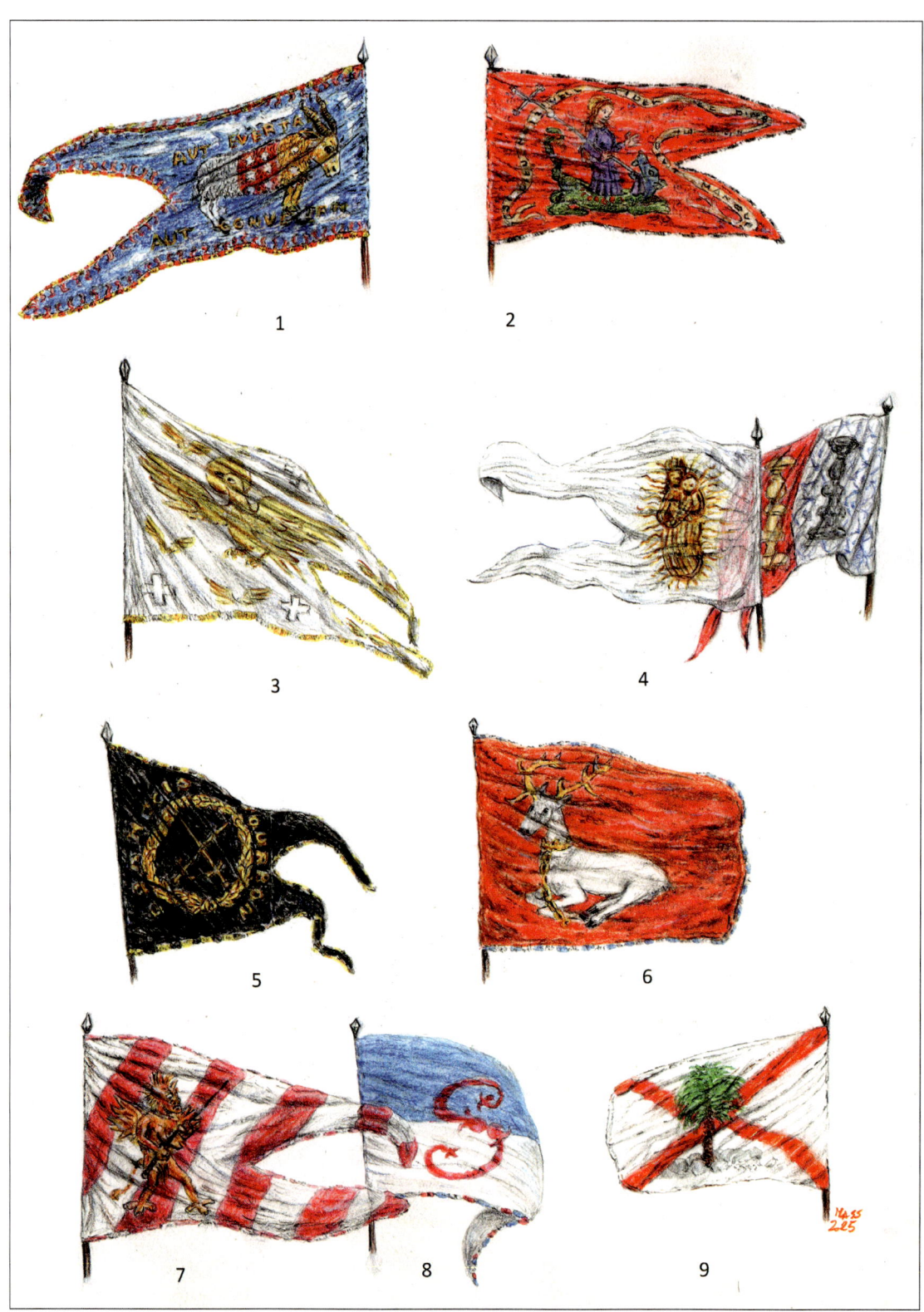

Plate H: Captains' Colours and insignia.
(Illustration by Massimo Predonzani © Helion & Company 2025)
See Colour Plate Commentaries for further information.

Plate I: The First Tapestry: 'Advance of the Imperial Troops and Attack of the French Gendarmerie Led by Francis I'
(Reproduced with the permission of the Ministero della Cultura, Museo e Real Bosco di Capodimonte)

Plate J: Second Tapestry: 'The Defeat of the French Cavalry. The Imperial Infantry captures the Enemy Artillery
(Reproduced with the permission of the Ministero della Cultura, Museo e Real Bosco di Capodimonte)

Plate K: Third Tapestry; 'The Capture of the King of France'

(Reproduced with the permission of the Ministero della Cultura, Museo e Real Bosco di Capodimonte)

Plate L: Fourth Tapestry: The Attack on the French Camp and the Flight of the Women and Servants of the Army of Francis I'
(Reproduced with the permission of the Ministero della Cultura, Museo e Real Bosco di Capodimonte)

Plate M: The Fifth Tapestry: 'The Escape of Civilians from the French camp. The Swiss refuse to advance despite the interventions of their leaders'
(Reproduced with the permission of the Ministero della Cultura, Museo e Real Bosco di Capodimonte)

Plate N: Sixth Tapestry: 'The Flight of the French Army and the retreat of the Duke of Alençon across the Ticino'
(Reproduced with the permission of the Ministero della Cultura, Museo e Real Bosco di Capodimonte)

Plate 0: Seventh Tapestry: 'The Sortie of the Besieged and the rout of the Swiss, who drown in large Numbers in the Ticino River'
(Reproduced with the permission of the Ministero della Cultura, Museo e Real Bosco di Capodimonte)

Plate P: Detail. The Knights of Charles III, Duke of Bourbon.
(Reproduced with the permission of the Ministero della Cultura, Museo e Real Bosco di Capodimonte)

SECOND TAPESTRY

Basque warrior from the **Trachtenbuch**. (Artwork by Massimo Predonzani)

Spanish arquebusiers, 1529. (Artwork by Massimo Predonzani)

Slashings are depicted in the artworks of the first quarter of the sixteenth century by Spanish painters such as Juan Ramirez, Juan Vicente Macip, Alejo Fernandez and Alcira's master. Doublets and jackets are reproduced with puffed sleeves and sometimes with slashings. Many examples of hose have slashings, and half–thigh length breeches are decorated with patterns or slashing. Lastly, berets are puffed and have a band.

The drawing of Spanish arquebusiers on the march at Charles V's coronation in Bologna in 1529 by an unknown artist in 1529 was drawn only one year later (see image 'Spanish arquebusiers 1529' below). The soldiers wear puffed-sleeved jackets, sleeveless coats and hoses, all without slashings. Lastly, they all wear burgonets. Arquebusiers used also helmets like the casquet or cabacete; artworks like the frescoes of the capture of Oran, executed in the cathedral of Toledo in 1514, and the tapestries of the capture of Tunis in 1535 document it well. Moreover, several soldiers depicted in these two works wear a breastplate for protection. The slashings on clothes, on the other hand, can be seen in the tapestries of the capture of Tunis but not in that of Oran.

THE BATTLE OF PAVIA 1525

Following this research, I have attempted a reconstruction of the Spanish arquebusiers in Pavia, with appropriate weapons and clothing of the time. (See colour plate E)

The upper part of the tapestry depicts the defeat and flight of the French heavy cavalry. On the left, the Imperial men-at-arms infiltrate the French formation and unhorse some cavalrymen. They all sport the St Andrew's cross on their clothing, but this one is white. Originally, these crosses were painted on the background of the tapestries, like other elements and heraldic symbols. Immediately below, another group of French gendarmes fall under the fire of the Spanish arquebusiers. A man-at-arms is shot three times – there are two wounds on the horse, bleeding, and a third on the cavalryman's armour. This was intended to represent the effectiveness of the Spanish arquebusiers. The rest of the background depicts the fleeing French men-at-arms. Over their armour, they wear colourful skirts in combinations of beige, gold and yellow, while their plumes are white and gold.

They carry flags on their spears, most of them with no distinctive marks, with a field of various colours, white, beige, yellow and gold. Many are red with the white cross, and others are blue with the white cross. Several flags have a white background with a white cross, but they were painted at the time. This is even more evident on three much larger trumpet banners among the cavalry. They display the white cross on a white field. Probably, the field was painted red, since there is a glimpse of a pink tint visible in a magnification of the photo I was given by the Capodimonte Museum.

French insignia and two Landsknecht banners. (Reproduced with the permission of the Ministero della Cultura, Museo e Real Bosco di Capodimonte)

Almost in the centre of the fleeing army, there are three Standards larger than all the others. One is square with three lilies woven in gold in the centre, and the border and fringes also woven in gold. The field is white, certainly anachronistic because white insignias with golden lilies would appear later in French military heraldry. Originally, the field was painted blue and recalls the flag of France – the royal Cornette – that the Imperials captured in Pavia. Gustave Desjardins describes it as: 'large, square, made of blue-green velvet scattered with golden lilies.'[5] (see image 'French insignia…' below) To the left of this flag, there is a white banner hemmed with gold with a stripe across the centre. Similarly, the other Standard nearby is rectangular, reminiscent of a Standard but much larger. In both Standards, the colours of the field and stripe are barely visible – they could be blue and white or blue and red. It is an unusual flag, especially because it lacks the French symbol, that is, the cross and the lily.

All these Colours and Standards, French and Imperial, display symbols or emblems linked to their respective sovereigns. There are no insignia for the companies of the various captains, which at the time were widespread and are documented in texts and iconography. To give just two examples: the Standard with the wheel of Trémoille in the tapestry of the siege of Dijon, and the white and yellow Standards with red bars of Louis d'Ars in the miniatures of a chronicle by Auton.

On the right side of the tapestry, the Imperial landsknechts, after defeating the hated landsknechts of the Black Band, are shown capturing the artillery. Their clothing is perfect and colourful, with exaggerated puffed sleeves full of slashings. These Germans wear thicker beards than the arquebusiers seen before and have flat caps with feathers. None of them wear shirts, but they have a white and red identification scarf at the shoulder. Their weapons are mainly halberds and swords, there are almost no pikes – there is only one pikeman on the far right about to kill François de Lorraine. Among the Landsknechts is Frundsberg, their most famous commander. He wears 'Maximilian style' armour and holds a pole weapon – it should be a poleaxe. On his belt is his name: JORGE DE FRANSBURSK.

The Germans carry three Colours, all with the red St Andrew's cross but on different coloured fields. The cloth of the first Colour, at the left, flaps in the wind making it difficult to read, but it should display a red cross on a yellow field with blue reflections as shading. Just to the right, near Frundsberg, there is another with the field divided yellow and blue. The last one, higher and in the middle, has a rounded fly and displays the red St Andrew's cross on a yellow field with flints and sparks – probably, there were four as the quarters of the field. It is the Burgundian flint and sparks, an emblem inherited by Emperor Maximilian and widely used on landsknechts Colours. (Cf colour plates G.1 and G.2, 'Landsknecht Colours at Pavia')

---

5   G. Dejardin, *Recherches sur les drapeaux français*, Paris 1874, p.59.

In the scene, the landsknechts are massacring what remains of the Black Band and capturing the French cannon. The Germans on the French side wear the same clothes but with a white cross; almost all of them are shown either already dead or about to be killed. In the background, many others are fleeing, some with their weapons on their shoulders, but most are unarmed and are joining with the fleeing French cavalry. Among them are some Colours, but their colours are unclear and they display no emblems. These too were probably painted.

The stradiots that enter the battlefield from the right are peculiar. They are a part of the Imperial Army as is clear from the white band with a red stripe in the middle that they sport across their chest (see image 'Imperial stradiots' below). They differ slightly from the stradiots depicted in older iconography, such as from the Battle of Fornovo or the Conquest of Genoa by Louis XII. The stradiots at Pavia have hats of oriental fashion and round, heart-shaped or almond-shaped Arab-style shields embellished with tassels. For the rest, they are like the other stradiots: they ride small horses with no decoration only plain harness, and wear long garments, boots, carry a spear and have their trademark beards.

Imperial stradiots. (Reproduced with the permission of the Ministero della Cultura, Museo e Real Bosco di Capodimonte)

Finally, placed purposely in the lower right corner of the tapestry, is the killing of two noble landsknecht commanders of the Black Band. The first, about to be killed by a landsknecht pikeman, is François de Lorraine, Conte de Lambesc and brother of the Duc de Lorraine Antoine II, identified by the inscription on his horse's harness: FRANCOYS M DE LORAIN.[6] He

---

6   The line – above the A stands for N.

wears a beige or gold skirt with red slashing, has a white cross on his chest and has red and black feathers on his helmet. The other captain, to his right and laying on the ground in agony, is identified with the inscription LA BLANSE ROSE. This is Richard de la Pole, Duke of Suffolk, known by the soubriquet of the 'White Rose'. He was the last Yorkist claimant to the Crown of England. He wears a crimson skirt with white slashings and shows a white cross.

15

The Rout of the French Nobles and the Capture of the King

While the Black Band was slaughtered, the Spanish infantry and Imperial cavalry annihilated the French gendarmerie. Although defeated, the French cavalry did not abandon their King and tried to hold back the assault of Spanish arquebusiers, pikemen, and cavalrymen. Many French captains rushed to defend their King, abandoned by his own squadrons.

Louis de la Trémoille, a 75-year-old captain, was fighting alongside the King when his horse was shot dead by an arquebusier. He was saved by his page, Jacques de Brosse, and two of his men-at-arms, Louis Bonnin and Jehan du Bourget. Brosse gave his horse to his lord, and Trémoille attempted to reach the King but was killed by two shots to the head and to the heart. His biographer, Jean Bouchet, reports that several men of Trémoille's company fell alongside their captain including Jean de Jancourt, Sieur de Vilarnou and Trémoille's Standard bearer, Jaques de Salézart, Jean, Sieur de Layre, Marçon 'The Breton' Arras, and many others. Among the victims, there were also some younger gentlemen of the House of Trémoille: Jehan le Poix, the younger son of the Seigneur de Villemor; the younger brother of Lord Odet de Chazerat; the only son of Jehan de Poix and Adam du Ravenel, brother of Sieur de La Rivière.[1]

The Maréchal La Palice, at the head of the right wing of French cavalry, twice defeated the attack of the Italian Castaldo's cavalry. However, when Imperial reinforcements arrived, La Palice's men-at-arms were defeated. Clermont d'Amboise, his lieutenant, was killed, as was La Palice's horse. La Palice, although cut off and hindered by old age and armour, attempted to reach the Swiss but was captured by Castaldo. According to some Spanish chroniclers, it was Cuchar or Zucharo, captain of the light cavalry, who captured La Palice. However, infantry captain Buzardo, called 'The Cruel',

---

1 Jean Bouchet, 'Panégyric du chevallier sans reproche, Louis de La Trémoille' in Mémoires pour servir a l'Histoire de France, tome quatrieme (Paris: J.L.F. Foucault, 1837), pp.476–477. M. Du Bellay, *Memoires* (La Rochelle: 1573), p.212.

THE ROUT OF THE FRENCH NOBLES AND THE CAPTURE OF THE KING

envious of Castaldo's prisoner and his rich bounty, killed La Palice with an arquebus shot to the chest.[2]

Galeazzo da Sanseverino, *Grand écuyer de France*, was shot while trying to defend his King. Giovio writes that a bullet went straight through him and he fell, wounded. The Sieur de Langery went to his help, but Sanseverino refused, and in his agony, begged Langery to leave him to his destiny and go to help the King. Jean Giono recounts another bizarre version of the *Grand écuyer's* death. Amid the fight, the captain was hit by his companion's sword, which destroyed the upper part of his helmet. Half-dead and without a helmet but still in the saddle, Sanseverino rode towards the enemy. The Spanish arquebusiers shot him multiple times, but he remained seated. His soldiers thought it a miracle, but then he fell.[3]

The fight had turned into a massacre of the French cavalrymen and nobles. The King remained with 50 men-at-arms out of his initial 200. Giacomo da Nocera writes that the King could not withstand the Imperial forces and retreated to Mirabello with the Seigneurs de Lescun and de Saint-Pol; during the fight, the enemy broke three lances in a vain attempt to wound or kill the King, but his well-made armour resisted all blows.

Meanwhile, Amiral Bonnivet rode far and wide to try to stop the fleeing soldiers – infantry and cavalry alike – but he knew that it was in vain and that defeat was imminent. He understood it was his suggestion that led to their defeat since he had convinced the King to besiege Pavia. Thus, he resolved to die honourably in battle; he spurred his horse into the German infantry and faced them with his visor lifted, offering his throat to the enemy's pikes. This is how the Amiral de France met his end.[4]

The sources cite many other French nobles among the fallen of that day, such as the Lord of Maraphin, the First Squire of the King. Claude de Husson, Count of Tonnerre, was so disfigured by the blows that it was impossible to identify his body at the end of the battle. Just, Count of Tournon, was hit as he tried to aid Francis I; he fell and choked under his horse's weight. Louis d'Ars, an old captain who had distinguished himself in the War of Naples, suffered the same fate. See Plate E: Spanish arquebusiers defeat the French gendarmes.

Jacques d'Amboise, Lord of Bussy, died in battle, while René, the Bâtard of Savoy, was captured with Claude, his 17-year-old son; René died of his

---

2　A. Varillas, Histoire de François I (Paris; 1685), tome I, p.408. P. da Sandoval, *Historia del Emperador Carlos V* (Madrid: Madoz, 1846), volumen IV, p.210.

3　P. Giovio, *Vite del Gran Capitano e del marchese di Pescara* (Bari: Gius, Laterza & Figli, 1931), pp.428–429; A. Varillas, Histoire de François I (Paris; 1685), tome I, p.407; Jean Giono (Franco Pierno, trans.) *Il disastro di Pavia,* (Milan: Ed. Settecolori, 2023), p.224.

4　The account of the Battle of Jacomo da Nocera, 'Orador veneciano e Paulo in D. Testi, La batalla de Pavia, Fuentes historiograficas y epistolares del siglo XVI, (Madrid: Ministerio de Defensa 2024), pp.64, 66 & 68; P. Giovio, *Vite del Gran Capitano e del marchese di Pescara* (Bari: Gius, Laterza & Figli, 1931), p.429, *Histoire Bonnivet* in *Encyclopédie Méthodique Histoire* (Paris: 1786), ome II, p.724.

injuries about a month later. Maréchal Thomas de Foix, Lord of Lescun, suffered the same fate; he was looking for Bonnivet on the battlefield to kill him and avenge France's defeat caused by his ill advice when he was shot in an arm and shoulders by Spanish arquebusiers. He would die a prisoner a couple of days later. François of Bourbon-Vendôme, Count of Saint-Pol, suffered 13 injuries and was abandoned on the battlefield to die; a Spaniard found him and noticed a fine ring he was wearing; as he tried to steal it by cutting his finger, the Count came to his senses. The soldier recognised him and brought him to Pavia, where Saint-Pol recovered. Other prisoners were Roche du Maine, Lord of Tercelin and lieutenant of Alençon, and Antoine Clermont, Lord of Tallart.[5]

King Francis and the few survivors of his guard tried to rejoin the Swiss retreating towards the south-east of Mirabello. Surrounded by Imperial cavalry and infantry, the King kept three or four enemies at bay with his sword – he is said to have fought so valiantly that some French chroniclers compared him to Roland at Roncesvalles (see colour plate A). These sources report that he killed seven men in battle and wounded many more. Eventually, his last companions were either killed or captured; among them, there was Guiche, his Standard bearer, who was wounded and had to surrender to Tavannes, a 16-year-old page who had taken an enemy sword. The page was Gaspare de Saulx, Seigneur de Tavannes, who would later become famous in the Wars of Religion and in the St Bartholomew's Day Massacre in France.[6]

Once alone, Francis fought his way to the bridge, trying to ford the moat, but his horse was killed. According to some German chroniclers, it was captain von Salm who killed the horse, while Spanish, and some Italian, chroniclers credit this to Spanish arquebusiers. Fery de Guyon, a Burgundian chronicler, mentions a certain Louis Mérey of the Franche-Comté as responsible for the death of the King's horse and adds that it was the third mount the King had lost in the battle. The King fell with his horse on him and was promptly surrounded by enemy cavalrymen and infantrymen. Fearing for his life, Francis shouted, "Spare me! I am the King!"

Numerous men claimed the honour of having captured the King of France, especially Spanish soldiery. The sources mention three men in particular: Diego de Avila, man-at-arms of the Viceroy; Juanes de Urbieta,

---

5   M. Du Bellay, *Memoires* (La Rochelle: 1573), p.212; A. Varillas, Histoire de François I (Paris; 1685), tome I, pp.407, 411 & 417; R. de la Marck Florange, *Mémoires du Maréchal de Florange* (Paris: Renouard, H. Laurens, successeur, 1924), tome II, p.229; Comte de Panisse-Passis, Les comtes de Tende de la Maison de Savoie (Paris: Firmin-Didot, 1889), p.40; Blaise de Monluc, *Commentaires et lettres* (Paris: Mme Ve J. Renouard, 1864), tome I, p.163.

6   P. Charles Fleury, *Historie du cardinal de Tournon*, Paris 1728, p.47; 'Relazione sulla battaglia di Sébastien Moreau' in D. Testi, La batalla de Pavia, Fuentes historiograficas y epistolares del siglo XVI, (Madrid: Ministerio de Defensa 2024), p.94; M. Michaud (ed.), Nouvelle collection des Mémoires *relatifs à l'histoire de France...* (Paris: Didier,1854), p.71.

THE ROUT OF THE FRENCH NOBLES AND THE CAPTURE OF THE KING

The Capture of the King of France. (Reproduced with the permission of the Ministero della Cultura, Museo e Real Bosco di Capodimonte)

man-at-arms of Mendoza or a common soldier; and the Knight, Alonso Pita de Veiga. The first two are mentioned in several chronicles, while de Veiga is cited only by Oznajo. Other sources report different names for this event, such as Juanes Sandoval, an infantryman named Cordova, Cesare Ortolano of Forlì, Castaldo, or the Burgundian Montmartin. Recent Spanish studies, however, credit Alonso Pita as the King's true capturer, earning him the title of 'Hero of Pavia' among the Spanish.[7]

Other chroniclers, instead, mention German or Italian soldiers as capturers. Alexandre Gauthier cites some chronicles from Burgundy in his writings and reports that the company of Bailly d'Amont attacked the King, the arquebusier Luis Mérey shot his horse, and the Bâtard of Montmartin and Étienne de Grospain disarmed him.[8]

---

7   Gabriel Pita Da Veiga Joyanes & Joaquin Pita Da Veiga Subirates, 'La prison del rey de France: consideraciones sobre la captura de Francisco I y sus verdaderos protagonistas' in *Revista de Historia Militar*, no. 12 (2020), pp.143–192.
8   A. Gautier, 'Personaggi della Franca Contea alla battaglia di Pavia del 1525' in Pavia 1964 n. 1 & 2–3, pp.20–28.

In the following chapter, where the third tapestry of Capodimonte is discussed, is yet another version of the capture of the King.

However, it went, the Imperial troops freed the King from under his horse and stripped him of weapons and clothes – a prize to show off and to sell for a rich reward. Francis was wounded to the left thigh and hand, but nothing severe; his sturdy armour had shielded him from bladed weapons and arquebuses, recording only several dents. When the captain of Bourbon's cavalry, La Motte des Noyers, arrived, he offered the King a surrender in the name of his captain. According to Martin du Bellay, the King had been captured by Captain Pompèran, another of Bourbon's men. Francis I retorted indignantly that he would not yield his weapons to a traitor and asked to see Lannoy. While La Motte was looking for Bourbon, Lannoy passed by, recognised the King and accepted his surrender. The Viceroy loaned the King his surcoat since Francis had been left half-naked by the enemy soldiers.[9]

Sanudo reports a letter by a Venetian writer about the plundering of the King's garments:

> A Spaniard servant of the Abbot of Nazaret got his golden spurs. A light cavalryman took a sleeve of white brocade with fringes and slashings. Another Spanish soldier took his estoc encased in crimson velvet, and yet another one got the scarf that the Most Christian King wore across his chest. This scarf was in gold brocade and, like a priest's stole, scattered with white silk crosses; among them was attached a gold cross with an emerald, diamond, and a pearl in each arm. In the last arm, a small case encased a gold cross enshrining a splinter of Christ's True Cross. It is estimated that this cross is worth about 1,000 ducats without the relic.[10]

---

9   More texts on the capture of the King: 'Relazione sulla battaglia del Frundsberg' in D. Testi, La batalla de Pavia, Fuentes historiograficas y epistolares del siglo XVI, (Madrid: Ministerio de Defensa 2024), p.48; J. de Oznajo, 'Batalla de Pavia y prison del rey de France Francisco I' in Coleccion de documentos inéditos para la historia de Espana, (Madrid: Imprenta de la Viuda de Calero,1846), volumen IX, pp.470–472; Fery De Guyon (A.L.-P. Robaulx de Soumoy ed.), *Mémoires* (Brusells: Société de l'Histoire de Belgique, 1858, pp.16–18; Loys Gollut, *Les Mémoires historiques de la République Séquanoise* (Arbois: Auguste Javel, 1846), p.1584; M. Du Bellay, *Memoires* (La Rochelle: 1573), p.213; Antonio Grumello, *Cronaca* in *Raccolta di cronisti e documenti storici lombardi*, (Milan: Francesco Colombo, 1856), tomo I, p.375; P. Giovio, *Vite del Gran Capitano e del marchese di Pescara* (Bari: Gius, Laterza & Figli, 1931), pp.429–430; M. García Cerezeda, *Tratado de las campañas y otros acontecimientos de los ejércitos del emperador Carlos V en Italia, Francia, Austria, Berbería y Grecia*, tomo I (Madrid: Impresores de Cámara, 1873), pp.126–127; M. Mambrino Roseo, Historie del Mondo, (Venice: 1592), III, p.90.

10 M. Sanudo, *I Diarii* (Venezia: M. Visentini, 1893), tomo XXXVIII, p.41.

THE ROUT OF THE FRENCH NOBLES AND THE CAPTURE OF THE KING

Once the King was captured, the Imperial troops began shouting 'Victory! Victory! Spain! Spain! The King is captured!'

Some sources, like Ramazzotto's report and Cerezeda's chronicle, mention that after the capture of the King of France, the King of Navarre was taken prisoner as well. Prudencio de Sandoval describes this capture but does not explain exactly where it took place. Henri d'Albret, King of Navarre, was fleeing the battlefield after the French defeat, but three Spanish soldiers spotted him: a veteran man-at-arms from Portilla, near Valladolid, named Ruy Gòmez, a light cavalryman named Cristòbal de Cortesia, and Juan de Pernia, an infantryman from Carrion. The three soldiers chased the King of Navarre not because they knew who he was but because of his rich weapons and horse barding. The light cavalryman rode first; the man-at-arms came second due to problems with his horse's reins; lastly, the infantryman, who was still a good runner. Cortesia reached the King and engaged in a fight; then, the arrival of Ruy Gòmez made d'Albret surrender. Sandoval writes that the King surrendered to the two cavalrymen, not to the infantryman. The King of Navarre gave his mace, his estoc and his horse caparison of brown velvet with golden stripes to Ruy Gòmez.

Juan de Oznajo gives another version of this story and writes that the King of Navarre fought only against Cristòbal Cortesia and surrendered only to him with a promise of 20,000 ecus to spare his life. Sandoval concludes that Pescara ordered that the King of Navarre be brought to him and gave 1,000 gold florins to Gòmez as a reward, another 1,000 to Cortesia, and 800 to Pernia.[11]

11　P. da Sandoval, *Historia del Emperador Carlos V*, volumen IV (Madrid: Madoz, 1846), pp.223–225; J. de Oznajo, 'Batalla de Pavia y prison del rey de France Francisco I' in Coleccion de documentos inéditos para la historia de Espana, (Madrid: Imprenta de la Viuda de Calero,1846), volumen IX, p.473.

16

Third Tapestry
The Capture of the King of France

See Plate K

Third Tapestry. (Reproduced with the permission of the Ministero della Cultura, Museo e Real Bosco di Capodimonte)

This tapestry depicts the climatic event of the battle: the capture of the King of France. The place is not easily identifiable: according to some sources, Francis I was captured near Cascina Repentita as he attempted to leave the western side of the park in order to take the road to Milan. The building at the centre of this tapestry could be the Repentita; it looks more like a palace than a farmhouse, but it is an architectural interpretation by the Flemish tapestry makers. In the background, the park wall goes from left to right with several tents and camps behind, with a group of soldiers. It is unclear whether these soldiers are Imperial or French because their tents are too far in the distance and there is no flag or identification symbol visible. It should be an Imperial camp since the group of soldiers entering from a breach in the wall have

THIRD TAPESTRY

the St Andrew's Cross. This cross, although white, was originally painted red. As I highlighted in the previous chapters, many similar insignias in the tapestries' backgrounds were painted, not embroidered.

In the foreground on the left, the King of France is helped from his dying horse by Imperial troops. Francis wears beautiful armour, a silver surcoat and the golden brocade scarf described by Sanudo and cited in the previous chapter. On the hem of his garment, there are the crowned initials F and S, and the long plume is in the colours white, red and tenne. Giovio and Brantôme describe this same silver surcoat and flamboyant panache.[1]

The dying horse is represented with several bleeding wounds. His peytral is decorated with the fleurs-de-lys of France as is his beautiful shaffron, ornamented with panaches in the same colours as that of the King. The shaffron and peytral lay on the ground with the harness cut to free the King, all alongside a landsknecht's sword and an arquebus – symbolising the weaponry used to bring down the horse.

There are several Imperial soldiers pulling the horse's tail to get at the King, supported by three cavalrymen identified by names embroidered on their figures (see image 'The Capture of the King' above). The first bearded cavalryman on the left has no helmet and has the writing LA MOTE on his neck; he is Charles, Seigneur de La Motte des Noyers en Bourbonnais, who according to certain sources saved the King's life from Spanish infantry. This man, called La Motta by Italians, partook in the Challenge of Barletta during the war between France and Spain for the Kingdom of Naples.[2] The second cavalryman is dressed in yellow and red plumes on his helmet and has the writing Co De SALM on his gorget; he is Graf Nikolaus von Salm, commander of the auxiliary men-at-arms of Archduke Ferdinand. German chroniclers mention him as the one who killed Francis' horse. The last cavalryman on the right in a golden and red *saione* holds the King by the shoulders and has the name BMON MARTIN on his sword scabbard; he is Jean Bâtard of Montmartin, a Burgundian knight, cited in the chronicles of Franche-Comté as one of the capturers of the King.

The presence of these three cavalrymen in the tapestry is proof that the tapestry weavers favoured the Flemish-German version of the capture of Francis in place of the Spanish one with Avila, Urbieta and Pita de Veiga as main characters.

Right behind the three cavalrymen, there are two soldiers holding the Imperial captains' horses as another cavalryman above La Motte raises the King's sword in triumph.

On the left of this group, Viceroy Charles de Lannoy is dismounting from his horse helped by a page or a landsknecht. The Viceroy has the

---

1   P. Giovio, *Vite del Gran Capitano e del marchese di Pescara* (Bari: Gius, Laterza & Figli, 1931), p.423; Pierre Brantôme, *Oeuvres complètes*, tome III (Paris: R. Sabe, 1869), p.141.
2   M. Predonzani, *The Italian Wars,* volume 5: *The Franco-Spanish War in Southern Italy 1502.1504* (Warwick: Helion & Co,.2024), pp.37–42.

THE BATTLE OF PAVIA 1525

Charles de Lannoy. (Reproduced with the permission of the Ministero della Cultura, Museo e Real Bosco di Capodimonte)

writing VISSEROV on the blade of his sword. Over his armour, Lannoy wears a brocade surcoat in red, blue, and gold, and wears a panache of red, white and gold. Behind him, his Standard bearer holds the Imperial Standard and wears a crimson *saione* with gold and white hems. This Standard is crimson and displays the black double-headed eagle near the staff, the Pillars of Hercules on the left, and the following elements in gold: the steel flints with the ragged Cross of Burgundy, and Emperor Charles' motto *PLUS OVL TRE*. Lastly, the Standard edge has red, yellow, and white fringe – The Emperor's livery. Chapter 26 'The Heraldry of the Battle' digs into the livery and arms of Charles V.

On the right-hand side of the tapestry and beyond the group with the King, are three men-at-arms with swords. The two Imperial cavalrymen in crimson surcoats are watching the French cavalryman in the middle. The Frenchman wears a beret and a black surcoat with a white cross over his armour and is bleeding from a wound to his left arm. It must be a captured French soldier, but other than the white cross, he carries no other symbols or identifying marks. What strikes the audience most is the knight's stance, still with his sword in hand as if he were not a prisoner. Scholars have formulated several hypotheses on his identity: Sanseverino, Bonnivet, or even Bourbon. However, the first two had died before the capture of the King, and Bourbon is already depicted in this same tapestry on the right.

Luigi Casali indicates two intriguing, possible identities in his book. The French soldier could be Henri d'Albret, King of Navarre, who was captured by three Spanish soldiers – see Chapter 15 above. According to Casali, the School of Jean Clouet made a portrait of Albret like the man in the tapestry. Casali's second hypothesis is the French poet Clement Marot, who took

Three knights. (Reproduced with the permission of the Ministero della Cultura, Museo e Real Bosco di Capodimonte)

part in the campaign in Italy with the Duc d' Alençon; according to this poet's writings, he was wounded in the left arm and captured at Pavia.[3]

Though intriguing, these hypotheses clash with the mature appearance of the soldier in black and his full beard. Albret and Marot were respectively 22 and 29 years old, thus much younger than the depicted man.

The sources do not report many important, elderly captains among the captives: Charles Tiercelin, Seigneur de La Roche du Maine was 43 years old; Galiot de Genouillac, Grand Maître d'Artillerie was 60 years old; and the Marchese di Saluzzo was 50 years old. Additionally, Saluzzo was in Savona on the day of the battle, though some chroniclers do mention him at Pavia. The mysterious soldier could be one of the captains, but I have another theory – see below, at the end of this chapter.

At the right of the three cavalrymen, there is an Imperial cavalryman in a red coat dismounting from his horse, and two landsknechts – one holds the reins of a captured horse and points out the captive King to his companion.

Above this scene, there are the most important Imperial captains, aside from Pescara. The first one is Charles Bourbon with the writing BOURBON on his horse reins and the coat of arms of his House on the caparison, gold

---

3   Luigi Casali, *Gli arazzi della battaglia di Pavia nel Museo di Capodimonte a Napoli* (Pavia: Edizioni ViGiEffe, 1993), pp.35–36.

like the harness and surcoat; he wears a red and white panache. Behind him, the Marchese di Vasto rides a horse with an iron shaffron; the legend on his horse's chest identifies him as MAR. D. Vsto CAP.no DI CAVALLI ANNI SUI. Vasto wears a red coat and has a blue panache. The last captain on the right, near the tapestry edge, has identifying writing on his horse reins, but it is unclear. Thanks to the high-resolution photos from the museum, I could decode it enough to read MOSSOR.ALL. A.ONT – *Monseigneur Alarcont*.

The Three Captains, Bourbon, del Vasto, and Alarcón. (Reproduced with the permission of the Ministero della Cultura, Museo e Real Bosco di Capodimonte)

The soldier could be Hernando de Alarcón, commander of the Imperial rearguard. His horse has a gold and silver harness, and the captain wears a dark coat and has a red and white panache.

Behind the commanders, there are three men-at-arms with peculiar surcoats; their left sleeve is decorated with three triangles in red, yellow, and blue – these are the colours of a livery. At the time, the livery carried on a sleeve was worn by German cavalrymen. In a watercolour album by Herzog William IV and Herzog Albrecht V von Bavaria, there are several cavalrymen depicted with the Herzogs' liveries on their right sleeves. In the Capodimonte tapestry, the three men-at-arms are Bourbon's guard, also depicted on the first tapestry. In both scenes, they wield spears shorter than those carried in battle and with a wide spearhead; they also wear the same yellow-beige surcoat. In the first tapestry, the cavalrymen show their right sleeve without livery, in the third one they show the left sleeve with yellow, red, and blue triangles. These colours recall Bourbon's coat of arms – gold fleurs-de-lys and a red bend on a blue field. See the image above. 'The Three Captains, Bourbon, del Vasto, and Alarcón.'

In the upper part of the tapestry, fighting takes place among the woods and farmhouses of a North European architectural style. Above the captains on the right, a group of landsknecht pikemen with pipes and drums carry a Colour displaying the St Andrew's Cross. The field of this Colour is divided into three stripes of white, yellow, and red; the cross appears to be white, but originally it was red, the Imperial colour – since it was painted and not embroidered, it has lost its original hue.

To the left, a long line of men-at-arms and some infantrymen parades near the large building at the centre of the tapestry – it should represent the Repentita. Some of them have a St Andrew's Cross on their clothing or have red scarves, identifying them as Imperials.

On the left side of the tapestry, Swiss infantry or Black Band landsknechts turn away still armed. They are carrying a banner with the white cross and the field striped red and blue.

Under this scene, there is a depiction of two fights. To the left, two Imperial cavalrymen kill a French man-at-arms with swords at his throat. The Frenchman was also present in the first tapestry and has a coat and horse barding with the manna impresa – I identify him as Conte Just Tournon. The Imperial cavalryman behind him pulls back Tournon's head by his hair, offering his throat to the other Imperial soldier. Several knights of Francis I met their end in this fashion. To the right, two men-at-arms fight against two infantrymen; none of them have any badge of recognition, but the two cavalrymen are Frenchmen going to aid Tournon.

If we compare these French cavalrymen with those in the first tapestry, we easily find that they are the same soldiers accompanying the King – in the same tapestry, they are depicted twice. The cavalryman with the manna impresa (Tournon) rides before the King, and behind him rides Montpezat in his red surcoat and Pomereux in a beige coat. These men are identical to

The knights of the King from the first tapestry. (Reproduced with the permission of the Ministero della Cultura, Museo e Real Bosco di Capodimonte)

those fighting the two infantrymen; and they wear the same colours over their armour. Furthermore, in the first tapestry, there is a fourth cavalryman, wearing a black surcoat, between Montpezat and Pomereux, whom I believe to be Montingend or Montjean. He could be the cavalryman in black with the white cross and the unsheathed sword standing near the captive King in the third tapestry. Painter Jean Clouet made a portrait of Montjean looking like the man in the tapestry, especially his full beard.

Carefully analysing the figures depicted multiple times in the tapestries shows that there are some differences.

The cavalryman in black has golden embroidery on his vest absent in the first tapestry, and his horse has a different harness. Even the other three cavalrymen differ in the colour of their panaches and horse barding. Even so, these differences or discrepancies are present in every figure depicted more than once in the tapestries. King Francis is depicted three times: his horse has different bardings and accessories each time, and even his garments differ in decoration. Small details differ also for Bourbon and his guard, who are depicted twice. Even the 'Lady in Red', shown in two tapestries, and two Imperial captains present twice in the last tapestry show some differences.

It is important to remember that scholars have established that this set of tapestries was woven in Brussels after the designs of Flemish painter Bernard van Orley between 1528 and 1530. The workshop that directed the production belonged to the brothers Dermoyen, and several collaborators worked on this commission. Being woven by several artists, these tapestries have differences or variations in detail or single figures. However, these variations do not invalidate the study of the depicted symbols and characters.

In conclusion, the multiple depictions of the four French cavalrymen until the scene of the King's capture suggest that they were at the King's side until the very end. This confirms, once more, that the tapestry weavers preferred the Flemish-German account of the battle.

17

The Rout of the Swiss

As the French heavy cavalry and the Black Band were defeated, the Spanish infantry drove back the Swiss of Florange. However, the exact order of events differs across the various chronicles.

Giovio sets the defeat of the Swiss before that of the Black Band, while according to Juan de Oznajo and Sandoval, the Germans were defeated first then the Swiss, and lastly, the King was captured. Florange and Frundsberg, like Giovo, mention the defeat of the Swiss followed by that of the Black Band and finally the capture of the King. Luzascho and Cerezeda report the Swiss defeat by the Spanish without mentioning the Germans. Marco Guazzo wrote that the Swiss fled, abandoning the Black Band and the Italians.

However, it happened, after the Swiss bands of Florange had fled, the main group from the five abbeys made the same choice. Giovio reports that this numerous body of 4,000 to 5,000 men stopped with no intention of moving. Targeted from a distance by the Spanish arquebusiers, these infantry suffered significant losses among their captains in the front ranks. In addition, the Swiss witnessed the defeat of the King's cavalry, but instead of rushing to its aid, they threw away their pikes and fled. Their most valiant commander, Jean de Diesbach, tried to stop their flight with angry shouting and by hitting the fugitives, in vain. Unable to bear this shame, he threw himself into the midst of the enemy, choosing an honourable death. These actions are represented in the fifth tapestry.

Giovio continues his report correctly, writing the Swiss version of the cause of their retreat. The Swiss blamed the Duc d'Alançon, who, with the rearguard, had stopped to watch the battle until he realised that fate was against the French forces. Thus, he promptly escaped with his cavalry and crashed into the advancing Swiss square, disrupting its formation.

Several chroniclers point out that the Swiss fled almost without putting up a fight, some even accuse them of cowardice. Two eighteenth-century Swiss historians, however, tried to give a different, and even opposite, analysis of this event.

The historian Baron de Zurlauben, who wrote his report in 1700, reports only the casualties. He writes that the Swiss lost most of their captains that day: other than Jean de Diesbach of the Canton of Bern, who was at the head of the troops, also among the fallen there were the Grisons Florin Tack and Jean Scheck and Conrad de Zurlauben of Zug. Out of 7,000 men who fought in the battle, the Swiss suffered 3,000 losses and 4,000 prisoners. Among the prisoners, were the captains Jacques de Cré, Jacques and Jean Rudolphe, sons of the Procurator d'Erlach, Jean-Jacques de Watteville, and François Armbruster, all came from Berne. The two d'Erlach were mortally wounded and died shortly after the battle. Jean-Jacques de Watteville was also wounded, and the Grison captain Pierre de Zaun was captured.

May de Romainmotier, another Swiss historian and also from the eighteenth century, recounts a different version from those reported so far. He writes that the Swiss fought bravely in Pavia, and after the defeat of the landsknechts of the Black Band, they were in a square formation when they faced the attack of the Spanish troops of del Vasto, who attacked them from the front. The *gendarmerie* led by Bourbon attacked them from the right, and the landsknechts and the cavalry of Lannoy charged into the back, left uncovered after the escape of the Duc d'Alençon and the French rearguard. Having lost most of their captains and 4,000 men, the Swiss had to accept the honourable conditions for surrender offered by Bourbon – 2,500 men were taken prisoner. In addition, Romainmotier mentions the courage of the men of the *Cent Suisse* of the guard of Francis I, who died defending the King. This is the only source that defends the Swiss who fought in the battle, but it still reports unreliable events.

In other sources, it is reported that the cavalrymen of de Leyva left Pavia and attacked the Swiss of Diesbach, causing them heavy casualties and forcing them to surrender[1].

---

1 P. Giovio, *Vite del Gran Capitano e del marchese di Pescara* (Bari: Gius, Laterza & Figli, 1931), pp.426–426; J. de Oznajo, 'Batalla de Pavia y prison del rey de France Francisco I' in Coleccion de documentos inéditos para la historia de Espana, (Madrid: Imprenta de la Viuda de Calero,1846), volumen IX, pp.466–468; R. de la Marck Florange, *Mémoires du Maréchal de Florange*, tome II (Paris: Renouard, H. Laurens, successeur, 1924), pp.228–232; M. le Baron de Zurlauben, *Histoire militaire des suisses au service de la France* (Paris: Desaint and Saillant et al,1751), tome IV, pp.173–174, M. May de Romainmotier, *Histoire militaire de la Suisse et celle des suisses dans les différens services de l 'Europe*, (Lausanne: J.P. Heubach et cie., 1788), tome V, pp.185–187; 'Relazione sulla battaglia di Zuan' in D. Testi, La batalla de Pavia, Fuentes historiograficas y epistolares del siglo XVI, (Madrid: Ministerio de Defensa 2024), p.59.

18

Fourth Tapestry
The Attack on the French Camp and the Flight of the Women and Servants of the Army of Francis I

See Plate L

Fourth Tapestry. (Reproduced with the permission of the Ministero della Cultura, Museo e Real Bosco di Capodimonte)

This tapestry depicts the fugitives of the defeated French Army who arrived at the camp and warned it of the defeat, instilling panic among both civilians and military, causing them to flee.

On the left of the tapestry, the first Imperial pursuers appear, and at the bottom, five landsknechts defeat and kill five French infantrymen. In the foreground, a French soldier with a broken pike is about to be hit by the two-handed sword of a *doppelsoldner* – he wears a burnished infantry

THE BATTLE OF PAVIA 1525

The 'lady in red.' (Reproduced with the permission of the Ministero della Cultura, Museo e Real Bosco di Capodimonte)

armour with golden inlay. Among the infantry of the time, only the most valiant and wealthy owned armour.

Immediately above, there are other fights: some Swiss infantrymen manage to kill an enemy stradiot, while an Imperial cavalryman disarms a French man-at-arms, hitting him with his spear at the throat. You can even see pieces of wood flying around the helmet of the stricken cavalryman. To their right, several Swiss infantrymen flee the field by crossing a stream. One uses his pike to jump over the waterway, probably the Vernavola that crosses the entire park from north to south. Other fugitives run to the only building near the stream, which Luigi Casali identifies as Mirabello Castle.[1] Casali points out that this building is identical to the one painted by Jörg Breu in his Battle of Pavia, and to the one reproduced by Sebastian Munster in his book Cosmographia. The Vernavola depicted in the tapestry should flow from left to right. Instead, it flows in the middle, crossing the tapestry and the park, starting on one side of the wall and arriving at the opposite side. In addition, chronicles and letters about the battle agree that the Imperials of del Vasto took Mirabello at the beginning of the clash, provoking the French counter-attack. In this scene, however, the decisive clash is already over. Another hypothesis is that the building represents Cascina Repentina,

---

1   Luigi Casali, *Gli arazzi della battaglia di Pavia nel Museo di Capodimonte a Napoli* (Pavia: Edizioni ViGiEffe, 1993), pp.37–38.

FOURTH TAPESTRY

where the King's main camp was. In the tapestry, the French camp is to the right, immediately after the building. It is protected by a deep moat and rows of gabions interspersed between the artillery pieces. Tents and pavilions stretch towards the horizon. A golden pavilion near the bridge on the moat bears France's coat of arms. It is the King's pavilion, displaying three golden lilies on a white field – originally, the field was painted blue.

In the middle of the camp are groups of fleeing soldiers, civilians, mules and horses. They have abandoned heavy weapons and any hindrance, carrying only the vital things on their shoulders or on mules. The mules, all with mesh muzzles, are loaded with boxes and bags with straps with coloured fringes decorated with golden rattles. Overall, the scene is chaotic. Powder barrels explode, terrorising the nearby infantry, while two soldiers with halberds are about to kill another infantryman on the ground, perhaps a thief.

In contrast to the scenes of panic, under a canopy near the wall, men and women are cooking meat on a spit, as if nothing was happening.

In the centre of the tapestry, in the foreground, there is a mishmash of people, military and civilian, trying to leave the park through a breach in the wall. A white greyhound leads the way, followed by a girl with her dog in her arms and, to her left, a halberdier carrying a wicker basket on his shoulders. Behind them, women and men in a hurry lead mules loaded with baggage, followed by soldiers with halberds. Among this group is a woman dressed in a lavish red dress with blue and gold sleeves, embellished with numerous jewels. She rides a white mule which has a crimson harness with gold decoration. Perhaps she was a grande dame, a noblewoman belonging to the King's entourage. Jean Giono, in The Battle of Pavia (Fr. Le Désastre de Pavie), focuses on this female figure. He writes that no source mentions her, and that the artists of the tapestry highlighted her figure because of the popular opinion saying that the King was in sweet company the night before battle. Giono mentions some of these rumours about a lady of Pavia leaving the city to give herself to the King. Other rumours identified her as a noblewoman Isabella Visconti who never existed however. He then mentions the famous Clarice, one of the most beautiful ladies in Milan, with whom Bonnivet had fallen madly in love years earlier. Then he mentions other ladies; undoubtedly, this last is the result of gossip made to enhance King Francis' reputation as a great lover.

Finally, Giono mentions the King's only known mistress at the time, Emmeline du Flech, a lady-in-waiting to the Duchessa di Savoy, who had an affair with Francis months earlier when he was in Turin. Giono says that she was with the King at the Charterhouse of Pavia when, in November 1524, the King received the nobles of the Duchy of Milan.[2] There is no other information about this 'lady in red.'

---

[2] Jean Giono (Franco Pierno, trans.) *Il disastro di Pavia*, (Milan: Ed. Settecolori, 2023), pp.200–201.

Behind the lady are her ladies-in-waiting and two mules with elaborate and precious trimmings and harnesses, loaded with trunks. One wears a head collar adorned with plaques decorated with red hearts. Two Swiss infantry lead the mules; the one on the right, particularly energetic, spurs the animal with a stick and flaunts his large codpiece which blocks his sword. Behind them, there are other women, elderly, civilians, perhaps officials, and soldiers. They all look shaken and scared. The only person who shows no fear is the lady in red, whose face seems indifferent and annoyed, disdainful, as a gentlewoman should be.

19

The Fifth Tapestry
The Escape of Civilians from the French Camp. The Swiss refuse to advance despite the interventions of their leaders See Plate M

Fifth Tapestry. (Reproduced with the permission of the Ministero della Cultura, Museo e Real Bosco di Capodimonte)

The scene depicted in this tapestry, like the previous fourth tapestry, represents the escape of civilians and soldiers from the French camp. At the upper left, the Imperials sack the camp, and the fire highlights the disastrous event. Under this scene, a long row of gabions protects and marks the limits of the camp, stretching towards the horizon. In front of it, the wall of the park, with gaps in it, runs parallel. Between the gabions and the wall, the fugitives try to escape. There are soldiers, women and children, civilians and mules loaded with goods; among them, 'the lady in red' on a mule repeating the lady from the fourth tapestry.

In the foreground below, another group of fugitives is crowding to cross a gap in the wall, next to a stream. An infantryman armed with a pike, who has just crossed the gap, looks at the spectator and seems almost satisfied. He has two chickens tied by their legs on his pike and next to him, is a woman with a child dressed in landsknecht fashion, perhaps the soldier's family. Behind them, are other soldiers and civilians, women, two ladies riding two small horses, a donkey with two trunks and a monkey with an iron chain. Lastly, two friars close this group. One of them, with a tonsured head, rides a horse with an iron shaffron with a coat of arms in the centre – a gold cross on a red field. Near him, a soldier drives a mule carrying a trunk covered with a costly fabric embroidered with fleur-de-lis, a rampant lion and the repeated motto *AVANT* on its border.

The motto *Avant* and the lady in red. (Reproduced with the permission of the Ministero della Cultura, Museo e Real Bosco di Capodimonte)

On the right-hand side of the tapestry, the scene enclosed by the wall of the park depicts the Swiss bands' surrender to the Imperial cavalry.

The setting is the south-eastern part of the park, near Pavia. The stream in the foreground is the Vernavola, that flows out of the park under an arch in the wall. Thanks to this clue, Luigi Casali states in his book on the tapestries of Pavia that the depicted area faces the monastery of San Paolo and the nearby Torretta (see map in Chapter 10). According to Casali, the building near the wall is the Torretta, however this is located inside the park

THE FIFTH TAPESTRY

on maps[1]. The building, which has other constructions around it, could, instead, be the monastery. The military camp that extends towards the horizon is that of Floange and the Swiss, located in the five abbeys. The field on the left behind the gabions should indicate the lodgings of the French infantry, where captain La Palice, the Duc de Longueville who died in the siege, and the *Grand Maître de France*, René the Bâtard de Savoy, all were. In the scene, there should also be a view of Pavia in the background and the Vernavola running south, in the centre. However, as was previously stated, the tapestries are not always faithful to the geography.

There are two other details that do not coincide with this representation, highlighted in the catalogue Art & War in the Renaissance.[2] On the left-hand side of the tapestry near the frame, is a tent with the Imperial Eagle, and, among the civilians, some infantrymen sport a red cross.

Consequently, according to the catalogue, this group of soldiers who enter the park from the left should be Imperials. Romano presents as evidence the accurate engraving by Jörg Breu of the Battle of Pavia, where a large group of civilians with a Colour displaying a St Andrew's Cross appears on the far right of the Imperial Army, behind the wall of the park. However, the civilians of Breu are running away from the park and the battle, as before the fighting Lannoy had sent the civilians and the luggage half a mile from the camp to protect them. The civilians of the Capodimonte tapestry enter the park while the battle is far from over, fleeing from a looted camp on the left. There are soldiers who either fight or steal chests and other goods; if the eagle were accurate, it would be an Imperial camp! However, this is unlikely.

The black double-headed eagle. (Reproduced with the permission of the Ministero della Cultura, Museo e Real Bosco di Capodimonte)

In this regard, I put forward a possible explanation. Usually, the Imperial Eagle of Charles V has the Pillars of Hercules as support, but the eagle arms on the tent is supported by a lion and an animal like a greyhound. The double-

---

1 Luigi Casali, *Gli arazzi della battaglia di Pavia nel Museo di Capodimonte a Napoli* (Pavia: Edizioni ViGiEffe, 1993), pp.45–46.
2 Carmine Romano (ed.), *Art & War in the Renaissance: The Battle of Pavia Tapestries* (New York: Rizzoli International 2024)

THE BATTLE OF PAVIA 1525

Coat of arms of René, Bâtard de Savoy. (Artwork by Massimo Predonzani)

headed black eagle was also on the coat of arms of other noble families such as the Pallavicini and the Coreth, as well as on the arms of René, the Bâtard de Savoy – who according to Florange was positioned nearby. René was the natural son of Philip II of Savoy. He was a skilled and energetic politician who helped his father govern the duchy and, after his father's death, also aided his brother Philibert, who did not have an inclination to rule. In 1501, René married Anna Lascaris di Tenda, daughter of Gian Antonio Lascaris di Ventimiglia, Conte de Tenda, thus becoming one of the most powerful men in the duchy. From that moment, René quartered his coat of arms – the cross of Savoy crossed by the black bend sinister as a mark of illegitimacy – with the Lascaris' arms, a black double-headed eagle.

Unfortunately, in the same year, his brother Philibert II married Margaret of Habsburg, daughter of Maximilian and fiercely anti-French. Margaret despised her brother-in-law, most especially because he had always backed the French. So much did the Duchess dislike her brother-in-law that in 1503 René was expelled from Savoy and deprived of all offices and fiefs, and was left with only the territories of the Lascaris.

The Grand Bâtard sought shelter in France, where he was well received, and put to use using his excellent political skills; in 1519, Francis I appointed him *Grand Maître de France*. René distinguished himself in several French military campaigns and the financial policy of the state, becoming one of the King's closest advisers. Still, he would never regain possession of his assets, not even when Duca Charles II took over the rule of Savoy after the death of Philibert. In his will, therefore, the Grand Bâtard left his eldest son Claudio, in addition to all his assets and the county of Tenda, his family name and the coat of arms and insignias of the House of Lascari.[3] Consequently, if René left his heir the Lascari coat of arms, it is obvious that he could have sported the black eagle on his tent, like the one in the picture. The Lascari double-headed eagle was black on a yellow or white field.

In addition, the coat of arms above the shaffron of the friar's horse recalls the Savoy coat of arms, while the motto *AVANT* on the fine cloth of the nearby mule is an ancient and traditional motto of Savoy.[4]

---

3   Comte de Panisse-Passis, *Les comtes de Tende de la Maison de Savoie* (Paris: Firmin-Didot, 1889).
4   J. Gelli, *Motti, divise, imprese di famiglia e di personaggi italiani* (Milan: Ulrico Hoepi, 1916), p.610.

THE FIFTH TAPESTRY

Finally, the red crosses sported by some infantrymen may have been used to deceive, but more likely are the badge of the Grisons Swiss. The Milanese chronicler Giovanni Andrea Prato tells the story of the peoples of Switzerland and their insignia in his Milanese chronicle of the early sixteenth century. He mentions the Grisons and their banner, a red cross on a white field.[5] According to the chronicles, the Grisons abandoned the French Army a few days before the battle, as the Sforza Army had attacked their homeland. Francis I offered to double their pay if they remained, but most refused. Some Swiss, however, did remain like the good mercenaries they were.

For these reasons I believe Casali's interpretation of the places represented in the tapestry to be the more reliable.

Chains with coats of arms, and Captain Diespart. (Reproduced with the permission of the Ministero della Cultura, Museo e Real Bosco di Capodimonte)

The right side of the tapestry is more precise and clearer in its depiction of the events. It represents the Swiss bands who no longer want to fight and throw their weapons on the ground, raising their arms in surrender. They all have the white cross on their chest and back, and their Colour also displays the white cross with the field divided into stripes of white and yellow, yellow and red, or yellow and blue. Some Colours only have a yellow

---

5 G. Andrea del Prato, *Storia di Milano*, in Archivio Storico Italiano III° 1842, p.232.

field. These are the banners of the Swiss in the pay of France, devoid of the traditional symbols of the cantons. Among the Swiss, there are the Imperial cavalry with their white and red shoulder scarves. They all have the visor raised and threaten with swords those Swiss who have not yet surrendered. Most likely, these Imperial cavalrymen came from Pavia.

In the foreground, is faithfully represented a group of Swiss infantry. A doppelsoldner with a sword, a Standard bearer with a Colour on the ground, a drummer and a piper. The drummer and piper wear chains with shield-shaped plates painted with coats of arms. The first coat of arms on the left, sported by the drummer, is the arms of Robert de la Marck, Seigneur de Fleurange, commander of the Swiss. The coat of arms had a yellow (gold) field with a chequered white and red band in the centre and a red rampant lion above[6]. The next coat of arms on the right displays the lilies of France, and the one after the lilies with the dolphin. The last coat of arms on the piper's chain is difficult to identify. It displays a red, rampant animal, perhaps a lion, on a blue and white field. It is probably the coat of arms of a Swiss captain, but it is not that of the commander, Jehan Diespart – he used two gold lions divided by a golden ladder on a black field. Diespart or Diesbach stands to the right of the group with his pike raised and wears white landsknecht clothing with gold slashing. Acknowledging the futility of calling his infantrymen to order, he offers his head to the sword of the Imperial cavalryman next to him, choosing death over dishonour. Both Giovio and other chroniclers report this fact.

---

6   M. de la Chesnaye-Desbois, *Dictionnaire de la Noblesse* (Paris: Vve Duchesne 1775), tome IX, p.519.

20

The Escape of the Duke of Alençon

The Duc d'Alençon was the sole French captain who saved himself from the battle.

Charles Valois Alençon was a Prince of the Blood, married to Margaret de Valois, sister of the King. He took part in several campaigns in Italy; was at the capture of Genoa in 1507, at the Battle of Agnadello in 1509, and at Marignano in 1515. Francis I trusted him and appointed him commander of the rearguard. Still, in all chronicles about the Battle of Pavia, he is remembered for his retreat. Even the Swiss held him accountable for their shameful rout.

According to Italian chronicler Taegio, when the duke saw the rout of the Swiss and the death and capture of a great many French soldiers, he brought together 400 lances and took the road for France, saving himself. Other Italian chroniclers, from Giovio to Guicciardini, write that Alençon retreated without fighting. The only difference in sources is the number of troops that followed him: some report of 300 men-at-arms, others of 400 lances, or 500 soldiers. Paolo Luzascho from Verona fought at Pavia with the Imperial forces and wrote that the duke retreated with 400 men-at-arms, 2,500 French infantrymen, and 2,000 Italian soldiers deployed on the other side of the Ticino River. Luzascho reported that the infantry saw the Swiss rout and joined them, instead of fighting. French chroniclers also report their compatriot's retreat.

Du Bellay wrote that 'the Duc d'Alençon, at the head of the rearguard, witnessed the defeat of the army and the capture of the King; disheartened and without hope in a turn of tide, he followed the recommendations of his advisers and retreated via the bridge over the Ticino River.' Florange is the sole chronicler who had words of praise for the duke. 'Monseigneur Alençon fulfilled his duty the whole day.' La Roche du Maine, his lieutenant, saw the French defeat and said to him, 'Monseigneur, all is lost. Save yourself. I shall remain here and block the way to those who would pursue you.' La Roche faced the enemy to save his lord, who withdrew across the bridge; many followed the lieutenant's example. La Roche du Maine was subsequently captured alongside the Monseigneur de Nanthoulet, son of the French Chancellor, and several others.

As for Spanish chroniclers, the most respected ones, such as Oznajo and Cerezeda, reported that Alençon and his men-at-arms had fought since the beginning of the battle. They record that it was Alençon who attacked the Italians of Cesare Maggi and captured their artillery; however, this is incorrect. It was lieutenant La Roche du Maine, with his light cavalry and part of the duke's gendarmerie who defeated the Italians; they wore the badges and livery of the Duc d'Alençon, which probably made the Spanish believe, albeit erroneously, that it was the duke who led the attack.

As the battle progressed, the French were defeated. The Spanish chroniclers described accurately the duke's rout across the Ticino. Once across the river, the French captain had the bridge destroyed to block the Imperial's pursuit. Oznajo wrote that Alençon gave this task to Pedro de Guevara and his Spanish infantry in the pay of France, but de Guevara was under orders to guard the bridge built northwest of Pavia, near San Salvatore. With the French Army in disarray, de Guevara attempted to defend the passage and rally the fugitives to save them; then, he destroyed the bridge and the boats on which it stood. Some sources on the battle report that it was the Imperial troops of de Leyva who destroyed the bridge, after having defeated the French Italian garrison who guarded the exits from Pavia.

Whatever the situation, the collapse of the bridge resulted in the death of many fugitives, who drowned in the Ticino trying to escape. Sources report that more than 500 Swiss alone drowned.

In conclusion, Charles d'Alençon saved himself and a great number of men-at-arms and infantry, a military force vital to protect France, that had been left defenceless. However, the duke was accused of having abandoned the King to favour his political ambitions – in the King's absence, he would rule the Kingdom in his place as Regent. Giovio wrote that Alençon fell ill, shocked by the defeat and false accusations, and died of pleurisy shortly after on 11 April.[1]

---

1   F. Taegio, Rotta e prigionia di Francesco primo re' di Franciasotto Pavia l'anno 1525. Composta dal Taegi, e dal latino tradotta dal Cremonese Cambiago, Pavia 1655, p. 62; P. Giovio, Vite del Gran Capitano e del marchese di Pescara,Laterza, Bari 1931, p. 432; F. Guicciardini, Storia d'Italia, Milano 1844,vol. III p. 161; J. de Oznajo, Batalla de Pavia y prison del rey de Francia Francisco I, in Coleccion de documentos inéditos para la historia de Espana, Madrid 1846,tomo IX, pp. 457,460, 468; M. García Cerezeda, Tratado de las campañas y otros acontecimientos de los ejércitos del emperador Carlos V en Italia,.., Tomo I. Madrid 1873, pp. 124-125, 128.

21

Sixth Tapestry
The Flight of the French Army and the Retreat of the Duke of Alençon across the Ticino See Plate N

This tapestry illustrates the flight of the French beyond the Ticino. The scene occurs west of the city, perhaps near San Lanfranco, which could be the building at the bottom left with the round towers. A French flag flies on the main tower, barely visible because it displays a white cross on a white field, the field was originally painted. The river flows in the foreground under a bridge of boats on the right, then curves to the left and reaches behind the building. In the background is a beautiful landscape with hills and woods, a castle on a hill, and some peasant houses in the countryside. However, the buildings are in North European style.

Sixth Tapestry. (Reproduced with the permission of the Ministero della Cultura, Museo e Real Bosco di Capodimonte)

Fighting horses and cavalry dominate the scene from the river in the foreground to the building with the towers. Imperial light cavalry is chasing the French men-at-arms. On the left, some frightened infantry run among the cavalry – judging by their clothes, they are Swiss but could also be French, who were camped nearby. As mentioned before, Flemish iconography of the time depicted all infantrymen's clothes in landsknecht fashion, regardless of the soldiers' origin.

On the left side of the tapestry, there is a large squadron of Imperial light cavalry. There are two groups of cavalry; most of them are Spanish jinetes, with burgonets or simple caps secured with a kerchief. They are armed with a spear or sword and do not carry shields. The other group consists of stradiots, easily recognisable by their distinctive caps in the shape of a truncated cone, sometimes worn with a turban. They have shields and do not wear any armour – the jinetes, however are wearing armour. In the centre of the tapestry, a captain of the stradiots is shown from behind, he is carrying a heart-shaped shield and has a burgonet as his only protection. Next to him is a light cavalryman in full armour dressed in red, green and white. The stradiots chase the French gendarmes, many of whom raise their arms with open hands in surrender.

The Duc d'Alençon. (Reproduced with the permission of the Ministero della Cultura, Museo e Real Bosco di Capodimonte)

In the foreground to the left of the bridge, a French man-at-arms is about to be overwhelmed by two jinetes. He attempts to defend himself with his broken spear. From this group can be seen the difference in their horses: the French horses are powerful like those of the other gendarmes,' while the Spanish horses are smaller, but would have been agile. In addition, the French wear full armour with beige or gold, or even red, surcoats. There are countless lances bearing white or red flags with the cross. The crosses are dark, while they should be white – the French colour.

SIXTH TAPESTRY

To move to analyse the scene on the bridge. Here infantry are demolishing the wooden structure with halberds or bare hands. They are dressed in the landsknecht fashion, but as per the previous chapter, it was the Spanish infantrymen of captain Guevara, in the pay of France, who destroyed the bridge. Two Swiss infantrymen run on top of it, a drummer and a Standard bearer, trying to cross it as quickly as possible. They are preceded by a man-at-arms with a beige and gold surcoat and a red and blue plume on his helmet.

Finally, on the right, the French rearguard marches away after crossing the river. The first horseman who leads the group is Alençon, with the inscription DA LENSON on his horse's harness. The sign – above the letters SO stands for the letter N.

Imperial Light Cavalrymen. (Reproduced with the permission of the Ministero della Cultura, Museo e Real Bosco di Capodimonte)

All these French cavalrymen wear gold or beige garments similar to those of Alençon. They also have white flags with the French cross on their lances, similar to those carried by the large group on the left described above.

117

22

The Sortie of de Leyva with the Garrison of Pavia

Leaving the action of Antonio de Leyva's men for last is my preference as an author, because once again, chroniclers disagree on the time of the intervention and even the direction in which they attacked.

Taegio and Marco Guazzo wrote that de Leyva left the city quite early, during the clash between the French right wing and Cesare Maggi's Italian infantry. Taegio writes that de Leyva defeated a band of French light cavalry and some infantry on watch outside the walls. Cerezeda mentions the Imperial group leaving Pavia at the beginning of the fighting, without further details.

Most chronicles, however, say that the intervention of the troops from Pavia happened after the defeat of the French men-at-arms and the landsknechts of the Black Band or simply that de Leyva simply left the city late. The previously mentioned anonymous author, who wrote of the siege of Pavia, reports that the night before the battle, de Leyva gathered six pieces of artillery and several sappers with hoes and shovels, as well as infantry and cavalry. However, there was a problem: as shown in the iconography of the battle, the city gates had been reinforced with an additional wall built in front of them (see image at the end of Chapter 10). These defensive walls were designed to allow small groups of men to exit, but not thousands of men at once. To facilitate the operation, the sappers had to demolish them, delaying the exit of the soldiers. In addition, they lost more time moving the cannons because of the mud.

200 men-at-arms and 5,000 Germans with some cannon left the city through the castle gate; Antonio de Leyva left in a litter because of his gout. These men attacked the Italians of Giovanni Medici, who were guarding the siege lines, but without their recently wounded commander. The Venetian Orator writes that the Imperial sally defeated the Italians after only 20 minutes of fighting, killing them all, then looting the enemy camp of the five abbeys. Giovio and Florange report that de Leyva's soldiers were ruthless; they killed fugitives and were largely responsible for the slaughter of the Swiss in Ticino (cf colour plate F). The two chroniclers highlight how these

soldiers were also the greediest when it came to looting the camps, and it appears that de Leyva plundered Florange's tent. During this fighting, Blaise de Monluc, who had joined the company of captain Castille of Navarre, was captured. Monluc wrote that he was taken by two cavalrymen of Antonio de Leyva's company.

Some chroniclers write that the garrison of Pavia continued north towards Mirabello after destroying the enemy garrison, while others write that they moved west to destroy the French bridges over the Ticino. Probably, both things happened, as the seventh tapestry analysed in the following chapter argues. It shows the infantry and cavalry leaving Pavia and moving in two directions, one towards the French camp to the east and the other on the opposite side towards the river.

As we have already seen, Alençon's cavalry survived the French debacle along with several thousand infantry. In addition to these men, captain Clarmont saved himself because he was guarding Montmorency's quarters on Gravellone Eyot. Having witnessed the defeat, this Clarmont resolved that helping the King was useless and withdrew with his troops. Passing the Gravellone River, he destroyed the bridges, continued towards Mortara, and arrived in France unscathed. The French in Milan, who were besieging the castle held by the Sforza's men, did the same. Their commander, Teodoro Trivulzio, kept the news of the defeat secret and actually announced that the French had won the battle. Undisturbed, he had weapons and luggage prepared and left Milan with his troops. Thus, he arrived unmolested at Lake Maggiore.[1]

---

1 F. Taegio, *Rotta e prigionia di Francesco primo re' di Francia sotto Pavia l'anno 1525. Composta dal Taegi, e dal latino tradotta dal Cremonese Cambiago* (Pavia:1655), p.58; M. Guazzo, *Historie* (Venice: 1549), p.8; A. Bonardi, *L'Assedio e la battaglia di Pavia. Diario inedito* (Pavia: Poulailler,1895), p.22; R. de la Marck Florange, *Mémoires du Maréchal de Florange*, tome II (Paris: Renouard, H. Laurens, successeur, 1924), pp.231–232; M. García Cerezeda, *Tratado de las campañas y otros acontecimientos de los ejércitos del emperador Carlos V en Italia, Francia, Austria, Berbería y Grecia,* tomo I (Madrid: Impresores de Cámara, 1873), p.122; P. Giovio, *Vite del Gran Capitano e del marchese di Pescara* (Bari: Gius, Laterza & Figli, 1931), p.430; J. Baader, 'Die Schlacht bei Pavia, nach dem Bericht eines Augenzeugen' in Anzeiger fur kunde der deutschen vorzeit, November 1868, p.348; 'Relazione sulla battaglia del Frundsberg e Zuan Moro' in D. Testi, La batalla de Pavia, Fuentes historiograficas y epistolares del siglo XVI, (Madrid: Ministerio de Defensa 2024), pp.51 & 59.

23

Seventh Tapestry
The Sortie of the Besieged and the Rout of the Swiss, Who Drown in Large Numbers in the Ticino River

See Plate O

Seventh Tapestry. (Reproduced with the permission of the Ministero della Cultura, Museo e Real Bosco di Capodimonte)

As per the title of this chapter, this seventh and final tapestry represents the sortie of de Leyva's Imperials from Pavia and the rout of the Swiss and other soldiers of the French Army, who drowned in great numbers in the Ticino River. The scene places the city of Pavia in the centre, seen from the west; on the left, there is the Visconti castle and, on the opposite side, the covered bridge that crosses the Ticino. The river occupies the entire right side of the work, starting from the front, passes under the bridge, touches the island of Gavellona and then twists and turns towards the horizon. In the background, there are hills, woods, houses and camps. The vegetation is as lush as in the other tapestries, which is unlikely considering that the events took place in February.

SEVENTH TAPESTRY

Luigi Casali writes that the depicted city recalls the Pavia of Jörg Breu's engraving on the Battle of Pavia. The castle, just like the square towers and the walls, is crenellated in Ghibelline fashion, although in Breu's work, there are towers with square crenelation. Even the buildings of the city are the same up to their truncated-cone chimneys. In both works, the walls are medieval and damaged by the blows of the French artillery. For this reason, there are numerous embankments close to the walls to reinforce the weakest points, such as the semi-circular embankment that protects the entrance to the castle[1].

However, this depiction of the city is not accurate. In the late Romanesque church of San Teodoro, in the centre of Pavia, there is a fresco attributed

Sortie from the castle of Pavia. (Reproduced with the permission of the Ministero della Cultura, Museo e Real Bosco di Capodimonte)

to Bernardino Lanzani with a view of sixteenth-century Pavia. The fresco was executed in 1522, just three years before the battle. The architecture of this Pavia is quite similar to that of the tapestry, but with some substantial differences. The towers are similar, square-based with squared crenelations, and the same goes for the battlements of the city walls. The Visconti castle in the fresco differs above all in the towers for their masonry corbels covered by roofs, and in the masonry-covered walkways along the front. Then, the covered bridge over the Ticino has a simpler aesthetic to that shown on the tapestry, which is more 'imaginative'. Finally, the houses are similar in terms of the roofs in brick tiles, but in the tapestry, they have a North European

---

1   Luigi Casali, *Gli arazzi della battaglia di Pavia nel Museo di Capodimonte a Napoli* (Pavia: Edizioni ViGiEffe, 1993), pp.59–62.

style of architecture with truncated-cone chimneys. The fresco houses, on the other hand, are simpler in design with small chimneys on the roofs.

Returning to the scenes of the seventh tapestry, the Imperial cavalry leaves the city through the castle gate and attacks the French troops left behind on guard. The chroniclers Capo de Capino and Florange report that the Imperials left the castle gate, and Giovio confirms this version adding that part of the troops also left Porta Nuova. The cavalry are all well-armed men-at-arms who have white, yellow and red plumes and carry spears with banners displaying the Burgundian Cross. The infantry is further back.

The cavalry takes two directions; on the left, it clashes with the French infantry who are guarding against any sorties. These infantry were part of the bands of Giovanni Medici, but in the tapestry, they have the usual landsknecht dress and diplay the white cross. Behind them, in the background, other infantry are fleeing with donkeys and waggons, abandoning shelters and small towers.

In the foreground of the tapestry, Swiss infantry are fleeing from left to right towards the Ticino. The first two on the left, with hats adorned with beautiful plumes, could be captains. One holds a two-handed sword, while the other, in infantry armour, holds a Colour with the French cross and the bottom of white and yellow stripes. In front of them, other Swiss armed with halberds and pikes flee and climb over the west wall of the park, which ends in the Ticino on the tapestry.

Between these soldiers and the city walls, many other Swiss are fleeing – there are also women with them. They leave the small circular towers or shelters of the French trench line and go towards the river. On the left, two Imperial cavalrymen chase a drummer and a Standard bearer, while on the far right, other cavalrymen push the fugitives into the Ticino and kill them using lances. Terrified, the soldiers throw themselves into the water.

Monfort and Sucre. (Reproduced with the permission of the Ministero della Cultura, Museo e Real Bosco di Capodimonte)

Many drown, while on the other shore, some try to help their drowning comrades. In these scenes, the tapestry makers have well represented the death of the hundreds of Swiss in the river, as reported by the sources.

In this tapestry, there are two prominent figures indicated with an inscription of their names: two men on horseback in the centre of the scene, chasing the Swiss. The one on the left is a man-at-arms with the inscription MONFORT on the bridle of his horse, the other is a light cavalryman wearing a burgonet and with the inscription SVCRE on the bridle of his horse. They are the same two men who chased the drummer, and the Swiss Standard bearer described above, with only slight differences in the horses' harness and the colours of the plumes. This is a peculiarity of these tapestries when it comes to representing the same character several times, something already analysed in the chapter on the third tapestry (see image 'Sortie from the Castle' above).

Until now, scholars have not been able to correctly identify these two cavalrymen, misled by the name Monfort.[2] There are various hypotheses, such as he was François Laval, Comte de Montfort, thought to be mentioned among the casualties of Pavia – he actually died three years earlier in the Battle of Bicocca.[3] Another hypothesis suggests him to be Guy, Comte de Laval et Montfort, Governor of Brittany under Francis I – the chronicles of Pavia never mention this nobleman. Finally, he is sometimes thought to be another Montfort, captain of the Provencal infantry, who, although he was at Pavia and took part in the battle, was actually at the head of the French pikemen who joined the square of the landsknechts of the Black Band – they were almost all killed or taken prisoner[4].

It is possible that, looking for this character among the French Army has misled the scholars, confused by the name Monfort. These two cavalrymen, although without recognition signs, are fighting for the Imperials. They chased the two infantrymen with the drum and banner, and in this same tapestry, they attack a Swiss infantryman, who raises his open hand in surrender. In this regard, Luigi Casali points out an interesting detail. Comparing the tapestry with the preparatory drawing made by van Orley and the other artists and preserved in the Louvre, he found that in the drawing, the two cavalrymen do not hit the infantryman but hold their spears vertical. It is evident that the scene was modified in the tapestry,

---

2   Luigi Casali, *Gli arazzi della battaglia di Pavia nel Museo di Capodimonte a Napoli* (Pavia: Edizioni ViGiEffe, 1993), pp.63–64; N. Spinosa, *Gli arazzi della battaglia di Pavia* (Milan: Bompiani, 1999), p.74; Carmine Romano (ed.), *Art & War in the Renaissance: The Battle of Pavia Tapestries* (New York: Rizzoli International 2024), p.117.
3   M. Couanier de Launay, *Histoire de Laval* (Laval: Mary-Beayghêne,1894), p.225; P. Giovio, *Vite del Gran Capitano e del marchese di Pescara* (Bari: Gius, Laterza & Figli, 1931), p.293.
4   M. de la Chesnaye-Desbois, *Dictionnaire de la Noblesse* (Paris: Vve Duchesne, 1775), tome X, p.361, F. B. Barthold, *George von Frundsberg* (Hamburg, Perthes, 1833), p.320.

but the surrender of the infantryman is visible in both the tapestry and the preparatory drawing, as is the confident action of the two cavalrymen, who are not fleeing as all French cavalry do from the second tapestry onwards.

In my opinion, this man-at-arms is Guillaume de Montfort, a gentleman of Emperor Charles V and a descendant of the ancient Taillant d'Yvorie family. He was from Burgundy and was part of the cavalry of the same county, becoming a great squire of The Emperor and his most trusted confidante. Charles V assigned to him a delicate mission, as evidenced by the letters that The Emperor wrote to him, today preserved in the Granvelle Collection.

These documents, dated from 1528 to 1529, contain a list of Montfort's missions. He was sent to Germany with 20,000 ducats to hire 3,000 German infantrymen, then he went to Flanders to talk with the Archduchess Margaret, The Emperor's wife, and travelled to Hungary with messages for The Emperor's brother, Ferdinand. Monfort died in Mantua in March 1530 while accompanying Charles V.[5] I have not found quotes about him in the sources on the battle, however his important role and his closeness to The Emperor leads me to deduce that he could be this person on the tapestry.

As for the other cavalryman, this man's horse has no protection while the man wears a full armour with a beige saione on top. He has a burgonet with a white plume, and the bridle of his horse has the inscription SVCRE. This was an Imperial captain of light cavalry named Sucre, mentioned by Monluc in his account, while, after the battle, he talks with the prisoner Federico Bozzolo about the clash and the mistakes made by the French.[6] This captain was the most important commander of the Imperial cavalry after Civita Sant'Angelo. Marin Sanudo calls him Zucharo, commander of 150 light cavalry, while Spanish chronicler Prudencio Sandoval calls him Alvares Chuchar, commander of a company of Cappelletti (stradiots). Finally, Florange mentions him as Jacques de Succre, Seigneur de Bellaing, a Burgundian captain fighting for The Emperor.[7]

The identification of this character confirms that these two cavalrymen fought for the Imperials and not the French, as it was previously thought.

---

5 *Charles-quint a Montfort* in *Papiers d'Etat du Cardinal de Granvelle*, Paris 1841, pp.347, 425, 439 et seq.
6 Blaise de Monluc, *Commentaires et lettres* (Paris: Mme Ve J. Renouard, 1864), tome I, p.73.
7 M. Sanudo, I Diarii (Venice: *M. Visentini*, 1893), tome XXXVII, p.499; P. da Sandoval, *Historia del Emperador Carlos V*, volumen IV (Madrid: Madoz, 1846), pp.169–170, 210; R. de la Marck Florange, *Mémoires du Maréchal de Florange*, tome II (Paris: Renouard, H. Laurens, successeur, 1924), pp.43, 166 and 318.

24

The Casualties of the Battle

According to the accounts of the battle it ended between 9:00 and 10:00 in the morning. Corpses and wounded lay on the ground for two or three miles. In this regard, Spanish historian Ulloa gives the following description:

> On that day, soldiers had little mercy, until they were tired from much killing. Throughout the countryside, nothing could be seen but the bodies of the dead, some of which caused great compassion, because, being mortally wounded and groaning, they called for help. Others, who were dying, screamed miserably and turned in their own and others' blood, praying their enemies to finish them. Many were without arms, others without legs and others without heads. It was a gruesome fact of arms. More than 10,000 men died in combat, and many drowned in the river.[1]

According to Paolo Giovio, a total of 10,000 people died. Caspar Wintzerer and Santa Cuz report the same number, but write it as French casualties and do not consider the drowned soldiers.

According to Francesco Guicciardini, more than 8,000 men and about 20 of the premier lords of France died in the French ranks, between those killed in combat and drowned in the Ticino River while fleeing. About 700 Imperials died, but no captain except the Marchese di Sant'Angelo.

---

1   Llonso de Ulloa, *Vita dell'invittissimo, e sacratissimo Imperator Carlo V* (Venice, 1566), p.99; P. Giovo in La vita del s. Don Ferrante d'Avalos Marchese di Pescara (Florence: 1556), p.245; J. Baader, 'Die Schlacht bei Pavia, nach dem Bericht eines Augenzeugen' in Anzeiger fur kunde der deutschen vorzeit, November 1868, p.350; A. de Santas Cruz, 'Relazione' in D. Testi, La batalla de Pavia, Fuentes historiograficas y epistolares del siglo XVI, (Madrid: Ministerio de Defensa 2024), p.152.

Two other Italian chroniclers, Passero and Grumello, agree in saying that the French Army suffered 15,000 dead. Passero adds that '3,000 men drowned in the Ticino, and the French lost 33 pieces of artillery.'[2]

Another Italian chronicler, friar Jacopo Filippo, writes that about 800 of The Emperor's men were killed, and on the French side, almost all the Italians and the landsknechts of the Black Band died. In addition, they lost 1,500 Swiss, and the others surrendered to the Imperial Army, except for 500 who drowned in Ticino. Thus, on both sides, 8,000 men remained on the battlefield.

In a letter from Armaciotto Ramazzotti to Guicciardini, the Italian captain writes that 14,000 French had died in battle. The Imperials suffered fewer losses, but lost a number of captains: the Marchese di Civita Santangelo, the lieutenant of the Marchese di Pescara, two Spanish captains, four landsknecht captains, and six Spanish and Neapolitan gentlemen.

According to Spanish historian Prudencio de Sandoval, 15,000 French but only 700 Imperial troops died in Pavia.[3]

Capino de Capo reports 12,000 French casualties, 8,000 prisoners and 29 captured cannons. Other Italian chroniclers, on the other hand, register lower numbers. Politiano and the Anonymous report about 6,000 dead, Bernardino Barba writes of 4,000, whereas Donado, Zuan Moro and the Venetian Orator report 3,000 casualties between the two armies.[4]

French chroniclers du Bellay, Monluc and Florange do not report the overall losses of the battle. Instead, they list the names of the French captains and nobles who died or were taken prisoners. Florange was the most exhaustive in this regard; thus, the choice to report his list.[5]

Prisoners:

King Francis; the King of Navarre;[6] the Monsigneur de Saint-Pol and Knight of the Order[7]; François Talmont, Prince de Tallamont;

---

2 Francesco Guicciardini, *Histoire d'Italie de l'année 1492 à l'année 1532,* tome 5 (Paris: A. Desrez 1837), p.168; G. Passero, *Historie* (Naples: Vincenzo Maria Altobelli, 1785), p.320; Antonio Grumello, *Cronaca* in *Raccolta di cronisti e documenti storici lombardi,* (Milan: Francesco Colombo, 1856), tomo I, p.375.

3 J. Philippo, *Supplementi delle croniche del Venerando Padre Frate Jacobo Philippo, dell'ordine* Heremitano, (Venice: 1535), p.ccclxvi; 'Lettera del capitano Ramazzotto a Francesco Guicciardini' in *Archivio Storico Italiano,* tome V (Florence: Presso G.P. Vieusseux, 1851), p.319; P. da Sandoval, *Historia del Emperador Carlos V,* volumen IV (Madrid: Madoz, 1846), p.245.

4 Reports on the Battle of Pavia can be found in D. Testi, La batalla de Pavia, Fuentes historiograficas y epistolares del siglo XVI, (Madrid: Ministerio de Defensa 2024), pp.52, 56, 58, 59, 62 & 67.

5 R. de la Marck Florange, *Mémoires du Maréchal de Florange,* tome II (Paris: Renouard, H. Laurens, successeur, 1924), pp.235–241.

6 Henry of Navarre escaped from the castle of Pavia with a rope ladder on the night of 25 December 1525.

7 Knight of the Order of St Michael.

THE CASUALTIES OF THE BATTLE

Louis de Clèves, Monsigneur de Nevers; François de Saluce; René, the Bâtard de Savoy and Knight of the Order;[8] the Monseigneur de Lescut, *Maréchal* de France and Knight of the Order; the *Maréchal* de Montmorensy, Knight of the Order; the Monsigneur d'Aubigny, Captain of the Gardes Écossaise, and Knight of the Order; Monsigneur de Florenges, Capitaine Général des Suisses and Knight of the Order; the Monseigneur de Bryon, Knight of the Order; Gallice Viconte (Galeazzo Visconti); Sieur Frederyc de Beauge (Federico da Bozzolo), Knight of the Order; Lord Pol Camille (Paolo Camillo Trivulzio), captain of 100 gentlemen of the King's Household and Knight of the Order.

Captured Officers who were neither Princes nor Knights of the Order:

Monseigneur Vyame de Chartres, captain of a band of 100 gentlemen of the King; Monseigneur de Sainte, captain of 50 men-at-arms; Viscomte de Vanedent, captain of 50 men-at-arms; Monseigneur de Savigny, captain of a band of archers of the guard; Monseigneur de Nansot, captain of a band of archers of the guard; La Rochepot, brother of *Maréchal* de Montmorency, captain of 50 men-at-arms; La Roche du Maine, lieutenant of Alençon; Savigny, lieutenant to the *amiral*; the lieutenant of Monsieur d'Aubigny; the Viscomte d'Estoges; Monseigneur Gabriel de Lignac, lieutenant of Monsieur de Lescout; Baron de Creton, lieutenant of *Maréchal* Cabannes; the lieutenant and son of Monsigneur de Tournon de Tournon; the lieutenant of de Saint-Pol Maulgiron; Captain Parys, lieutenant of Monseigneur de Bryon; the lieutenant of Monseigneur de la Trimouille d'Estampes; Noirfontaine, who bears the insignia and pennon of Monseigneur de Florenges; the Bailly de Dijon, who carried the King's Cornet.

Nobles taken prisoner who did not hold Court or Army positions

Monseigneur de Montigaut (Montigend) de Bretagne, who was seriously wounded; Monseigneur de Carignant, son of the Sieur Saint Vallier; Monseigneur de Boysy (Tristan Gouffier); Monseigneur Gabriel de la Guiche; Monseigneur de Barbesieuix; Monseigneur de la Gruytheuse (Louis de Bruges, Sieur de la Gruthuse); Monseigneur de Bussy; Monseigneur Antoine de Hallwin, Sieur de Piennes; Antoine de Lettes, Seigneur de Montpezat, gentleman of the King's Chamber; the Bailly of Paris (Jean de la Barre, commander of Paris); the Sieur de Bessansy; Pier Ortys; Pommereaulx, *Maître d'Artillerie*;

---

8   According to several sources, he was not at Pavia during the battle.

Hugues de Lanoye; La Chambre; Francisque, a squire; Marin de Monchenu, *Premier Maître* of the King's Palace; Ghynegatte, *Maître* of the Palace; Monsignor des Bonnes, *Maître* of the Palace; *Général* Ponthieu; Poton; Montmort; Marfontaine; Monsigneur Jean-François de la Rocque, Sieur de Roberval; Gruffy; *Trésorier* Jean Grollier; the treasurer of Milan and other four treasurers.

Captains of the French infantry:

Monseigneur Dancy, lieutenant of *Monsieur* de Bussy; captain Miracle; captain Castille Lagruez; captain Labborde; captain Sainte Jullien.

Italian Captains who were captured and killed:

Captured: captain Garnet, captain Bagart, Marcque Antoine d'Escusant.[9]

The Landsknechts:

Graf Wolfz, Captain General and three or four other captains who were with him.

19 Swiss captains taken prisoner.

As for the casualties, the most famous names come first:

François, brother of the Duc de Lorraine, captain of a band of landsknechts; the Duc de Suffort, captain of another band of landsknechts; Galeazzo da Sanseverino (Galliace de Saint-Severin,) *Grand écuyer de France*, Knight of the Order; the Sieur La Tremouille, Governor of Burgundy and *Amiral* de Bretagne, First Chamberlain to the King, Knight of the Order; the Sieur de Bonnivet, *Amiral* de France, Governor of Daulphinez, Knight of the Order; the Sieur de Lescut, *Maréchal* de France;[10] *Maréchal* Cabannes, Sieur de La Palice, Governor of Bourbonnois, Knight of the Order; the Sieur de Chaulmont (Georges d'Amboise, Seigneur of Chaumont); the Sieur de Bussy (Jacques d'Amboise), Captain of the French mercenaries; Comte Tonnoire (Claude de Husson, Comte de Tonnerre); the Sieur de Istella; the squire Narasin of the King's squires; the Bâtard

---

9   Unidentifiable names.
10 He also figures among the prisoners.

THE CASUALTIES OF THE BATTLE

of Luppe (Michel, Bâtard de Luppe, *Maître de lePalace du Roi*); the *Maître* of the palace Saint-Severin and many other gentlemen.

We have seen the disparity of numbers in contemporary sources regarding the losses of the French. Modern scholars, on the other hand, agree on around 10,000 dead; only Piero Pieri gives a lower figure, estimating 6,000 deaths among the French. For the Imperial forces, on the other hand, ancient and modern texts cite losses of 800 men or less, only Johann Newald cites a total number of Imperial losses from 400 to a maximum of 1000.[11] An accurate calculation is impossible, but in my opinion, the Imperial casualties would have been more than 1,000. The sources that cite these losses, however, are all written by chroniclers on the winners' side, who had the evident interest of reporting low numbers. In this regard, it is necessary to consider the events that occurred, such as the defeat and slaughter of Cesare Maggi's Italian infantry, the bombardment of the French artillery and the charge of the King's gendarmes; all actions that had a heavy impact on the Imperial Army. In addition, the German Black Band was annihilated in the fight, but many of its enemies also fell. For these reasons, I believe that the Imperial casualties were far more than those registered in the reports – and additionally there were at least a few thousand wounded.

---

11 J. Newald, *Niclas Graf zu Salm, eine historisch studie* (Wien: Gerold, 1879), p.47.

25

The Aftermath of the Battle

Portrait of Charles V by Titian. (Wikipaedia)

At the end of the battle, Francis I was taken to the Certosa of Pavia and the next day to the fortress of Pizzighettone to prevent any attempts to free him and to keep him safe from assaults by Imperial soldiers or the citizens of Pavia, who had endured painful months of siege at his hands. Meanwhile, the soldiers ransomed the bodies of dead French nobles to their servants or family representatives, and Lannoy released many prisoners who could not pay their ransom. Among the German mercenaries, there were attempts to revolt in the Imperial camp because of the usual lack of wages. Lannoy resolved the matter, promising payment soon.

On 3 March, the Imperial Army entered Milan, to where Pescara, Bourbon and Lannoy moved their headquarters.

On 10 March, however, the news of the victory reached The Emperor's court in Madrid, along with a message from Bourbon advising Charles V to organise the invasion of southern France and to resume the alliance with King Henry VIII of England.

Francis began negotiating with the Imperial commanders, while in France, the government had passed into the hands of Louise de Savoy, the King's mother. She reinforced the country defences, paid the Swiss mercenaries in full to ensure their loyalty, and reorganised the remnants of the defeated army in Lyon, reinforcing it with additional troops.

Then, she refused the conditions imposed by Charles V to free her son, especially the cession of Burgundy and the lands confiscated from the Duc de Bourbon. In Picardy, there was fear of an

THE AFTERMATH OF THE BATTLE

English attack, so, due to the death of the Duc d'Alençon, Charles, Duc de Vendôme, was sent to organise the defence of the cities. At the same time, Louise sent ambassadors to warn King Henry VIII against the danger of a too-powerful Emperor.

On 10 June 1525, Francis was put on a Spanish galley in Genoa to be taken to Naples. A small fleet escorted him as French warships followed, but at some point, the Spanish changed course and headed for Spain. After disembarking in Barcelona, the French King was taken to Madrid, where he arrived on 17 July.

On 11 August, Henry VIII and the regent Louise signed a treaty in which the English King undertook not to attack Picardy. At the time, England had no funds to sustain a new war in France and concerns over an overly powerful Spain had grown in Henry, who also requested The Emperor to free King Francis in return for heavy ransom.

Meanwhile, the Pope, Venice, Florence and other minor states created an anti-Imperial alliance in Italy.

The King's imprisonment, although more like a sojourn, was not particularly pleasant because Charles V refused to receive Francis on several occasions. To make matter worse, Francis I fell suddenly ill – the cause being claimed to be to his sorrow over Charles' constant denials. The illness, of an unspecified nature, worsened to such an extent that The Emperor decided to visit him on 28 September 1525, fearing his imminent death. Whether the illness was due to sorrow is unknown, but, after Charles' visit, the King's health improved until he was completely well.

In November, Margaret of Angoulême, Duchesse d'Alençon and sister of the King, arrived in Madrid. She tried in every way to plead for her brother's release, but in vain.

Finally, the ambassadors of both parties reached an agreement, which was signed on 14 January 1526 in Madrid. Francis I ceded Burgundy to The Emperor and renounced his interests in the Duchy of Milan and the Kingdom of Naples. He also agreed to leave his sons, Francis and Henri, as hostages and to marry Eleonora of Habsburg, the sister of Charles V.

On 17 March, in Bidassoa on the border between France and Spain, the French King was released in exchange for his children. However, on 22 March, the Pope conceded to Francis the invalidation of his obligations under the Treaty of Madrid. In the meantime, in Italy, hostilities had begun afresh, and a new Imperial Army under Bourbon's orders ended the revolt of the Italian states and sacked Rome in May 1527. In August of the same year, the King of France sent a new army to Italy under the command of Odet de Foix, Comte de Lautrec. The French besieged Pavia, then captured and plundered it. But the following year, while besieging Naples, a virulent plague broke out in the army which killed many men, Lautrec among them, and forced the army to return to France.

Although he was again victorious, Charles V had to deal with a Turkish Army, which, after invading Hungary, was about to attack Vienna, as well as an imminent Protestant revolt in Germany.

THE BATTLE OF PAVIA 1525

Thus when Francis I asked to renegotiate the terms of the Treaty of Madrid, The Emperor agreed. The treaty, signed at Cambrai on 3 August 1529, saw the King of France renouncing his claims on Italy and paying a large war compensation. Charles V, for his part, renounced his claim on Burgundy and released Francis' sons.

Despite this treaty, the war between France and The Empire continued, although erratically, for another 20 years.

26

The Heraldry of the Battle of Pavia

A. The Heraldry of The Empire

The Heraldry of Charles V

This chapter initially presents the heraldry of Emperor Charles V. Born in Ghent in 1500 to Philip 'the Handsome' Habsburg and Joanna 'the Mad,' Charles was the grandson of The Holy Roman Emperor Maximilian and of the King of Spain, Ferdinand. On his father's death in 1506, Charles inherited The Netherlands, Artois, Luxembourg and Franche-Comté. In 1516, with the death of Ferdinand, he became King of Spain and also

Standard of Charles V. (Reproduced with the permission of the Ministero della Cultura, Museo e Real Bosco di Capodimonte)

gained the Spanish territories in Italy and the Americas. Then, in 1519, he inherited the Austrian lands from his grandfather Maximilian, and in the same year, was elected Emperor of The Holy Roman Empire.

His primary coat of arms was the Imperial black, double-headed eagle, visible in much of the iconography of the Battle of Pavia – in the third tapestry of Capodimonte or the painting by Ruprecht Heller. In his book *Teatro d'Imprese*, Giovanni Ferro mentions some coins of Charles V with the eagle holding in its claws a basilisk and a snake representing defeated enemies.

Charles V's impresa, on the other hand, was the Pillars of Hercules with the motto *Plus Ultra* – it alluded to Spanish sovereignty extending beyond the Straits of Gibraltar with the conquest of the Western Indies. According to Paolo Giovio, the sovereign's doctor, the Milanese humanist Luigi Marliani, invented this impresa. At times, the columns were depicted on flags accompanies by the double-headed eagle.

Another of The Emperor's emblems was the St Andrew's Cross, also known as the Burgundian Cross, that Charles V inherited from his father, Philip. It was usually red on a white or yellow field, but there were other colour variations recorded in the iconography. Under Charles V, this cross became the Imperial sign of recognition – and was used until the eighteenth century. The St Andrew's Cross could be simple or knotted – the latter was the Burgundian version. Sometimes, the cross was depicted with four flint steels, another impresa of the Ducs de Burgundy.[1]

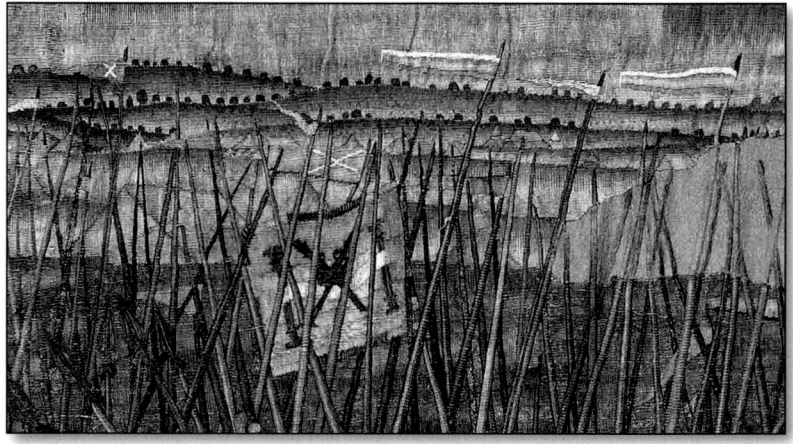

Imperial insignia from the first tapestry. (Reproduced with the permission of the Ministero della Cultura, Museo e Real Bosco di Capodimonte)

The following are the colours of Charles V's livery, which Sanudo mentions in his *Diarii* where he publishes the letters of the Venetian diplomat Francesco Corner to the court of Spain. These letters, dated December 1518, tell of Charles' arrival in Valladolid, where he me the

---

1 G. Ferro, *Teatro d'Imprese* (Venice: 1623), p.87; P. Giovio, *Vite del Gran Capitano e del marchese di Pescara* (Bari: Gius, Laterza & Figli, 1931), pp.46–47; C. Paradin, *Devises Heroiques* (Paris: 1614), p.52–53.

Cortes of Castille as the new King of Spain. In the letters, Corner describes the clothing of the nobles, clergymen and gentlemen who participated in the procession, as well as the clothing of servants, pages and guards of the sovereign.

Thus, we learn that the King's falconers were dressed in white, red and yellow cloth – the diplomat emphasises that these colours were Charles' livery. Then, Corner mentions 20 knights of the King dressed in crimson satin embroidered with gold and silver brocade, and 200 halberdiers who wore clothes in the same livery – 100 of them were Germans. Finally, he describes 10 grooms dressed in silk livery jackets, and 100 Burgundian archers in the same colours – white, red and yellow.

Charles would wear these colours even after he was elected Emperor in 1519, since the chronicler Prudencio de Sandoval mentioned this livery on the robes of The Emperor's knights at his entrance into Aachen in 1520.[2]

He still wore them at Pavia in 1525, as exemplified by the Capodimonte tapestries. In the first tapestry, the Imperial Army has numerous insignia coloured white, yellow and red, as noted in the above chapter on this tapestry.

This livery changed in 1530. In the chronicles about Charles V's coronation in Bologna in the same year, his pages are described as wearing velvet clothes in yellow, *bigio* (grey) and *morello* (dark purple) – the author writes that they were wearing The Emperor's livery. However, later in the chronicle, the author mentions 24 pages in Charles' livery but in yellow velvet with purple and the left sleeve chequered yellow and purple.

The halberdiers are described wearing yellow velvet jackets with purple lists and one quartered sleeve in the same colours.[3]

Other liveries are also mentioned in the texts, such as some servants of Charles wearing yellow and black clothes or other Spanish cavalrymen in a full yellow livery.

Two considerations in this regard. The use of the livery on one sleeve is interesting, a peculiarity of Bourbon's guard that I have already described in the chapter on the third tapestry. Then, the colour variety in the clothes of The Emperor's pages, servants and soldiers certainly differentiated the groups by importance. However, in that period, the sovereign's livery changed and adopted the predominant colours of yellow and red. His guard sported these colours as in the tapestries on the capture of Tunis in 1535, executed by Willem de Pannemaker. Clonard reconstructed this guard's garment in his 'Album dela Infantería española' in 1800.

---

2   M. Sanudo, *I Diarii* (Venice: M. Visentini, 1889), pp.128–129; P. da Sandoval, *Historia del Emperador Carlos V*, volumen III (Madrid: Madoz, 1846), p.275.
3   G. Giordani, *Della venza e residora in Bologna del somo pontefice Clemente VII per la coronación di Carlo V imperatore celebata nel anno 1530*, Bologna 1842, pp.28 and 31.

THE BATTLE OF PAVIA 1525

The Heraldry of the Imperial Captains

For this chapter, I used the description of the Imperial captains made before the battle by chronicler Juan de Oznajo, who participated in the Battle of Pavia and the campaign in the company of the Marchese di Vasto.[4]

I will compare Oznajo's descriptions with other sources on this subject, written before and after the Battle of Pavia, to paint a more realistic view of the captains' heraldry. Passero's chronicle is especially relevant among these texts for its heraldic content.

Captain Alarcón and Viceroy de Lannoy (Artwork by Massimo Predonzani)

Oznajo begins by describing Viceroy Charles de Lannoy's vanguard, preceded by six cornets dressed in red and yellow, with red taffeta trumpet banners displaying the Imperial coat of arms in gold. The Viceroy was armed with white and gold weapons and wore a *saione* in brocaded crimson satin over his armour and had white, red and gold feathers on his helmet.

Sigismondo from Naples also reported these colours in a letter published by Sanudo, in which he recounts the King of France's departure from Genoa to his captivity in Spain. Sigismondo writes that Francis I had taken his place in the galley of Viceroy Charles de Lannoy, recognisable by the velvet and satin tents in red, white and yellow – according to the writer, it was the livery of the Viceroy.

On the third tapestry, which depicts the King's capture, the Viceroy has dismounted with the help of an attendant. On his helmet, he has white, red and gold plumes. Over his armour, he wears a beautiful *saione* in gold, blue and crimson brocade. Behind him is his Standard bearer with the Imperial Standard, wearing a crimson *saione* with a gold and white edge.

Considering these elements, Lannoy's livery consisted of yellow, red

---

4   J. de Oznajo, Batalla de Pavia y prision del Rey de Francia Francisco I in *Coleccion de documentos inéditos para la historia de Espana* (Madrid: Imprenta de la Viuda de Calero,1846), volumen IX, pp.454–456.

THE HERALDRY OF THE BATTLE OF PAVIA

and white – the same colours as those of Emperor Charles. Unfortunately, the impresas adopted by the Viceroy remain unknown, but his coat of arms had three green lions on a silver field.

After the Viceroy, Oznajo describes the Duc de Bourbon, saying that he wore a brocade tunic over his armour but with no device. Paolo Giovio also reports this and explains that the duke, fearing a revenge from the French because of his betrayal, had his faithful friend Pompèran wear his insignia and clothes, and he dressed as a simple cavalryman instead.[5] In the Capodimonte tapestries, on the other hand, Bourbon is represented with the coat of arms on his horse's barding so as to be easily recognisable by the viewing audience. The first tapestry also depicts his knights in yellow livery and with a sleeve decorated with red, blue, and yellow triangles, the colours recalling his coat of arms, and with a Standard with the winged stag impresa. The duke did use other impresas and mottos, such as a strap with the motto *Esperance* or flaming swords with the motto *A Toujours Mais*.[6]

The Spanish chronicler goes on to describe the liveries of the Marchese di Vasto, captain Hernando de Alarcón, Castriota and Hernando de Avalos, Marchese di Pescara, and many others.

The impresas of Alfonso d'Avalos, the Marchese di Vasto, are well-known. Giovio mentions the world with the four elements, the Madonna and Child, and the Archangel Raphael with Tobias. In addition, two sheaves of wheat and the Temple of Juno Lacinia. Unfortunately, d'Avalos began to use these insignias after 1530, approximately when he became captain general of the Imperial Army, so they were not in use at Pavia. Only the Temple of Juno Lacinia was more contemporary but it was not used until 1527, still after the Battle of Pavia.[7] Thanks to Oznajo's chronicle, we know, at least, that in the fight d'Avalos wore a silver and light red robe, the same colours as his plumes and his horse's harness.[8] In short, it was a white and red livery. In the Capodimonte tapestries, on the other hand, in the third tapestry, he is represented in full armour with his horse's harness painted red and with blue plumes on his helmet. He has no beard, since at the time of Pavia, he was little more than 20 years old.

According to Oznajo, Hernando de Alarcón, the Spanish captain who led the rearguard, had a black velvet robe over his armour without any device. The Neapolitan chronicler Passero also mentions black and yellow as his livery in the description of a review of the men-at-arms and light

---

5   P. Giovio, *Vite del Gran Capitano e del marchese di Pescara* (Bari: Gius, Laterza & Figli, 1931), p.423.
6   Find a list of these impresas in my previous book on Pavia: M. Predonzani & V. Alberici, *The Italian Wars*, volume 3: *Francis I and the Battle of Pavia 1525* (Warwick: Helion & Company, 2022), pp.94–96.
7   For the heraldry of del Vasto: M. Predonzani & Simon Miller, *The Italian Wars, volume 4. The Battle of* Ceresole (Warwick: Helion & Company 2022), pp.66–69.
8   J. de Oznajo, 'Batalla de Pavia y prison del rey de France Francisco I' in Coleccion de documentos inéditos para la historia de Espana, (Madrid: Imprenta de la Viuda de Calero,1846), volumen IX, p.455.

cavalrymen present in the Kingdom of Naples on 4 October 1518. The description is precise and interesting, with a lot of details on the captains and their men. It does not list the main captains, but their lieutenants. The chronicler records that the parade of the company of Don Alarcón, Viceroy of Calabria, was led by his lieutenant, Captain Vigliega, and began with grooms dressed in yellow and black cloth who led by hand six horses dressed in multicoloured velvet caparisons. Some of these horses also had protections on their necks and wore a shaffron; one wore a steel harness covered in black velvet. Captain Vigliega rode a horse with a crimson velvet caparison with gold embroidery, the same colour of velvet that covered its neck and shaffron. The captain wore a crimson velvet *saione* over his armour. Around him, there were four other grooms dressed in black and yellow cloth. A standard bearer raised a large banner embroidered with gold; unfortunately, the chronicler does not report the impresa or emblem displayed on it. Finally, there were 50 well-armed Spanish men-at-arms wearing black and crimson velvet *saioni* on top of their armour and horses equipped with harnesses. It is interesting to note that Alarcón's men wore black and yellow, while the men-at-arms wore black and crimson.

Finally, this captain also participated in the coronation of Charles V in Bologna in 1530 with his soldiers, who wore velvet *saioni* in a yellow and turquoise livery.[9]

Ferrante Castriota, Marchese di Sant'Angelo, commanded the light cavalry and, according to Oznajo, wore light armour and rode a brown horse. Castriota wore a crimson coat over his armour, and his horse's harness was of the same colour. In his review of 1518, Passero writes that this company was led by a gentleman named Vincenzo da Sorrento, who rode a large horse with a barding, peytal and shaffron of grey (*pardo*) velvet. He wore a *saione* of the same colour over his armour. In front of him, four pages proceeded on horseback, dressed in brown cloth; the grooms also wore brown cloth. Behind them, 50 Italian cavalrymen rode barded horses and wore garments in various colours over their armour.[10]

Other captains, also mentioned, and their companies who later fought in the Battle of Pavia, are mentioned by Passero in the review at Naples.

The company of Giovanni Guevara, Conte di Potenza, was led by his lieutenant Ludico de Baldaia at the review. The latter had three horses: one with barding, shaffron and peytral covered with black velvet; another with golden harness with the Italy impresa painted on it.[11] Both were led by pages on foot. Baldaia rode the third horse; its harness, peytral and shaffron were covered in crimson velvet with golden fringes. Baldia wore a covering of brocade and velvet, always crimson, over his armour. Grooms and pages wore the count's device, but Passero does not describe the colours. Then,

---

9   G. Passero, *Historie* (Naples: Vincenzo Maria Altobelli, 1785), p.275; G. Giordani, cit. p.31.
10 G. Passero, *Historie* (Naples: Vincenzo Maria Altobelli, 1785), p.274.
11 It should depict the turreted Italy, a woman with a mural crown on her head.

there were 50 men-at-arms, well-armed and dressed in golden clothes; the golden bardings were painted with various impresas or devices. Their Standard was blue and gold, but the impresa it displayed is unknown.

Then there was the company of the Conte di Culisano, or Gollisano, of the House of Cardona. According to Passero, this nobleman was killed in the Battle of Bicocca in May 1522, while Sanudo mentions him among the Imperial Army in the campaign that led to Pavia. The captain who led the company was Juan Velasco, who had a black *saione* and his horse's barding was black. His 90 cavalrymen also wore black velvet.

There followed Pierto Osorio or Uxoria, captain of the Granada *Adelantado* (governor). Osorio would serve at the Battle of Pavia. For the review, he paraded with four horses: two had black velvet harnesses, and the other two were covered in black velvet but embroidered with silver shells. Of these last two horses, one was led by a page with a silver-painted spear; the other was led by Osorio himself, with a surcoat over his armour in black velvet with shells. The grooms were dressed in yellow, black and white, while the 100 cavalrymen of the company wore multicoloured velvet *saioni*.[12]

Many captains, or rather lieutenants, paraded showing the horses in their possession, and often these horses were barded with different emblems or impresas. This is because, at the time, impresas were widely used by nobles and captains; the most important persons adopted several impresas in their lifetime. For example, for Pescar I have found eight impresas carried by him at various times.

Hernando de Avalos' most famous impresa as Marchese di Pescara was the Spartan shield with the motto Aut Cum Hoc Aut In Hoc (Either With This or on This). This impresa, painted on a Standard, was lost at the Battle of Ravenna in 1512, when Avalos was taken prisoner. In Question de Amor, a romantic literary composition written by an anonymous Spanish author and published in 1513, there is an accurate description of the clothing of the noble Spanish and Italian cavalry in the Army of the Holy League before the Battle of Ravenna. On this occasion, Pescara brought four horses, three of which had bardings and saioni of brocade. The primary horse had a crimson satin caparison with gold decorations, spaced one hand apart. Between decorations, the crimson satin was embroidered with gold threads, and every three fingers, there was a small gold knot.[13]

Pescara also appears in the account of the 1518 review written by Passero. His lieutenant was Ugo of Cardona, one of the few Imperial captains who died at Pavia. He had before him six horses; Passero calls two of them ginetti (light horses) led by two grooms dressed in yellow and purple. Another horse had a caparison, peytral and shaffron of crimson velvet;

---

12 G. Passero, *Historie* (Naples: Vincenzo Maria Altobelli, 1785), p.278.
13 Anonymous, *Estudio edicion y notas de Clara Perugini, Question de Amor* (Salamanca: Ediciones Universidad Salamanca, 1995), p.164.

THE BATTLE OF PAVIA 1525

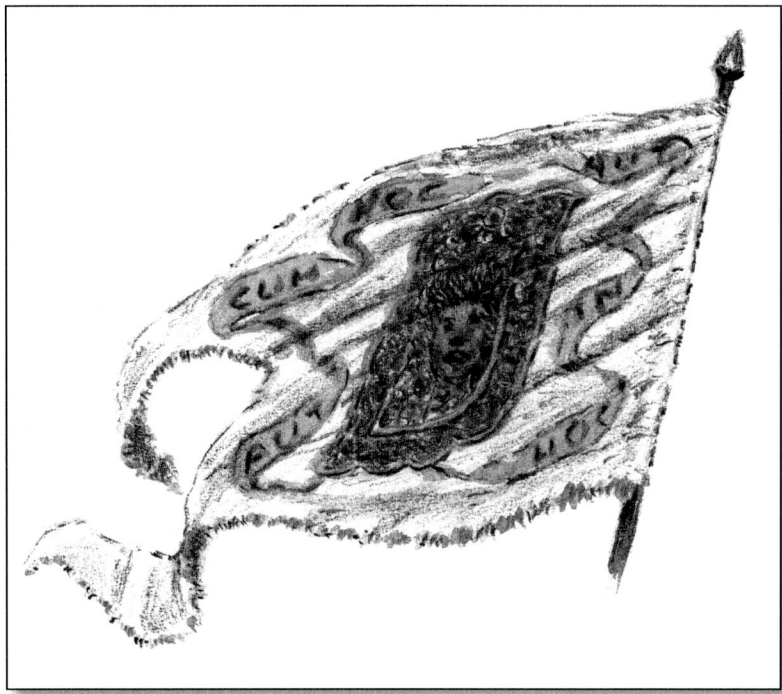

Standard displaying Pescara's shield. (Artwork by Massimo Predonzani)

a page rode it dressed in yellow and purple satin. A page dressed in purple and yellow satin rode another horse with caparison, peytral and shaffron of purple and gold satin. The fifth horse had a steel caparison, neck protection and shaffron. Cardona was mounted on the sixth horse, with a caparison covered half in silver cloth and half in gold cloth with silver buckles. The captain's saione had the same livery. Around Cardona, were four grooms dressed in yellow and purple satin. The men-at-arms of Cardona's company were Italians with golden harnesses with various emblems, their clothes were in more than one colour.[14] (Cf colour plate B, 'Cardona falls from his horse'.)

This text demonstrates that the livery of Pescara's company at that time was yellow and purple. Oznajo would mention the Marchese dressed in similar colours before the Battle of Pavia. Pescara wore cochineal hose, a crimson satin jacket and a rich shirt adorned with gold and pearls.[15] The figure of Pescara in the second Capodimonte tapestry is also very similar: he wears a crimson red jacket, yellow hose and a corselet with gold decoration. He wears a normal infantry cap with white feathers and is armed with a spear.

His impresas are all described by Scipione Ammirato in his book Il Rota overo delle imprese.[16] The Italian scholar mentions eight impresas embroidered on Pescara's funeral cloth when he died, as was customary in Naples for deceased nobles. There was the Spartan shield, mentioned above, on the Standard lost at the Battle of Ravenna; then two other impresas without a motto: a crucible for melting metals and a table with weights and pulley – both belonging to the Avalos family and visible in their chapel in the church of Monteoliveto in Naples; there are three bird wings tied

---

14   G. Passero, *Historie* (Naples: Vincenzo Maria Altobelli, 1785), pp.273–274.
15   J. de Oznajo, 'Batalla de Pavia y prison del rey de France Francisco I' in Coleccion de documentos inéditos para la historia de Espana, (Madrid: Imprenta de la Viuda de Calero,1846), volumen IX, p.465.
16   Scipione Ammirato, *Il Rota overo delle imprese* (Florence: Filippo Giunti, 1598).

THE HERALDRY OF THE BATTLE OF PAVIA

together by a lace at the base, thus forming a triangle, this impresa is also without a motto.

Ammirato dwells on a description of the impresa of the viper who gives birth to three snakelets with the motto Hac Fatum Me Ratio Necat (This Fate Is Killing Me For A Reason). At the time, it was believed that the viper killed the male during their union, and that the snakelets tore the mother's belly at birth, killing her too. The impresa represents the viper as the cause of her fate, but Ammirato sincerely admits that he does not know the reason behind the Pescara choice. It is not known when Pescara adopted this impresa.

Another impresa displayed on the canopy was the triumphal arch, with the motto Quae Devia Nunc Pervia (What Deviations Are Now Accessible). This Arch stood atop a high, steep mountain reachable via a spacious road. The monument had an arched door in the middle and two small ones at the sides. In the middle was the Latin motto; on the sides, F and A were written. On the right of the arch, a river came from the mountain that descended to the valley. According to Ammirato, this impresa represented the Marchese passing the Alps, recognisable by the letters F (Franciscus Ferdinandus) and A (Avalus Aquinius). The river was the Rhone, probably referring to Avalos' feat at Marseilles in 1524.

The next impresa was a pike on a rock with an olive wreath on top and the Spanish motto A La Honra Y No A La Vida (To Honour And Not To Live).

As well as Ammirato the philologist Vincenzo Borghini claims that the last impresa described was the most beautiful; it was the ram, gold at front, red in the middle and silver at the back. The ram had 19 stars on his body, seven on the red part, one on his tail, one on a front hoof, one on a hind hoof and the remaining nine were on the front, painted gold. The field was blue with clouds and flames around it. The motto was Aut Evertam Aut Convertam (Either Inverted or Transformed).

Ammirato writes that the symbol of the ram was used in war by the Etruscans and other ancient peoples; it was also one of the symbols of Mars, the God of War. Borghini recalls it as an emblem of The Emperor Octavian Augustus. Humanist Giovanni Pontano, who had been Pescara's tutor, said that Pescara had Mars as his natal chart. According to Ammirato, as a result, Avalos used the ram as a symbol of war and victory against his enemies.[17]

Colour plate H.1 is the reconstruction of the banner with the ram that belonged to the Marchese di Pescara.

Antonio de Leyva used an impresa considered beautiful by many contemporary writers. It was a beehive with the motto Sic Vos Non Vobis (Thus You [do something] Not For Yourselves). After the Battle of Pavia,

---

17   S. Ammirato, *Il Rota overo delle Imprese*, Florence 1598, pp.96–102; V. Borghini, *Lettere* in *Raccolta di prose fiorentine*, volume IV, 1751, pp.90–99; G. Ferro, *Teatro d 'Imprese*, Venice 1623, pp.101 and 392; E. Tasso, *Della realtà e perfettione delle imprese*, Bergamo 1612, p.42.

the captain became Governor of Milan and held that position for four years against the attacks of the French and Italians. Antonio hoped The Emperor would leave him in the city government, but in 1529, the state was returned to Francesco II Sforza. The year after, de Leyva participated in the coronation of Charles in Bologna, presenting himself with the beehive impresa of bees making honey not for themselves but for others, as he had done by preserving the duchy for others. Giovio writes that the impresa was visible on the barding of his lieutenant, since Antonio, suffering from gout, had to attend the coronation in a carriage.

I have found no other impresas of this captain; even the coins he minted during the siege to pay the landsknechts had only a cross with his initials A.L. The only mention of his heraldry is in the literary composition Question de Amor, which I have mentioned above with respect to Pescara.

Among the many captains, the description of Antonio de Leyva is as follows. He had four horses: the first had a barding of orange and white satin. The second had a crimson satin barding and a saione. The third had a white damask brocade barding decorated with brocade chequers thinly lined with stripes. In the middle of the squares, there were two Cs.[18] The fourth horse, the primary one, had a bard of white and crimson brocaded velvet, also quartered. In each square were two crossbars with three painted candlesticks in each bar. The candlesticks in the white square were silver, and those in the crimson square were gold. But this was de Leyva's clothing more than two years before Pavia. (see colour plate H.4 'Standard with the Virgin Mary and Standard of de Leyva'.)

Other Captains.

The Neapolitan captain Cesare Maggi commanded the Italian infantry at Pavia. He was born in Naples of humble origins; Luca Contile writes in his book on impresas that he adopted the palm tree precisely to highlight his birth. This plant grows and bears fruit in arid and stony soils and does not dry out; in the same way, Maggi wanted to show that although he was born in relative poverty, thanks to his strength and courage, he had and would prevail over the dangers of war. The motto that accompanied this impresa was *Nec Arvit* (Without Ploughing).[19] (See colour plate H.9.)

Giovan Battista Castaldo was a member of Pescara's company; he was his *famiglio*. Some texts on the Battle of Pavia mention him for capturing La Palice and killing the King's horse. He has three known impresas; however, he used them all after the Battle of Pavia. Mount Vesuvius was designed by Giovio after 1536, the tiger with the mirror was carried during the expedition against the Turks in Transylvania in 1551, and the laurel plant

---

18   The letter C is for the initial of his bride, Castellana de Villaragut y Bellvis.
19   L. Contile, *Ragionamento di Luca Contile sopra la proprietà delle imprese*, Pavia 1574, pp.83–84.

was used around 1560. His coat of arms was that of his family: wavy of seven, argent and azure.[20]

In the Battle of Pavia, Graf Nikolaus von Salm led the Burgundian and Upper Austrian cavalry, and his coat of arms was gules, two salmon argent, nine crosses argent.

Jehan d'Andelot, a gentleman of Franche-Comté, fought against King Francis at Pavia, who wounded him in the face. According to the historian Lois Gollut, the King had this episode represented in one of his tapestries at the Louvre. Andelot was depicted with a green velvet coat over his armour, showing his coat of arms: chequey azure and argent, a lion gules armed, langued, crowned or.[21]

Georg von Frundsberg, the commander of the landsknechts, wore a quartered coat of arms: 1 and 4, or a mountain sable; 2 and 3, sable a swan argent.

Marck Sittig von Ems's family crest was a gold ibex on a blue field.[22]

B The Heraldry of the French

King Francis I

The salamander among fire was King Francis I's device, inherited from his father Charles, Comte d'Angoulême. At the time, the salamander was believed not to burn in fire but to feed on it. According to Paolo Giovio and Claude Paradin, the King was prone to 'burn with amorous passion' and claimed to feed on it. Just as the salamander stands in the flames and is not consumed by them, so he burnt with love without being destroyed by it. The motto that accompanied the emblem was in Italian, *Mi Nutrisco* (I nourish myself), or in Latin, *Nutrisco et Extinguo*, (I nourish and extinguish).[23]

The crowned salamander is still visible in bas-reliefs of Francis' palaces, and at the time, it was sported on insignias and clothes. In a tournament held in Paris in 1514, Francis, who was not yet King but only Duc de Valois, is described by the sources as dressed over his armour with a coat of arms of satin in three colours, red, yellow and white, with golden embroidery. He had on his chest the impresa of a silver salamander among golden flames, with the motto *Nutrisco et Extinguo*. The chronicles again mention the salamander on a parade in Paris in February 1515, shortly after Francis'

---

20 G. Ferro, cit. pp.54, 495 and 692.
21 Loys Gollut, *Les Mémoires historiques de la République Séquanoise* (Arbois: Auguste Javel, 1846), p.1581.
22 For other elements of Imperial heraldry at Pavia, see: M. Predonzani & V. Alberici, *The Italian Wars*, volume 3: *Francis I and the Battle of Pavia 1525* (Warwick: Helion & Company, 2022), pp.90–105.
23 C. Paradin, Devises heroiques et emblemes, Paris 1614, p.14–15; P. Giovio, *Dialogo delle imprese militari e amorose*, Bulzoni 1978, p.50–51.

THE BATTLE OF PAVIA 1525

coronation, worn by his guard of 50 French archers wearing white cloth *saioni* with golden flames embroidered on their garments. The salamander, displayed on the archers' chests and backs, was surrounded by fire and poured water from its mouth. On the edge of the archers' collar was the motto *Nutrisco et Extinguo*. Each archer had a sallet, a spear and a taffeta pennon in the King's three colours of red, yellow and white.

The archers of the Gardes Écossaise, 24 men with halberds, wore white cloth *saioni*. Their hose and the plumes on their sallets were also white. Their Captain, Robert Stewart, Monsieur d'Aubigny, also wore white clothing with the crowned silver salamander on the chest and back.

Other soldiers of the Swiss Guard, the *Cent Suisse*, wore damask jackets half red and half white and yellow. They were armed with halberds and had hose, plumes on their hats and the insignia in the same three colours.[24]

Years later, the royal livery changed. A document describing the King's entry into Troyes on 22 April 1521 describes 80 of the King's companions on horseback dressed in velvet and silk in the colours white, tenne (a brown similar to leather) and black; some children who were part of the parade wore these same colours.

In Pavia, the livery of the royal guards remained unchanged. The Swiss Guard was dressed in white, black and tenne, while the Scottish Guards were in silver. King Francis also wore silver clothing, with his monogram embroidered, over his armour and high plumes over his helmet. He wore a golden scarf across his chest with numerous white silk crosses. On his chest,

King Francis and Royal Standard of France. (Artwork by Massimo Predonzani)

24　Paul L. Jacob, *Le Roi des ribauds, 1514* in *Romans relatifs a l'Histoire de France aux XV° et XVI° siècles* (Paris: E. Renduel, 1839), p.519; T. Godefroy, *Le Ceremonial de France* (Paris: 1619), pp.154–159.

in the centre, he had a golden cross embellished with pearls, emeralds, and a small box where a piece of Christ's cross was said to be enclosed.

In the Capodimonte tapestries, the King's attire is like that described in the sources. His main insignia was the flag of France, a large square of blue-green velvet with the field of three gold fleurs de lis, which the Imperials captured.[25]

The Heraldry of the French Captains

No contemporary sources accurately describe the clothing or heraldic colours of the French captains at Pavia. Oznajo recorded a brief quote of the main Imperial captains' description before the beginning of the battle. The Spanish chronicler begins with the description of the King: 'Over his armour, he wore a chequered coat of gold brocade and purple velvet with several F. F. letters along the edge, which were gold on the velvet and violet on the brocade.' This description of the King's coat contrasts with those of other sources that mention that the King at Pavia had silver clothing, as we have already seen.

The panache on the helmet has the same yellow and violet colours but with a high flag in the middle of the feathers of purple cendal (silk) with the golden salamander among fire. A large golden F is embroidered above the salamander, and on the entire edge around the insignia, is the motto *Esta Fu E Non Plus* (This Time Or Never Again). According to the chronicler, the motto referred to the decisive battle about to begin. The flag is unusual, or anachronistic, reminiscent of its use by some French knights during the Hundred Years' War.

Then, Oznajo describes the clothing of Henri d'Albret, King of Navarre. The chronicler says he wore golden armour with a green velvet tunic embellished with golden spheres. His horse had a brown velvet caparison with golden stripes. Sanudo mentions Navarre's clothing in the Amboise tournament of 1518. Navarre dressed in white satin with small golden roses. His men sported a livery that was blue-grey satin on the right side and purple satin and chevron white satin on the left side[26]. Another emblem used by this King was the letter H, the initial of the name Henri, visible on his coins and manuscripts.

The third and last Prince that Oznajo mentions is John Stewart, Duke of Albany, described as an 18-year-old Prince of Scotland, wearing a brocade tunic with multiple white crosses.[27] However, it is impossible that

---

25   Albert Babeau, *Les rois de France a Troyes au seizième siècle* in *Revue de Champagne et de Brie*, tome VIII, Paris: Léoold Lacroix, 1880). To explore the heraldry of François I see: M. Predonzani & V. Alberici, *The Italian Wars*, volume 3: *Francis I and the Battle of Pavia 1525* (Warwick: Helion & Company, 2022), pp.76–81.
26   M. Sanudo, *I Diarii* (Venice: M. Visentini. 1889), tome XXV, p.415.
27   J. de Oznajo, 'Batalla de Pavia y prison del rey de France Francisco I' in Coleccion

John Stewart was there, since he was part of the campaign to conquer the Kingdom of Naples. Moreover, in 1525, the Prince was already 44 years old. Considering that he was absent in Pavia, it is likely that the chronicler reported these clothes seen or reported to him in a period before Albany departed from the French camp before Pavia, about two months before the battle.

John Stewart's coat of arms was a quartered escutcheon: 1. the Lion of Scotland, 2. the Dunbar Lion, 3. the Triskellion of the Isle of Man, 4. Bruce's St Andrew's cross. His impresa was the unicorn crest of Scotland, but also the dove. It appears he used the dove on his clothes during the coronation of Francis I in 1515. For the occasion, he wore a garment in white satin and silver brocade scattered with gilded-silver bird wings. The hem of his garment was embroidered with the motto *Sub Umbra Alarum Tuarum* (Under The Shadow Of Thy Wings). His men-at-arms wore a livery composed of: the right side was in yellow velvet, and the left was divided into quarters of grey-yellow velvet and white cloth. We still find the wings in the Prince's manuscripts and on a medal that he commissioned in 1524. From these sources, I can surmise that Albany sported wings not only on his clothes but also on his emblem as his main insignia.[28] (See colour plate H.3, Standard of Albany.)

Other Noble Captains With Their Heraldry

Francis II of Bourbon-Vendôme, Comte de Saint-Pol, used black in his livery. He attended the marriage of Louis XII in 1514, wearing a cape in yellow taffeta and black velvet.[29] In 1515, for the celebration of the crowning of Francis I, the Comte de Saint-Pol wore a black velvet robe scattered with wreaths of golden cloth in the shape of a crown. At the centre of these wreaths were two golden estocs tied with a silver girdle and positioned like a saltire. Between embroidered crowns, several golden letters formed the name 'Francis Bourbon'. The barding of his horse displayed the same livery and colours. Another document, referring to a tournament in Paris in 1517, also mentions Saint-Pol dressed in black velvet with gold embroidery. His panache was black; the same livery was worn by the 12 knights who accompanied him.[30] (See colour plate H.5, Standard of Saint-Pol.)

---

de documentos inéditos para la historia de Espana, (Madrid: Imprenta de la Viuda de Calero,1846), volumen IX, p.462.
28 M. Sanudo, *I Diarii* (Venice: M. Visentini. 1889), tome XXV, p.414; T. Godefroy, *Le Ceremonial de France* (Paris: 1619), p.162; B. Coombs, *The artistic patronage of John Stuart, Duke of Albany, 1520–30* (Edinburgh: The Society of Antiquaries of Scotland, volume 147, 2018) p.207.
29 Paul L. Jacob, *Le Roi des ribauds, 1514 in Romans relatifs a l'Histoire de France aux XV° et XVI° siècles* (Paris: E. Renduel, 1839), p.520.
30 T. Godefroy, *Le Ceremonial de France* (Paris: 1619), p.163; G. Malacarne, 'La vetta dell'Olimpo' in *I Gonzaga di Mantova* (Modena: Il Bulino, 2006), tomo III, p.47.

THE HERALDRY OF THE BATTLE OF PAVIA

Guillaume Gouffier de Bonnivet, *Amiral de France*, had as his main impresa a dolphin wrapped in an anchor with the motto *Festina Lenta* (Hurry Slowly), in the sense of 'be cautious'. Another impresa of de Bonnivet was the bosun's whistle; Sanudo mentions it in his *Diarii* during the meeting of June 1520 between Francis I and Henry VIII, King of England, at Ardes. Sanudo writes that Bonnivet wore a *saione* of gold and silver quartered and decorated with precious embellishments and embroidery. He wore a golden whistle at his neck in the shape of a croissant decorated with jewels. According to the Venetian chronicler, this whistle was the sign of his rank.

The meeting between the two kings also saw a number of tournaments. At the tournament of 11 June, the de Bonnivet arrived with 12 companions dressed in *saioni* and with horse bardings of silver and gold cloth on the right side, and on the left, black velvet embroidered with sea anchors. The panaches were in the same colours. Days later, the *amiral* and his companions wore a slightly different livery: one side of the garment was chequered gold and silver, the other was in morello velvet (instead of black) with an embroidered anchor.[31] Cf the image of de Bonnivet in Chapter 4 above.

Charles Valois, Duc d'Alençon, was discussed in chapter 21 dedicated to the sixth tapestry, and was depicted while fleeing the battlefield with the French rearguard. He and most of his cavalry wear garments in beige or gold with silver embroideries over their armour. These colours differ completely from those worn by Alençon and his men in a tournament in March 1518 at Amboise. There, the Prince wore a *saione* of black cloth powdered with several golden artichokes over his armour, and his horse's barding was the same. His men-at-arms wore the same black livery with embroidered gold letters that read *Laudatus Sum In His Quae Dicta Sunt Mihi* (I Am Glad For The Things I Know).[32]

Richard de la Pole, Duke of Suffolk, claimed the Crown of England by right of descent from the House of York. In the Capodimonte tapestries, he appears in the second tapestry with the landsknechts of the Black Band, he was one of their commanders. De la Pole is portrayed dying with a crimson *saione* over his armour with silver slashing and a white cross on the back.

The de la Pole family used different emblems. Richard had the white antelope with the crown and gold chain around its neck. The antelope is an ancient badge of Lancaster dating to before Henry V (r.1413–1422). This antelope appears on a medallion in a contemporary portrait of the Duke of Suffolk.[33] (See colour plate H.6 Banner of the Duke of Suffolk.)

---

31 A. Seillier, *Maison Gouffier de Bonnivet* in *Mémoires de la Société Académique de l'Oise*, Beauvais 1892, Tome XV, p.116; M. Sanudo, *I Diarii* (Venice: M. Visentini. 1894), tome XXV, pp.23, 79 & 242.

32 M. Sanudo, *I Diarii* (Venice: M. Visentini. 1894), tome XXV, p.413.

33 M. Powell Siddons, *Heraldic Badges in England and Wales* (Martlesham: The Boydell & Brewer, 2009), vol. II, pp.231–233.

THE BATTLE OF PAVIA 1525

François de Lorraine, Comte de Lambesc, was the brother of Antoine II, Duc de Lorraine and Bar. He died at Pavia while fighting in the ranks of the landsknechts of the Black Band. He also appears in the second tapestry with the Duke of Suffolk; François wears a beige or gold coat with crimson edge and trim. Lambesc also participated in the Amboise tournament of 1518. Sanudo reports that he led the band of the Duc de Lorraine, and his coat was divided into one side of gold cloth, and the other of yellow satin. His men-at-arms had their clothing of one side of yellow satin and the other of white satin.[34]

La Palice. (Artwork by Massimo Predonzani)

Thomas de Foix, Seigneur de Lescun, known as 'The Shield', brother of Odet de Foix, fought at the Battle of Pavia, where he was mortally wounded. Sanudo mentions one of his liveries in the chronicle of the tournament organised in honour of Henry VIII on 14 June 1520. Sanudo says: 'the Monseigneur de Lescun was dressed in black velvet and brocade; the whole garment was jagged in quarters. Along with him were 10 of his cavalrymen dressed in the same fashion.'[35] This is the only mention of Lescun's livery.

Jacques de Chabannes, Sieur de La Palice, *Maréchal de* France. He participated in all the Italian Wars and died at Pavia. La Palice's coat of arms was gules, a lion ermine, crowned or. He is described as wearing a similar emblem on his clothes in the tournament of November 1514 in honour of the wedding of King Louis XII. *Monsieur* de La Palice wore a red velvet jacket with a large black lion on his chest, langued, armed and with a crown on its head.[36]

Robert de la Marck, Seigneur de Fleurange. In Pavia, he was Captain General of the Swiss. His men-at-arms wore a black coat with a white device. The historian Brantôme attributes to him the device of Saint Margaret with a dragon at her feet. The Romans had imprisoned the saint, and the devil visited her in the guise of a dragon, devouring her. However, Margaret tore the belly of the beast with a crucifix that she held in her hand, freeing herself. The device was accompanied by the motto *Si Dieu Ne Me Veul Ayder, Le Diable Ne Me Peut*

---

34 M. Sanudo, *I Diarii* (Venice: M. Visentini. 1894), tome XXV, p.415.
35 M. Sanudo, *I Diarii* (Venice: M. Visentini. 1894), tome XXIX, p.243.
36 Paul L. Jacob, *Le Roi des ribauds, 1514 in Romans relatifs a l'Histoire de France aux XV° et XVI° siècles* (Paris: E. Renduel, 1839), p.520.

Manquer (If God Does Not Want To Help Me, The Devil Shall Not Fail Me).[37] (See colour plate H.2, 'Standard of Fleurange'.)

René, the Great Bâtard of Savoy, Comte de Villars, and natural son of Philippe II, Duca di Savoy, *Grand Maître de France*. Villars died of his wounds at the Battle of Pavia. He is discussed in Chapter 19 on the fifth tapestry, and the black double-headed eagle visible on a field tent. The hypothesis is that the coat of arms was his, as the eagle was the coat of arms of his wife, Anne Lascaris of Tende. Marin Sanudo also mentions the Great Bâtard at the Amboise tournament of 1518, writing that he and his band wore a white satin livery with some *dopioni* (circles) of yellow and blue satin on the right side of the clothing, while on the left side there were half circles in yellow, blue and white.[38]

Louis de la Trémoille, *Amiral* de Bretagne, the King's first chamberlain and Governor of Burgundy. He died at Pavia.

Trémoille's impresa or device was a cogwheel with the motto *Sans Point Sortir Hors de l'Orniere* (Without Coming out of the Furrow). The motto and figure carried the meaning that Trémoille always served his King loyally and was never tempted by any other profit. The cogwheel is an iconographic attribute of Saint Catherine of Alexandria, as it was used in her martyrdom. We find an insignia with this impresa on the walls of Dijon besieged by the Swiss in 1513. This siege was commemorated in a magnificent tapestry executed shortly after the event. In this work, Trémoille's Standard has a split-tail fly, the cogwheel is gold, while the lower part of the Standard is horizontally striped blue, yellow and red. Sanudo mentions Trémoille, and his cogwheel impresa, at the entry of Francis I into Paris in 1515. On that occasion, the French captain wore a coat of gold cloth covered with gold canvas cogwheels and silver rays.[39]

According to several sources, Michel Antoine, Marchese di Saluzzo, was not at Pavia; others, however, cite him as being present. Saluzzo's banner was divided horizontally, blue and white, with a large gold S in the middle. A chronicle of 1507 describes the marquis' guard armed with halberds, with hose coloured: one leg all turquoise and the other striped in three colours: red, blue and white. The same chronicle reports that, in 1509, Saluzzo is described wearing dress made of gold cloth and crimson velvet. In his company were 20 gentlemen dressed in damask in his red, turquoise, and white livery colours.[40] (See colour plate H.8, 'The Standard of Saluzzo in his livery colours'.)

---

37 'Loyal Serviteur, Chronique de Bayart' in J. A. C. Buchon, *Choix de chroniques et memoires sur l'histoire de France* (Paris: Desrez, 1836), p.94; Pierre de Brantôme, *Oeuvres complètes*, tome III (Paris: R. Sabe, 1869), tome. III, p.190.
38 M. Sanudo, *I Diarii* (Venice: M. Visentini. 1894), tome XXV, p.415.
39 P. Giovio, *Dialogo delle imprese militari e amorose* (Rome: Bulzoni, 1978), p.102; Comte Louis de Bouillé *Les Drapeaux français, étude historique* (Paris: J. Dumaine, 1875), p.61–62; T. Godefroy, *Le Ceremonial de France* (Paris: 1619), 2 vol., tome I, p.271.
40 Vincenzo Promis, 'Memoriale di Gio. Andrea Saluzzo di Castellar dal 1482 al *1528*'

Teodoro Trivulzio, Italian captain. Appointed Governor of Milan in 1525 by Francis I, he had to abandon the city after the Battle of Pavia.

Pierre Le Moyne, a Jesuit writer of the seventeenth century, describes Trivulzio's device as follows: his device was modest, consisting of five ears of wheat without other figures and even without a motto. The bundle of ears was a company brought by the Trivulzio family of Milan[41].

Anne de Montmorency, *Maréchal* de France, since 1522. He was at the battles of Ravenna, Marignano and Pavia, where he was captured. His most famous impresa was an arm holding a sword with the motto *Sans Fraude* (Without Fraud).[42]

Galeazzo da Sanseverino, Grand écuyer de France. The Grand écuyer took care of the stables and the King's posts, but also organised tournaments, parties and was present at the court protocol. Sanseverino also commanded a company of 100 lances.[43]

As Grand écuyer in the service of the King of France, Sanseverino had the privilege of dressing like the sovereign and wearing the same livery, albeit with a few small differences.[44]

Giovanni de' Medici did not fight in the Battle of Pavia, as he was wounded and was in Piacenza for treatment. He belonged to a cadet branch of the Medici family but still used the *or, five balls in orle gules* as his coat of arms. The colours of his livery were white and purple; a letter of 1517 documents the order for a white and purple striped taffeta flag for his company. Even his men, infantry and cavalry alike, wore clothes in these colours. The name 'Black Bands' was given to this company after the death of the condottiero. In all chronicles, the captain is mentioned only as Giovanni Medici without the epithet 'of the Black Bands', which only appeared in historiography at the end of the nineteenth century.[45] On colour plate H.7 the Standard of Giovanni Medici has been shown displaying a devil. At the time, the condottiero was called the Gran diavolo (Great devil).

---

in Miscellanea di storia italiana (Turin: dalla Stamperia Reale, 1869), volo VIII, pp.466–467 & 482.

41 P. Le Moyne, *De l'art des Devises* (Paris: 1666), p.214.

42 C. Paradin, *Devises heroiques et emblems* (Paris: Jean Millet, 1614), pp.118–119; B. Pittoni, *Imprese di diversi prencipi, duchi, signori, e d'altri personaggi et huomini letterati et illustri* (Venezia: 1562), p.15.

43 G. Alonge, 'Galeazzo Sanseverino' in *Dizionario Biografico degli italiani*, vol. 90 (2017).

44 T. Godefroy, *Le Ceremonial de France* (Paris: 1619), pp.156–157.

45 P. Gauthiez, Nuovi documenti intorno a Giovanni de' Medici detto delle bande nere, in Archivio storico italiano, quinta serie, volume XXX, Florence 1902, p.93; M. Arfaioli, *Medici, Giovanni de'* in Dizionario Biografico degli Italiani, Vol. 73, 2009; M. Predonzani & V. Alberici, *The Italian Wars*, volume 3: *Francis I and the Battle of Pavia 1525* (Warwick: Helion & Company, 2022), pp.109–114.

27

The Infantry in Pavia

Among the French infantry engaged in Pavia, the landsknecht Black Band was undoubtedly the most mentioned for their sacrifice against numerous enemy forces. Although the name 'Black Band' would suggest that these Germans wore black clothing, this fact is not proven. In 1515, Superintendent Marco Contarini wrote in some letters to the Republic of Venice that these Germans came from Montenegro near Freiburg, where it was said that the inhabitants all dressed in black. However, the Black Band landsknechts came from various parts of Germany, primarily from Flanders and the towns around the Rhine, such as Freiburg.

Other letters from Venetian officials tell of the Black Band's arrival in Milan after the victory at Marignano; when described, it does not say that these landsknechts dressed in black. They talk about golden clothes and hose or red hose, and black is mentioned only for the captains' panaches of feathers among other white or yellow plumes. Even in the iconography of the Battle of Pavia, such as the Capodimonte tapestries and the works of Jörg Breu and Ruprecht Heller, the Black Band landsknechts wear colourful clothing devoid of black. However, this colour appears on their flags, documented in the work of Breu and a certain Andreas Wagner. You can see Colours with the white cross and the field divided into fesses, a Colour with black and green stripes, and another with black and red stripes, (cf colour plate G.4, 'Two Colours of the Black Band').

In this regard, the description of the Milanese chronicler Bernardino Arluno is interesting; he also writes of the entry into Milan of the Black Band after Marignano: Praecellebant phalanges elatis, nigrantibus vexillis conspicuae (The pikemen advance proudly, with blackened banners visible).[1]

---

1   M. Sanudo, *I Diarii* (Venezia: M. Visentini, 1842–1895), tome XX, pp.439 and 493, tome XXI, pp.25–26; M. Predonzani & V. Alberici, *The Italian Wars*, volume 3: *Francis I and the Battle of Pavia 1525* (Warwick: Helion & Company, 2022), pp.106–109; B. Arluno, *De bello gallico seu Historia Mediolanensis a Gallorum Victoria ad Marignanum usque ad Francisci I Gallorum regis captivitatem*, 1534,

THE BATTLE OF PAVIA 1525

These elements, taken from various iconography and sources, demonstrate that these landsknechts displayed black markings on their banners and in their captains' panaches. (See colour plate D, on the right, the Black Band landsknechts at Pavia led by Suffolk.)

The second part of the chapter on the fifth tapestry deals with the Swiss infantry. They all sported the white cross on their chest and back, and their Colours also displayed the white cross with the field divided into stripes of various colours. In the Capodimonte tapestries, we find combinations with stripes in white and yellow, yellow and red or yellow and blue. (See colour plate G.3, 'Swiss Colours from the Capodimonte tapestries'.)

French infantrymen. (Artwork by Massimo Predonzani)

The French infantry are almost absent in the iconographies of the battle. However, some images of the time depict them. In addition, Louis Susane and André de Brantôme described the infantry weapons and clothing in their texts.

Susane, a French military historian of the late nineteenth century, wrote in Histoire de l'ancienne infanterie Française about the Army of Francis I:

---

manuscript in the Biblioteca Ambrosiana, Milan.

All officers and pikemen were armed with a long pike and a straight sword; they wore burgonets or solid helmets with ear flaps, corslets or armours similar to those of today's cuirassiers, vambraces, gloves and knee-length hoses. The arquebusiers were dressed more lightly with Morion or small helmets, jackets and mail sleeves. They also carried a sword or dagger. Such was the French band, the only infantry corps at that time to have a regular and permanent organisation.

Brantôme, who was writing in the second half of the sixteenth century, recounts instead in Grands capitaines François the story of the clothing of the French infantrymen at the time of King Louis XII and Francis I:

> They wore long jackets with large sleeves like the Bohemians and the Moors, and kept them for two or three months without changing them. They show their bare and hairy chest and wear diverse shoes. They also wore colourful slashed hose that showed the bare thigh and the buttocks. Cleaner infantrymen used taffeta in large quantities but still showed one or both bare legs and tied their hose to the belt. Most of them were poor people or criminals marked with the fleur-de-lys on their shoulders. Their ears were cut, and they had long, thick hair and horrible beards.

These writings can be compared with the woodcut 'The Crusaders in Damietta' from François Regnaults' Grand Voyage de Jierusalem of 1522. The print depicts the army of Louis IX of France landing at Damietta, Egypt, in 1249 during the Seventh Crusade. Of course, the clothes and weapons depicted are from the beginning of the sixteenth century (cf image 'French infantrymen' above). On the left the French men-at-arms can be seen, similar to the gendarmes in the Capodimonte tapestries. At the centre is the French infantry marked by the inscription aventuriers, the word with which the French mercenary infantry is identified in the chronicles. On their right are the Swiss with their typical clothing: wide-sleeved jackets, tight hose with numerous cuts and slashings. Overall, clothes that were practical in comparison to those of the French. The latter are armed with pikes, halberds, long swords, crossbows and arquebuses. Then, the Standard bearer holds the Colour with a cross, accompanied by a drummer and a piper. They wear various types of cloth caps and war hats or sallets. As in the piece written by Brantôme, they wear jackets with wide sleeves, hose of various colours with cuts and slashings, and have bare thighs. Some have one bare leg and some both and they wear shoes of various shapes. In this woodcut, the aventuriers do not have beards, probably to further differentiate themselves from the Swiss you see on the right – most of whom have a beard.[2]

---

2   Lous Susane, Histoire de l'ancienne infanterie Française (Paris: J. Corréard, 1849),

THE BATTLE OF PAVIA 1525

Italian infantryman. (Artwork by Massimo Predonzani)

The Italian infantry is also not easily recognisable in the iconography of the Battle of Pavia, since those in the pay of both France and The Empire dress in landsknecht style. Accurate images of Italian soldiers' clothing of the time can be seen in the cathedral of Cremona in the frescoes of the Passion of Christ, painted between 1520 and 1522 by Romanino and Pordenone. The Roman soldiers depicted by these artists wear clothes and weapons from the first decade of the sixteenth century, i.e. infantry in half armour with faulds down to the knee and various types of helmets – sallets, burgonets or cervellieres. Many have no head protection or wear large cloth hats decorated with ostrich feathers. As clothing, they wear doublets or jackets with wide sleeves, sometimes with slashing from which the shirt underneath comes out, sometimes without slashings. The hose are all of various colours, and a good part of these have some slashings on the knee or thigh; only a few soldiers show the upper part of the legs with German-style slashings and padding. All shoes have a 'duckbill' toe. These frescoes from just before 1525 help identify and reconstruct the aspect of an Italian infantryman. As for French and Spanish clothes, the 'national' characteristics have not been undermined by the predominant influence of landsknecht and Swiss fashion. In this case, the tight-fitting hose in device colours are typically Italian, all still wear a codpiece (see image, Italian infantryman).

Finally, we come to the Imperial infantry, identifiable by the red St Andrew's cross on their chest or back, or by the white and red cross-body scarf. With regard to Frundsberg's landsknechts, I wrote extensively about them in the chapters on

---

tome I, p.106; André de Brantôme, *Oeuvres completes*, tome V (Paris: R. Sabe, 1867), pp.302–303; Xylography by Francois Regnaults, Grand Voyage de Hierusalem (Paris, 1522).

the first and second tapestries, describing their typical clothes and Colours. In those chapters, there is also some description of the Spanish, highlighting the difference between their clothing and that of the Germans, supported by Spanish iconography of the period.

Finally, as in my previous publications, this book includes various chapters on the two contending armies' military heraldry, with precise and previously unpublished information on the captains' liveries and devices. For example, thanks to the texts by Scipione Ammirato, I have verified that Hernando de Avalos, the Marchese di Pescara and victor of the Battle of Pavia, had as many as eight devices during his military career.

Colour Plate Commentaries

Plate A: King Francis I defends himself against the attack of Imperial troops. Two cavalry are just below him, a Spanish arquebusier and a man-at-arms of Bourbon's guard are on the ground. Behind the King, there are a landsknecht pikeman and four Imperial men-at-arms.

Plate B: A French gendarme unseats Don Hugo of Cardona, lieutenant of Pescara, during the clash of cavalries.

Plate C: Three knights accompanying the King in the first Capodimonte tapestry. Left to right:
René de Montejan, Jean Pomereux and Just, Seigneur de Tournon.

Plate D: Combat between Imperial landsknechts and the French Black Band. At the centre is the commander of the Black Band, Richard de la Pole, Duke of Suffolk.

Plate E: The Spanish arquebusiers defeat the French gendarmes.

Plate F: The French and Swiss infantrymen escape, pursued by a stradiot and a jinete.

Plate G: Infantry Colours.
1: Imperial Colours and Standards taken from 'The Battle of Pavia' by Jörg Breu and 'The Battle of Pavia' by Ruprecht Heller.
2: Landsknecht Colours from the Capodimonte tapestries.
3: Swiss Colours from the Capodimonte tapestries.
4: Two German Black Band Colours from Jörg Breu's work.
5: Three Spanish Colours from various images on the battle.

Plate H: Captains' insignia.
1: Standard of the Marchese di Pescara with the ram impresa.
2: Standard of Robert de la Marck, Seigneur de Fleurange.
3: Standard of John Stewart, Duke of Albany.
4: Standard with Madonna with Child of the Imperial command, the insignia of Antonio de Leyva.
5: Standard of Francis II of Bourbon-Vendôme, Comte de Saint-Pol.

6: Standard of Richard de la Pole, Duke of Suffolk, called 'The White Rose'.
7: Standard of Giovanni de' Medici.
8: Insignia of Michel Antoine, Marchese di Saluzzo.
9: Standard of Cesare Maggi.

Bibliography

Manuscripts

Bibliothèque Nationale de France, Paris

Valbelle, H., 'Histoire Journaliere d'Honoré de Valbelle', Manuscrit fr 5072

Printed Books

Biblioteca Ambrosiana, Milan

Arluno, B., *De bello gallico seu Historia Mediolanensis a Gallorum Victoria ad Marignanum usque ad Francisci I Gallorum regis captivitatem*, 1534

Published Books, Sixteenth Century

Bellay, M. du, *Memoires* (La Rochelle: 1573)
Contile, L., De fatti di Cesare Maggi da Napoli (Milan: Appresso Gio. Ant. degli Antoni, 1565)
Giovio, P., *La prima parte dell'istorie del suo tempo* (Venice: 1560)
Giovio, P., *La seconda parte delle historie del suo tempo* (Venice: 1555)
Giovio, P., *La vita del s. Don Ferrante Davalo Marchese di Pescara* (Florence: 1556)
Guazzo, M., *Historie* (Venice: 1549)
Philippo, J. *Supplementi delle croniche del Venerando Padre Frate Jacobo Philippo, dell'ordine Heremitano* (Venice: 1535)
Ulloa, Alfonso de, *Vita dell' invittissimo e sacratissimo imperator Carlo V* (Venice: Dalla Bottegha d'Aldo, 1575)

Later Published Books

Arfaioli, Maurizio, The Black Bands of Giovanni: infantry and diplomacy during the Italian Wars (1526–1528) (Pisa: Edizioni Plus, 2005)

BIBLIOGRAPHY

Bardin, Général Étienne Alexandre, *Dictionnaire de l'armée de terre*, tome 1 (Paris: J. Corréard, 1841)

Barthold, F. W., *Georg von Frundsberg und das teutsche Kriegshandwerk zur Zeit der Reformation* (Hamburg: Perthes, 1833)

Bonardi, Antonio, *L'Assedio e la battaglia di Pavia. Diario inedito* (Pavia: Poulailler,1895),

Bouchet, Jean, *Panégyric du chevallier sans reproche, Louis de La Trémoille*, in *Mémoires pour servir a l'Histoire de France*, tome quatrieme (Paris: J.L.F. Foucault, 1837)

Brantôme, Pierre de, *Oeuvres complètes*, tome III (Paris: R. Sabe, 1867)

Casali, Luigi, *Gli arazzi della battaglia di Pavia nel Museo di Capodimonte a Napoli* (Pavia: Edizioni ViGiEffe, 1993)

Cerezeda, M. García, *Tratado de las campañas y otros acontecimientos de los ejércitos del emperador Carlos V en Italia, Francia, Austria, Berbería y Grecia*, tomo I (Madrid: Impresores de Cámara, 1873)

Charrié, Pierre, *Drapeaux et étendars du roi* (Paris: Le Leopard d'Or, 1989)

Chesnaye-Desbois, M. *Dictionnaire de la Noblesse* (Paris: Vve Duchesne, 1775), tome IX (1774) & tome X (1775)

Desjardins, G., *Recherches sur les drapeaux français* (Paris: A Morel et Cie, 1874)

Florange, R. de la Marck, *Mémoires du Maréchal de Florange*, tome II (Paris: Renouard, H. Laurens, successeur, 1924)

Giono, Jean (Franco Pierno, trans.) *Il disastro di Pavia*, (Milan: Ed. Settecolori, 2025)

Giovio, P., *Vite del Gran Capitano e del marchese di Pescara* (Bari: Gius, Laterza & Figli, 1931)

Giovio, P. (Maria Luisa Doglio, ed.), *Dialogo delle imprese militari e amorose* (Rome: Bulzoni, 1978)

Godefroy, T., *Le Ceremonial de France* (Paris: 1619)

Gollut, Loys, *Les Mémoires historiques de la République Séquanoise* (Arbois: Auguste Javel, 1846)

Grumello, Antonio, *Cronaca* in *Raccolta di cronisti e documenti storici lombardi*, (Milan: Francesco Colombo, 1856)

Guicciardini, Francesco, *Storia d'Italia* (Milan: Borroni e Scotti, 1843)

Guicciardini, Francesco, *Histoire d'Italie de l'année 1492 à l'année 1532*, tome 5 (Paris: A. Desrez 1837)

Hare, Christopher, *Charles de Bourbon* (London: John Lane, The Bodley Head, 1911)

Jacob, Paul L., *Le Roi des ribauds, 1514* in *Romans relatifs a l'Histoire de France aux XV° et XVI° siècles* (Paris: E. Renduel, 1839)

Jähns, M., *GeschichtlicheAufsätze* (Berlin: Verlag von Gebrüder Paetel, 1903)

Lalanne, Lodovic, *Journal d'un bourgeois de Paris sous le règne de François premier (1515–1536)* (Paris: J. Renouard & Société de l'Histoire de France, 1854)

Mini, Constantino, *La Vita e le Gesta di Giovanni de Medici o Storia delle Bande Nere e dei celebri Capitani che vi militarono* (Florence: Coi tipi di P. Fioretti, 1851)

Monluc, Blaise de, *Commentaires et lettres* (Paris: Mme Ve J. Renouard, 1864)

Mure, J. de la, *Histoire des ducs de Bourbon et des comtes de Forez*, tome deuxième (Paris & Lyon: Potier, 1867)

Newald, J., *Niclas Graf zu Salm, eine historisch studie* (Wien: Gerold, 1879)

Panisse-Passis, Comte de, *Les comtes de Tende de la Maison de Savoie* (Paris: Firmin-Didot, 1889)

Paradin, Claude, *Devises heroiques et emblems* (Paris: Jean Millet, 1614)

Passero, G., *Historie* (Naples: Vincenzo Maria Altobelli, 1785)

Pieri, P., *Il Rinascimento e la crisi militare italiana* (Rome: Einaudi, 1952)

Predonzani, M. & Alberici, V., *The Italian Wars*, volume 2: *Agnadello 1509, Ravenna 1512, Marignano 1515*, (Warwick: Helion & Company, 2021)

Predonzani, M. & Alberici, V., *The Italian Wars*, volume 3: *Francis I and the Battle of Pavia 1525* (Warwick: Helion & Company, 2022)

Predonzani, M. & Miller, Simon, *The Italian Wars*, volume 4. *The Battle of Ceresole* (Warwick: Helion & Company 2022)

Predonzani, M. *The Italian Wars,* volume 5: *The Franco-Spanish War in Southern Italy 1502.1504* (Warwick: Helion & Co., 2024), pp.37–42

Romainmotier, M. May de, *Histoire militaire de la Suisse*, tome V (Lausanne: J.P. Heubach et Cie, 1788)

Romano, Carmine (ed.), *Art & War in the Renaissance: The Battle of Pavia Tapestries* (New York: Rizzoli International 2024)

Saincte-Marthe, Scevole et Louis de, *Histoire genealogique de la maison de France*, tome deuxième (Paris: Sebastien Cramoisy & Gabriel Cramoisy, 1628)

Sandoval, P. de. *Historia del Emperador Carlos V*, tomo III (Madrid: Madoz, 1846)

Santa Cruz, Alonso de, *Cronica del Emperador Carlos V*, volumen II (Madrid: Impr. del Patronato de Huérfanos de Intendencia é Intervención Militares 1920)

Sanudo, M., *I Diarii*, tomo XX, XXI, XXIII, XXXIII, XXIV, XXIX, XXXVI, XXXVI, XXXVIII, XLIII (Venice: M. Visentini, 1842–1895)

Scalini, Mario (ed.), *Giovanni delle Bande Nere* (Florence: Banca Toscana, 2001)

Spinosa, N., *Gli arazzi della battaglia di Pavia* (Milan: Bompiani, 1999)

Taegio (or Taigi), Francesco, *Rotta e prigionia di Francesco primo re' di Francia sotto Pavia l'anno 1525. Composta dal Taegi, e dal latino tradotta dal Cremonese Cambiago* (Pavia: 1655)

Testi, Dario, *La batalla de Pavia, Fuentes historiográficas y epistolares del siglo XVI*, (Madrid: Ministerio de Defensa 2024)

Varillas, A., *Histoire de François I*, tome premier (Paris: Claude Barbin, 1685)

Journals and Chapters

Arfaioli, M., 'Medici, Giovanni de' in *Dizionario Biografico degli Italiani*, tomo 73 (Rome: Istituto della Enciclopedia italiana, 2009)

Baader, J., 'Die Schlacht bei Pavia, nach dem Bericht eines Augenzeugen' in *Anzeiger fur kunde der deutschen vorzeit,* November 1868.

Bouchet, Jean, 'Panégyric du chevallier sans reproche, Louis de La Trémoille' in *Mémoires pour servir a l'Histoire de France*, tome quatrieme (Paris: J.L.F. Foucault, 1837)

Capino, C. de, 'Relazione del 28 febbraio 1525' in *Bollettino della Società pavese di storia Patria*, tome 7 (Pavia: 1907)

Oznajo, Juan de, 'Batalla de Pavia y prision del Rey de France Francisco I' in *Coleccion de documentos inéditos para la historia de Espana*, volumen IX (Madrid: Imprenta de la Viuda de Calero, 1846)

Pita Da Veiga Joyanes, Gabriel & Pita Da Veiga Subirates, Joaquin, 'La prison del rey de France: consideraciones sobre la captura de Francisco I y sus verdaderos protagonistas' in *Revista de Historia Militar*, no. 12 (2020)

Promis, Vincenzo, 'Memoriale di Gio. Andrea Saluzzo di Castellar dal 1482 al 1528' in *Miscellanea di storia italiana*, volo VIII (Turin: dalla Stamperia Reale, 1869)

About the author

Massimo Predonzani was born in Piran, Slovenia in 1959 and currently lives in Trieste, Italy. He is an illustrator and researcher. He specializes in military heraldry during the Italian and European Renaissance. He is the author of Anghiari 29 giugno 1440 (2010), Ceresole 14 aprile 1544 (2012) and Caravaggio 1448 (2013). Since 2019 he has been collaborating with the publishing house Helion & Conpany with which he has published a series of 5 books on the Italian wars of the Renaissance. He also has a website where he shares his research and his painted illustrations (www.stemmieimprese.it).

Other titles in the From Retinue to Regiment series:

No 1   Richard III and the Battle of Bosworth
       Mike Ingram
No 2   Tanaka 1587: Japan's Greatest Unknown
       Samurai Battle   Stephen Turnbull
No 3   The Army of the Swabian League 1525
       Doug Miller
No 4   The Italian Wars Volume 1: The Expedition of
       Charles VIII into Italy and the Battle of Fornovo
       Massimo Predonzani & Alberici Vincenzo,
       translated by Irene Maccolini
No 5   The Commotion Time: Tudor Rebellion in the
       West, 1549   E.T. Fox
No 6   The Italian Wars Volume 2: Agnadello 1509,
       Ravenna 1512, Marignano 1515
       Massimo Predonzani & Alberici Vincenzo,
       translated by Rachele Tiso
No 7   The Tudor Arte of Warre Volume 1:
       The Conduct of War from Henry VII to
       Mary I, 1485-1558   Jonathan Davies
No 8   The Ethiopian-Adal War 1529-1543:
       The Conquest of Abyssinia   Jeffrey M. Shaw
No 9   The Ōnin War: A Turning Point in Samurai
       History   Stephen Turnbull
No 10 One Faith, One Law, One King: French Armies
       of the Wars of Religion 1562-1598
       T J O'Brien de Clare
No 11 The Italian Wars Volume 3: Francis I and the
       Battle of Pavia 1525   Massimo Predonzani &
       Alberici Vincenzo
No 12 On the Borderlands of Great Empires:
       Transylvanian Armies 1541-1613
       Florin Nicolae Ardelean
No 14 The Art of Shooting Great Ordnance: A History
       of the Development, Manufacture and Use of
       Artillery, 1494–1628   Jonathan Davies
No 15 The Italian Wars Volume 4: The Battle of
       Ceresole 1544 - The Crushing Defeat of the
       Imperial Army   Massimo Predonzani &
       Simon Miller
No 16 The Men of Warre: The Clothes, Weapons and
       Accoutrements of the Scots at War 1460–1600
       Jenn Scott
No 17 The German Peasants' War 1524-26
       Douglas Miller
No 18 The Tudor Arte of Warre Volume 2: The conduct
       of war in the reign of Elizabeth I, 1558–1603:
       Diplomacy, Strategy, Campaigns and Battles
       Jonathan Davies

No 19 The Kalmar War 1611–1613: Gustavus
       Adolphus's First War
       Michael Fredholm von Essen
No 20 Hojo: Samurai Warlords 1487–1590
       Stephen Turnbull
No 21 The Battle of Castillon 1453: The Death Knell for
       English France   Peter Hoskins
No 22 The Tudor Arte of Warre Volume 3: The Conduct
       of War in the Reign of Elizabeth I 1558-1603:
       The Elizabethan Army   Jonathan Davies
No 23 Sweden's War in Muscovy 1609-1617: The
       Relief of Moscow and Conquest of Novgorod
       Michael Fredholm von Essen
No 24 'Of Kerns and Gallowglasses': Irish Armies of the
       Sixteenth Century, 1487-1587
       Robert Gresh
No 25 'The Italian Wars Volume 5: The Franco-Spanish
       War in Southern Italy 1502-1504
       Massimo Predonzani
No 26 The Sieges of Rhodes 1480 and 1522
       Jonathan Davies
No 27 The Swabian War of 1499: The first confrontation
       between Landsknechts and the Swiss
       Albert Winkler
No 28 'A Mighty Fortress of God': The Siege of Münster
       1534-35   Doug Miller
No 29 The Nine Years War 1593-1603 Part 1: The
       ascendancy of Irish arms and the road to Yellow
       Ford, 1593-1598   James O'Neil
No 30 Elephants and Gunpowder:Southeast Asian
       Warfare 1380-1700   Stephen Turnbull
No 31 The English Longbow - Investigating a Myth
       Volume 1: Performance and employment
       1298-1485   Jonathan Davies
No 32 The War of the Roses Volume 1: The Triumph of
       York 1455   David Grummitt
No 33 The Battle of Pavia 1525: From the Chronicles
       and Tapestries of the Capodimonte
       Massimo Predonzani
No 34 Oda Nobunaga: Samurai Commander 1534-82
       Stephen Turnbull